Burgess-Carpenter Library
406 Butler
Columbia University
New York, N. Y. 10027

The Pattern of Imperialism

The United States, Great Britain,
and the late-industrializing world since 1815

The Pattern of Imperialism

The United States, Great Britain, and the late-industrializing world since 1815

TONY SMITH
Tufts University

CAMBRIDGE UNIVERSITY PRESS
Cambridge
London   New York   New Rochelle
Melbourne   Sydney

Burgess
E
183.7
.S62

Published by the Press Syndicate of the University of Cambridge
The Pitt Building, Trumpington Street, Cambridge CB2 1RP
32 East 57th Street, New York, NY 10022, USA
296 Beaconsfield Parade, Middle Park, Melbourne 3206, Australia

First published 1981

© Cambridge University Press 1981

Printed in Canada

Library of Congress Cataloging in Publication Data
Smith, Tony, 1942–
The pattern of imperialism.
Includes bibliographical references and index.
1. United States – Foreign relations   2. Great
Britain – Foreign relations – 19th century.   3. Great
Britain – Foreign relations – 20th century.
4. Imperialism.   I. Title.
E183.7.S62   325'.32   80–39676
                                     AACR1
ISBN 0 521 23619 3 hard covers
ISBN 0 521 28076 1 paperback

For GWT

Contents

Contents

Preface

My interest in British and American imperialism grew from an investigation of the character of French colonialism, especially in Algeria.[1] This earlier work encouraged me to approach the subject of Western global expansion on a broader scale by persuading me that my studies would be parochial if I were unable to see more clearly how French affairs related to the greater historical movement of Western imperialism, and by concerning me in the moral questions of how power is exerted by the strong upon the weak in international politics. As I have come to appreciate more and more, these are particularly thorny questions. The forces behind great historical movements are invariably so complex that plausible rival interpretations may be advanced to account for them in such a fashion that it is doubtful any single study can hope to satisfy all schools of thought. This is all the more the case with respect to the study of imperialism, where passions rage so high not only among ideological camps, but among public and private actors as well, all of whom are anxious to justify their conduct. As a result, although I remain convinced of the importance of raising moral issues in historical studies, I have seen more than my share in works on imperialism of authors taking refuge in moralism to avoid the task (if not to block the pursuit) of serious analysis. Yet even if I am more aware now than when this work commenced of the difficulties in establishing a general agreement on the causes of British and American imperialism, or of raising moral questions with respect to broad historical

movements, this book will succeed, nonetheless, if it advances
the discussion of these questions and if it raises clearly certain
additional matters in the study of imperialism that are often
neglected. These issues include an effort to establish the separate identities of the chief historical forces leading to imperialism of the British and the American varieties, an appreciation of the manner in which such forces can be seen to
interrelate, and a sense of the alternate choices leaders might
have made within the bounds of the historically possible in the
conduct of their nations' foreign policies.

During the academic year 1975–6, I had the opportunity to
be a Fellow at the Lehrman Institute founded by Lewis Lehrman, and to lead a series of seminars there on some of the
topics raised in this book. Nicholas Rizopoulos, executive director of the institute, was particularly helpful to me in a setting most conducive to research and discussion. In addition,
my work that year was aided by support from the German Marshall Fund of the United States. Then, in 1978, the Rockefeller
Foundation made me a Fellow in their International Relations
program, thus allowing me substantial opportunity to complete this work.

Several persons were good enough to read portions of the
manuscript and to make critical suggestions for revisions. Jorge
Dominguez reviewed my analysis of dependency theory; Miles
Kahler discussed his work on European decolonization with
me; Donald Klein offered advice on my reading of the character
of Sino–American relations; Sally Terry furnished me with information on Soviet–American rivalry in regard to Eastern Europe; and Ronald Steel and Alan Henrikson made comments
on my overall account of American foreign policy. I am grateful
to Stanley Hoffmann, Barrington Moore, Jr., Michael Doyle,
Theda Skocpol, Charles Lipson, and Robert Keohane for reading an earlier version of the entire manuscript and for a great
number of general organizational and thematic suggestions.
Stanley Hoffmann and Barrington Moore, Jr., were helpful by
the example of their own work as well: Professor Hoffmann for
his sophisticated political realism combined with a conviction
that political ethics matter and therefore that political under-

standing is vital; Professor Moore for his congenital skepticism
of received truth from whatever camp and for his instruction
in the value of the comparative historical method. Walter Lippincott has been a tireless and conscientious editor with whom
it has been a pleasure to work; and Anne Richards performed
a valuable service by carefully copyediting the final version. I
especially appreciate the unflagging support my friend Gary
Tinterow has given me throughout this undertaking. Although
I know that all of these good people will remain unconvinced
by some of the positions I have taken here, it is a pleasure to
thank them again for the questions they raised and the insights
they shared.

A considerably earlier version of Chapter 2 appeared in
World Politics, January 1979, and much of Chapter 3 was published in *Comparative Studies in Society and History*, January
1978.

Boston   T. S.
January 1981

Introduction

This book works from the premise that it is possible to establish through comparative historical analysis certain useful generalizations about the factors that had the most importance in determining the character of British relations (from about 1815 to 1947), and later those of the United States (from about 1898 to 1980), with the preindustrial, or late-industrializing, worlds of Africa, Asia, and Latin America. Both Britain and the United States were for some years predominant in world affairs by virtue of their economic and military capabilities (even if this power was far more limited than terms like "Pax Britannica" or "the American Century" imply). Each country used its power to promote a framework for world order through defending certain basic principles designed to regulate conduct among the great powers as well as between the strong and the weak. With regard to the "southern" lands of Africa, Asia, and Latin America, the dominant and preferred policy of each country was to foster a liberal "antiimperialism" based on respect for the integrity of self-government in these regions and a corresponding opposition to the extension of rival great power spheres of influence there; and each announced a commitment to nondiscriminatory, multilateral economic relations with these regions as a complement to its political antiimperialism. In many instances, however, such a policy amounted to liberal imperialism. For the fragility or malleability of southern social and political systems confronted by the power of Western expansion sometimes made the contact imperialist

The British Empire and the United States before World War II even when this was not the intention of London and Washington. When, by contrast, each of these states "reluctantly" acted in contradiction to its liberal principles, the usual justification was that they could not be considered operative: Either local anarchy or the ambitions of a rival great power to expand (or both) nullified the preconditions for order, thus justifying "preemptive" imperialism on the part of London or Washington. And when in direct control of a foreign land, each country generally encouraged a capitalist economy, a pluralist society, and a democratic polity (at least in the long run) roughly in line with home institutions.

Moreover, compared with many other powerful countries, Britain and America were possessed of relatively weak states with respect to the social forces they had to control. There were instances of state imperialism on the part of each country – especially when political concerns about the international configuration of power were raised and issues of national security seemed at stake – when the government determined to try to dominate the organization or the conduct of weaker peoples in Africa, Asia, or Latin America. But as a pluralist society, each country was also party to another, more informal kind of imperialism as well (one not necessarily in harmony with that sponsored by the state), whereby its private agents (the most important being economic, although religious and ethnic groups played their parts) had a strong enough influence on these areas to influence the shape of local social processes or the outcome of local political contests. In such cases, however, imperialism was not so much the product of an explicit desire on the part of the British or American governments to secure effective domination of political life in these regions as it was a function of the fragility or malleability of these societies in the face of foreign influences, the most dynamic of which were born of the industrial revolution although they included as well the impact of new ways and ideas. Imperialism was thus the consequence of three analytically distinct, although historically interrelated, forces: the particularistic demands of private interest groups in the dominant countries; the perspective of the dominant states with respect to general concerns of national security; and the strength and stability of political organization on the periphery.

Obviously there were also substantial differences between these two countries in terms of both their conduct and the international environment they confronted. Thus, the British state at all levels was far more immune to the pressures of private, partisan interests than was the American state, even if foreign economic activity was significantly more important to British well-being. Or again, the United States since 1945 has exercised its power in conjunction with strong economic allies in Western Europe and Japan – unlike Britain, which for the most part acted without trying to harmonize closely its concerns with those of its economic equals. In addition, American military planning has been more costly, complicated, and (in the nuclear age) more menacing than was Britain's. Most importantly of all, perhaps, British difficulties in Asia and Africa usually had to do with political instability in peasant kingdoms, whereas the United States has faced an altogether different order of challenge in the form of peasant revolutions in Asia and (potentially) in Latin America. If British problems with these peasant kingdoms were compounded when rival local parties bid for French, German, or Russian support, American difficulties have been typified instead by circumstances in which peasant revolutionaries with decided notions of social reorganization seemed (at least to Washington) to have an elective affinity to the Soviet Union.

Despite such qualifications about the similarities between the British and American periods, the resemblance between these two countries is particularly apparent in terms of the basic factors that determined the aggressiveness of their respective imperialist activities. For in each case, the most determined expansionist political policies would be decided upon when conditions of "anarchy" or political instability in regions of the South whose international orientation was deemed of political importance to London or Washington intersected with instability in the evolution of relations with rival great powers. By contrast, Anglo-American imperialism was most muted – content to protect its interests in indirect ways without making developments in the South matters of "high politics" – when conditions in these regions were quiet and relations with other great powers stable. Of course, between these polar, "ideal" situations lies a complex range of circumstances more or less likely to incite imperialism, as well as exceptions to the rule no general pattern can hope to account for. But as generalizations serving both to organize and to explain the historical evidence, these observations can be used to classify British and American imperialism as related species.

How, then, might we define this troublesome word "imperialism" and justify its use? Since the nineteenth century, the term has gained such partisan and pejorative connotations that there are many who with some reason maintain that it would be altogether better to ban it from use in favor of a more neutral vocabulary or a terminology more historically specific. The argument in support of its retention, however, is that the literature on imperialism constitutes a tradition of some importance in the analysis of international relations and that no better, alternative grammar exists to describe such a category of relations between the strong and the weak. By banning the word, we would risk cutting ourselves off from the richness of that literature and impoverishing our debate. The assault on the term thus comes from two sides: from those who treat imperialism as a code word stripped of nuance or complexity, to be used more as a scream of rage than as a tool of historical analysis; and from those who find all this tiresome and would prefer a more "relevant" or "objective" language, and so threaten to sterilize discussion, losing sight of the distinctiveness of relations such as those this book will examine. Let us instead attempt to resuscitate the concept of imperialism, insisting on its complexity against those who would use it in an ideologically simplistic fashion, and on its reality against those who would prefer to invent a new vocabulary. At the same time, let us hope that debate over semantics does not obscure the effort to clarify patterns in the exercise of British and American power in Africa, Asia, and Latin America since the early nineteenth century, whatever the reader's preferred nomenclature.

Imperialism may be defined as the effective domination by a relatively strong state over a weaker people whom it does not control as it does its home population, or as the effort to secure such domination. What constitutes effective domination may be difficult to decide, as the imperial power typically concerns itself with a limited range of issues, leaving to the local population its practices in other respects. Nevertheless, on a political level, imperialism may be said to exist when a weaker people cannot act with respect to what it regards as fundamental domestic or foreign concerns for fear of foreign reprisals that it believes itself unable successfully to counter. On a socioeconomic level, by contrast, imperialism exists when the local division of labor and the corresponding class relations of the weaker people can be demonstrated to have originated or to be sustained by external forces to such a degree that, failing these foreign connections, the local socioeconomic structure could not survive. When imperialism manifests itself directly, its presence is unambiguous enough: A political authority emanating from a foreign land sets itself up as locally sovereign, claiming the final right to determine and to enforce the law over a people recognized as distinct from that of the imperial homeland. But when effective domination is achieved through indirect control, then the reality of imperialism becomes more nebulous, as it would seem there is no easily agreed-upon standard to distinguish weaker forms of influence from a threshold of control indicative of imperialism. Under international law, the status of protectorate may generally be recognized as one where the subordinate state retains its sovereignty despite the exercise of paramount power by another state insofar as certain delimited questions are concerned. The British practice of indirect rule (in India or Nigeria) might be seen as a variation on this theme. But in other circumstances, when the dominant state or its agencies work informally through military or economic leverage to secure what it considers to be its chief interests in a weaker land, distinctions over where influence ends and imperialism begins may be a matter of legitimate disagreement.

Not only is the ambiguity of indirect control a problem in

the identification of imperialism, but so is the tendency to see it, as its definition implies, as a strictly bilateral relationship. Yet it must be stressed that in the cases of Britain and the United States (as well as in those of most other great powers), imperialism reflects a concern for maintaining international rank or a specific form of world order. More often than not, particular weaker countries are only counters in this larger game whose primary focus is multilateral, turned toward a concern with geopolitical issues of the balance of power. When this feature of imperialism is ignored (as it often is), the search for its causes is invariably conducted within too narrow a context, as if the behavior of the strong toward the weak alone might explain what only a study of the relationships among the powerful will tell us.

Just as I am something of a traditionalist in wanting to maintain the concept of imperialism in our discussion of modern politics, so my sympathies are with those who regret the neologisms coined with such enthusiasm in the social sciences today. Nevertheless, it has proved impossible to avoid employing certain terms of common currency in the following pages: especially "West" and "North" to refer to the "core," advanced, industrial, capitalist states, and "South" or "Third World" to label the "periphery," or developing lands of Africa, Asia, and Latin America. Core and periphery connote the international spread of the industrial revolution (as, for example, they are used in W. Arthur Lewis's *Growth and Fluctuations, 1870–1913*); but their use here is not intended to suggest the relation between puppeteer and puppet, as though the industrial states held the developing world in an iron grip (although this is the meaning intended by some). West and North are admittedly confusing ways of referring to the world of industrial capitalism, but I have tried (not always successfully) to limit the use of the former to the period before World War I, the latter to the years since 1945 (reflecting the changed status of Japan).

The most serious objections are surely to the words South and Third World. Neither China nor Korea is geographically south, and there is not an international agency today that still lumps all the developing world into a single category: The Or-

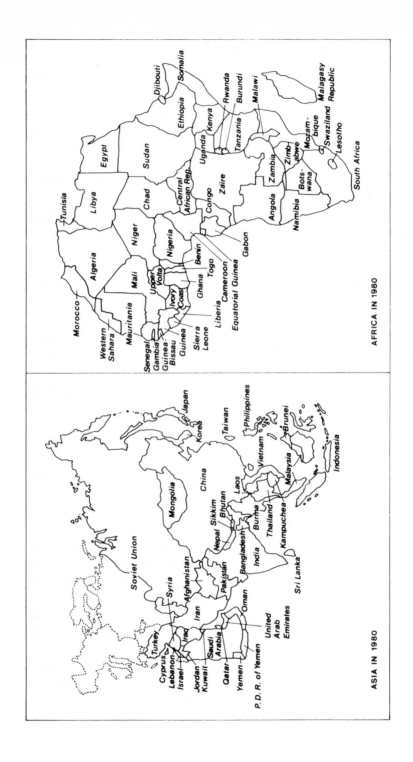

AFRICA IN 1980

ASIA IN 1980

ganization for Economic Cooperation and Development (OECD) and the World Bank presently distinguish among four or even five groups of developing countries, for example. Furthermore, it may be asked, what possible good can come from thinking about over 100 countries under a single rubric? The North may have some kind of unity in terms of its multiple joint economic agencies, its plans for a common military defense, its generally comparable political organization and (with reservations on Japan) social structures, but the unity of the South is far less tangible, despite efforts at the United Nations and through the Group of 77 and the Non-Aligned Movement. The social and political structures of, say, Brazil, Nigeria, and India exhibit far more differences than similarities, and economic indexes suggest distinctly different worlds of development: Latin America has a per capita output more than three times that of Africa (excluding South Africa), and more than five times that of East and Southeast Asia (excluding Japan), a lead reflected as well in terms of manufacturing output, energy consumption, and the like.[1] By what right can they all be referred to as South or Third World?

In important measure these objections are valid, and indeed the following chapters will try to amplify them, insisting over and again that the lands of the industrializing world are so distinct from one another that the fortunes of imperialism cannot be understood apart from careful reference to the variety of local circumstances attending there. What nevertheless unites these lands is what they are not: They are not industrially developed, regionally secure, or internally stable, for the most part, and they exist as part of an international system wherein strong states are ready to exploit these vulnerabilities in order to shape developments in these areas to their own ends. Thus, despite the relatively rapid growth of industry in the South in past decades, the some 2.15 billion people living there (excluding China), who in 1977 numbered over half the world's 4.12 billion people, probably produce no more than 10 percent of the world's total industrial output.[2] Per capita output statistics reflect this vividly: In 1976, the average per capita value of gross domestic product equaled $5,890 in the developed market economies, but only $510 in the less developed market economies ($1,220 in Latin America). More important than these economic figures, however, are the internal and regional political problems confronting virtually all Third World countries. Domestic class and ethnic conflicts have rarely or for long been contained by indigenous political institutions (although there are some important exceptions and some favorable developments), and old grievances have compounded new disputes to make for serious regional differences almost everywhere in the South. To be sure, specific structural problems are quite different; but these countries share a common situation in their need for political as well as economic development. In an international environment where great powers see interests to be realized in these weaker areas, and where deep and long-standing antagonisms exist between the superpowers, to be weak is to be threatened by imperialism. In this sense, it is appropriate to speak of the unity of the South or the Third World, even if in other respects these countries are radically dissimilar.

Chapters 1 and 2 deal for the most part with imperialism in the century before World War I, the period of British international hegemony. Chapter 3, on decolonization, reviews the decline of this order, chiefly through a survey of the kinds of Third World regimes created in the aftermath of European empire. Chapter 4 analyzes the pattern of American policy toward the South since the Republic's founding, but with emphasis on the years since 1940, and Chapter 5 looks at the state of these relations in 1980, following a decade of rapid change in the structure of world affairs. In an appended Note, I have considered the question of morality and American imperialism, an issue of concern to many in the United States who nonetheless appear to have limited empirical information at their disposal and whose discussions thus often appear rather abstract, if not irrelevant. Throughout this study, my effort has been to select the most significant determinants of British and American policy toward the South, to assign weights of relative importance to them, and to indicate the character of their interaction in a comparative historical manner. At the same time, I have given equal attention to patterns of political development in Africa, Asia, and Latin America, persuaded as I am that the countries of these regions have an identity of their own that affects not only their own condition but also the structure of the international system. This latter proposition is particularly neglected in the study of imperialism, to its detriment in analytical terms. For if there is nothing novel in calling attention to the ability of domestic interests to promote northern imperialism, and if it is becoming more common that analysts appreciate the role of the international system as such in influencing the course of imperialism, it is much less usual to find attempts to synthesize these two approaches, and rarer still that the contribution of southern areas is recognized in these processes.[3]

The approach adopted in the following pages is that of comparative history. In itself, such a method is able neither to evaluate the quality of a problem a researcher poses nor to suggest theoretical answers to its solution. It is equally at home with Marxist or psychoanalytic interpretations of history, as compatible with the pursuit of trivial as of significant questions. What the comparative historical method does provide, on the other hand, is a way of finding and sorting evidence and of checking the logic of propositions advanced to account for causal sequences. It is particularly useful in studies such as that of imperialism, in which a wide variety of cases calls out for some general ordering explanations that make sense of their diversity in terms of positing relatively consistent historical patterns. Two modes of analysis are most commonly practiced. One of these seeks to establish general propositions by finding evidence of their validity in a variety of separate cases. In other words, similar findings from otherwise diverse cases tend to confirm theoretical propositions. Thus, to establish the nature of political considerations behind American imperialism and their role relative to economic factors, we might examine a number of different situations to see what they have in common, what holds true from case to case. By contrast, the other mode of analysis looks for differences in spite of similarities and thereby seeks to ascertain the character of variations within the general pattern. For example, decolonization was a general historical movement, but the differences within it were significant. By admitting these variations and attempting to make sense of them, we may see the general pattern more complexly and hence, we may hope, more clearly and faithfully as well. In short, the first mode of analysis works best to establish the general features of imperialism, the second to delineate its more specific or individualized characteristics. In the pages that follow, both approaches will be used repeatedly.[4]

There is a tendency today in the social sciences, however, to rely too heavily on the comparative method and to miss a decisive isolated event or the force of a cumulative development that a more linear, historical approach alone provides. Consider, for example, the mark that the Korean War left on American policy toward radicalism in the Third World by seeming to seal the failure of America's China policy after 1945. Studies relying on comparisons alone might miss such a turning point. An appreciation of cumulative developments, on the other hand, obliges us to think in a global fashion, which the piecemeal approach of comparative studies might actually discourage (as if the parts adequately reflected the logic of the whole). In short, the comparative approach to the study of imperialism must not be separated from the historical account of its development, with due respect for the distinctiveness of time and place.

Whatever its inevitable shortcomings in the treatment of specific cases, this book will have achieved its purpose if it encourages more dialogue among those who are concerned with understanding the logic of imperialism but who tend to remain somewhat parochial in their approach, either by virtue of the analytical tools they choose to employ or as a result of the limited scope they give to their studies. A more fruitful debate should be on the agenda, one that would permit experts on the nineteenth century to talk with those on the twentieth century, Africanists with Latin Americanists, "structuralists" with traditional diplomatic historians, Marxists with those who favor more strictly political theories in the analysis of international affairs. Too often these various departments of knowledge fail to appreciate how much they have to learn from, and to offer to, one another. Work on the study of imperialism will best proceed when these barriers to exchange have fallen so that new investigations, based on a cross-fertilization of the wealth of approaches and on evidence already on hand, will be encouraged to appear.

Of course the effort to view affairs more complexly may result in an unfortunate eclecticism of explanations that confuses as much as it clarifies. For example, perhaps the best-known American college textbook on modern history presents the reasons for European overseas expansion in the nineteenth century in the following terms: "Imperialism arose from the commercial, industrial, financial, scientific, political, journalistic, intellectual, religious and humanitarian impulses of Europe compounded together."[5] Clearly, depending on time and place, very different factors predominated in this movement: economic agencies (as in the Congo or South Africa); strategic considerations (as in the occupation of Egypt); bureaucratic – usually military – initiatives (as in French West Africa); and domestic political calculations (as in German East Africa). But the major problem is to give relative weights to these factors, to see their interrelationships over time, and to develop the ability to recognize the general movement and its specific autonomous parts without losing sight of either.

The essential analytical problem is at once to avoid different forms of reductionism and yet to keep balance and proportion among the manifold factors that are to be considered. Two forms of reductionism are the most prevalent: that which collapses the political dimension into the economic (or vice versa); and that which insists on seeing the "part" (for example, local developments in the South) in terms of the "whole" (the developmental logic attributed to the workings of the international system). Reductionism is by no means a simpleminded affair, however. Part of the problem in coming to any general agreement on the nature of British and American imperialism lies in the ability of different reductionist camps to spin out concepts supple enough to account for virtually any piece of history according to their respective orthodox canons. This proclivity is compounded by the inherent complexity of the issues under consideration. Thus, geopolitical matters pertaining to the common good may sometimes be seen as clearly distinct from particularistic interests such as private economic concerns. At other times, however, these separate domains – the public and the private, the political and the economic – may become so interwoven that they can only be understood in combination, even if the degree of their relative importance can still be debated.

These observations might be kept in mind in efforts to analyze three distinct areas of action that, this study suggests, best classify the multiple forces contributing to the patterns of British and American imperialism: the character of private, domestic forces in Britain and the United States and the pressures they can mobilize to secure a foreign policy that suits their interests; the perspective of the British and American states on the nature of the international balance of power and on what would best be done for the sake of the national interest; and the political stability of governments in Africa, Asia, and Latin America in the face of internal, regional, and global challenges to their rule. Each of these analytically distinct areas exercises its pressure on the others, setting in motion a chain of reciprocal causation whereby each transforms the others as it too is transformed. Yet, at the same time, each dimension reveals its own concrete organizational form with its own internal "laws of motion," be they economic, political, or psychological. Each dimension must therefore be understood in its own terms as well as in conjunction with the others. To admit the partial separateness of these areas, however, opens the door for accident or coincidence in the intersection of forces, and thus for randomness or chance in the history of imperialism. Yet to admit this is not to deny the existence of structure or pattern in British and American imperialism in the years since 1815. What the chief traits of these imperialisms are, and how they might best be explained, is the subject of this book.

1

The dynamics of imperialism: the perspective of a century, 1815–1914

The intention of this chapter is not so much to bring new evidence to bear on the character of European, primarily British, imperialism before World War I as it is to sort through once again the material already collected by a number of distinguished historians for the purpose of addressing the perennial question of the forces lying behind imperialism. Such an effort may be useful to sharpen the focus of the debate over the character of imperialism between 1815 and 1914, as well as to enrich the categories by which we analyze the relations since World War II between the United States and the countries of Asia, Africa, and Latin America.

What makes the century prior to World War I so interesting for comparative study is that it divides rather neatly into two periods, during each of which a different mode of influence was dominant in shaping the relationships between the industrial (or fast-industrializing) core countries of Europe and North America and the preindustrial world. These periods may, then, be compared with one another as well as with the years of American international hegemony following World War II. The first period corresponds to London's international preeminence, which based itself on the supremacy of the British navy and the dynamism British commerce drew from the industrial revolution. It lasted from Napoleon's defeat in 1815 until approximately the last quarter of the century. During this time, the dominant processes shaping the relationship between the two areas were economic, stemming from the overseas expansion of the industrial revolution begun in England at the end of the eighteenth century.

During these years, British policy toward the preindustrial world progressively came to be characterized by the practice of concluding nondiscriminatory commercial agreements (the "open door" typified by most-favored-nation clauses) and by an opposition to territorial annexations. According to the beliefs of the time, an international division of labor in production based on comparative advantage would work to create a better-integrated, richer, and more harmonious world. In the process, Britain articulated a doctrine that had meaning for its concept of world order and its relations with the other great powers as well as for its conduct toward different parts of Africa, Asia, and Latin America. Peace and progress would complement one another as the nations of Europe cooperated, drawing up to them the peoples of other lands. Yet if in theory British policy were "antiimperialist," in practice the political regimes of many southern regions proved so fragile (as in the Ottoman Empire) or so malleable (as in Argentina) that the impact of British commerce backed by its navy amounted to liberal imperialism despite the genuine aversion of the British state to a forward policy there. Economic expansion was transmuted by circumstance into imperialism.

By the last quarter of the nineteenth century, however, the weight of these economic pressures began to be superseded by an imperialism inspired by political calculations, the so-called new imperialism, which by its name harkened back to the centuries before 1815 when European states were mercantilist, annexationist, and belligerent. As Britain's relative strength declined, the pace of contests among the Europeans accelerated, and in the process issues concerning the preindustrial world became matters of great power rivalry, of "high" politics. More active European intervention thus came to replace the relatively passive policies and indirect economic means of influence characteristic of the earlier years of the century. Accordingly, the dominant processes shaping the relationship between the strong and the weak became predominantly political, reflecting especially balance of power considerations. Thereafter, by a process of political adaptation, the same power factors in international relations that encouraged alliances among the strong also prompted imperialism toward the weak. To make matters worse, at somewhat the same time – and despite the efforts of Britain, in most cases, to stabilize the situation – the disintegration of political regimes in much of Africa and Asia became more acute for reasons independent of the European rivalry, thereupon feeding the fires of European competition while aggravating local conditions by prompting intensified foreign interventions. In short order, London's antiimperialism gave way to a deliberate new policy of preemptive annexations.

The juxtaposition of these two periods is particularly interesting as each illustrates rather dramatically the force of processes that often are so intermixed as to be difficult to distinguish. In the case of American policy toward the Third World since 1945, for example, there are those who stress the influence of the country's capitalist economic structure, whereas others insist on the nature of the confrontation with the Soviet Union in an effort to explain Washington's role. Each party tends to minimize (if not to debunk entirely) the analysis of the other. By seeing that economic and political processes in the North and South are to a certain extent independent of one another, as a study of European imperialism in the century before World War I demonstrates, it may be possible to present more fruitful accounts of United States policy since 1945, taking into account the variety of forces in operation. Such an undertaking will be postponed until Chapter 4, however. Here and in the following chapter, the concern is the review the wealth of literature assembled on imperialism between 1815 and 1914 with the hope of better understanding these historical developments in their own right while seeking to establish in a comparative fashion certain useful generalizations about both this period and the conduct of the United States in later years.

The course of economic imperialism

Whether it was in the service of God or for the pursuit of gold – the quest for the kingdom of Prester John or for that of El

Dorado – the tremendous overseas expansion of Europe that began in the fifteenth century was intended to promote the power of the states that sponsored it while satisfying the personal ambitions of the men who carried it forth. But the long-term consequence was far more complex and dramatic than was understood at the time. In 1492, as every schoolchild knows, Christopher Columbus discovered the route to the Western Hemisphere; five years later, Vasco da Gama rounded the tip of Africa and arrived in India. Although the earlier trade routes from Venice through the Arab Middle East rapidly declined as a result of these contacts, it soom became apparent that far more than a simple reorientation of trade was at issue. First as Portuguese and Spanish, then as Dutch, later as French and British, and finally as North Americans, the "Europeans" were drawing all parts of the world into an increasingly integrated political and economic whole.

From the very beginning, the basis of European imperialism was superior force: From the gunned ship of the sixteenth century to the gunned helicopter of today, advanced military technology has undergirded this expansive drive. Within the ring held by European military superiority, these southern areas were penetrated, when it was possible, politically and economically. The political dimension of the process primarily involved the fostering of networks of local native actors willing to work with the international system and, in areas of direct control, the creation as well of elaborate bureaucracies (in Latin America in the sixteenth century, in Asia and Africa in the nineteenth). But it was through the incorporation of these lands into the world economy through specialization in the division of labor that Europe affected these lands most deeply and permanently.

Plunder, such as that of the Aztecs and the Incas in the sixteenth century, or of Bengal in the eighteenth, was on the whole exceptional. Rather, in order better to serve their own needs, the Europeans tried to encourage forms of local social organization appropriate to international commerce. Of course, this too occasioned great human suffering, from the silver mines of Mexico to the slave coasts of Africa to the famines in Ireland.

But unlike plunder, these reorderings of society profoundly influenced the social organization of the world as we know it today. Such developments were gradual, to be sure; but today, half a millenium since these contacts were first made in the late fifteenth century, the northern states of Western Europe and the United States, associated now with Japan, remain at the heart of world affairs, their political, economic and military might continuing to be of decisive importance to a South still relatively backward technologically and thus still vulnerable to their demands.

In the sixteenth century, the European overseas impact was greatest in Latin America, where, in a remarkably short length of time, the Spanish and Portuguese had organized the region politically and had either pressed the local population into supporting their conquerors through the *encomienda* system (in the Spanish territories) or developed plantations based on slave labor (as in Brazil and the Caribbean). In the East, by contrast, local forces were far too strong at this time to permit much of a European occupation. Instead, following the strategy devised by Alfonso Albuquerque, the Portuguese contented themselves with beachheads established in certain key places: Ormuz, Goa, Malacca, and Macao were set up under their rule between 1498 and 1514. Sailing west from South America, the Spanish took the Philippines in 1521 (although it was nearly five decades before the profitable trade link between Manila and Canton developed). The seventeenth century saw the displacement of the Portuguese in the Orient by the Dutch, whose headquarters was at Batavia, and it witnessed as well the gradual expansion of slavery. But it was not until the eighteenth century that the slave trade reached its height, serving as the basis for the so-called Triangular Trade between Europe, Africa, and the West Indies, and deeply affecting the society and economy of the west coast of Africa and the Americas from Virginia to Brazil. It was in this century as well that the Dutch and the British began to shape the Orient more significantly than before, the Dutch by the promotion of plantation crops such as sugar and coffee on Java, and the British by their military victories in 1757 and 1764, which destroyed the Great

Mogul in Delhi and set them up as the paramount power on the Indian subcontinent. During the nineteenth century, the resistances of the rest of the southern parts of the globe to European influence were decisively breached: The Chinese and Ottoman empires found themselves unable to counter the foreign advances (now including those of Russia), Japan was opened, and Africa partitioned. By the close of the nineteenth century, four hundred years of Western expansion had united the globe so that local histories and world history became increasingly difficult to discriminate from one another.

To speak of world history in the nineteenth century is to speak of Great Britain. Despite Britain's inability to maintain control over its North American colonies after 1783, victory over Napoleon in 1815 left no other power present around the globe. In addition to the territories held before the Napoleonic Wars – including Canada, India, the Straits Settlements, Australia (New South Wales), Gibraltar, forts along the west coast of Africa, and numerous islands in the West Indies as well as in other waters – the struggle had given Britain control of additional lands as well: principally the Cape of Good Hope, Ceylon, Malta, and Mauritius. With the addition of Singapore (1819) and Aden (1839), Britain possessed a network of strategic bases that commanded the sea lanes of the world and that knit the lands under its rule into the most far-flung empire in history. How was it that such an extended range of commitments worked to Britain's advantage and did not instead tend to overtax it?

Three major historical factors explain the preeminence Britain could enjoy in world politics on the basis of these possessions during the three-quarters of a century following Waterloo. There was first the unquestioned supremacy of the British navy. Despite the magnitude of the area the navy had to patrol, it could concentrate its forces so as to maintain an overwhelming superiority whatever the challenge.[1] British land forces, by contrast, were quite modest in size so that the regions under London's influence, exception made for India with its large army, tended to be those where naval strength could be brought to bear with relative ease. Secondly, Britain was homeland of the industrial revolution, so that well into the nineteenth century its machine-made goods dominated world markets. Overseeing until the last quarter of the nineteenth century nearly one-third of the world's commerce, and commanding a far greater total of the capital available for loans and investment, London was the economic capital of the world.[2] Because the needs of its industry called for more raw materials and a wider market than the home islands could provide, Britain's economic vocation complemented its naval supremacy. And finally, Britain's position depended on the fragmentation of political power on the Continent, whose unity and opposition alone seemed able to threaten the British order of things. Acting as the "balancer" in European politics, as it had done in the past, London helped to ensure the division of the Continent throughout the century.

What, then, of British conduct toward Africa, Asia, and Latin America: Is it possible, or useful, to characterize it as imperialist? During this period no military caste or great power rivalry existed to spur imperialism on, so that if it existed its motive would appear to be largely economic. This is not to deny how important political considerations may be for imperialism, or to assert that the British state was simply the tool of domestic economic interests. But it would tend to establish that private and national economic concerns possessed enough importance to secure the active support of the state abroad. This had been, of course, a basic assumption of mercantilism before the rise of free trade, and it would seem that the practice survived in modified form even if the rhetoric of the times tried to disguise it.

In their 1953 essay on the "imperialism of free trade," John Gallagher and Ronald Robinson argue that in the midnineteenth century, Britain created an "informal empire" characterized by economic linkages that served the needs of economic actors in Europe at the same time as they served those of client elites on the periphery.[3] The process was especially successful in Latin America, where local social organization proved able to adapt to the opportunities provided by British trade and investment. In other areas, however, penetration with the assistance of local elites was less likely and instead the established political systems tended to disintegrate, as in China, the Ottoman Empire, and the west coast of Africa. Thus, for example, Britain hoped to build up the Ottoman Empire against Russia by means of international trade and investment, as well as by timely interventions, such as that against Mehemet Ali (1840–1) and against Russia during the Crimean War (1854–6). By 1878, however, when Turkey showed itself too weak to stop renewed Russian advances, the powers decided on a limited partition in order to guarantee the job for themselves. By the terms of the Congress of Berlin, Austria took Bosnia and Herzegovina, Britain received Cyprus, and the French were promised Tunisia. Four years later, the British felt obliged to occupy Egypt. "Informal empire" had proved a frail reed in Mediterranean politics. Whether the process was successful, as in Latin America, or not, as in the Near East, the economic impact of Europe on these lands was of such intensity that, according to this view, it should be called imperialist.

The most pertinent objections to be made to such usage of the terms "imperialism" and "informal empire" have to do with their definitions as well as with the reality of the process they claim to describe. Do Gallagher and Robinson not exaggerate the political and economic strength available to, or mobilized by, the British in mid-Victorian times, and do they not overestimate the capacity of elites in any of these peripheral areas to integrate themselves at all securely into such a system? Lenin, it might be recalled, used the term "semi-colony" somewhat like "informal empire" is used, to refer to countries such as Argentina whose dependence on Britain was great whatever the juridical status of the relationship. But Lenin was writing of the period after 1880.[4] As D. C. M. Platt cogently points out, case after case may be cited where the British government refused to intervene on behalf of its traders or bondholders abroad during this time, preferring to avoid the liabilities of direct involvement rather than to secure the immediate interests of its petitioners:

It is not true, for example, that H.M. Government was prepared to exercise informal control in Latin America, whatever the provocation, and the examples quoted by Gallagher and Robinson go nowhere to prove their case. Nor could it be said that "informal control" applied even to China; officials confined themselves to objectives (in opening China to world trade) well below the expectations of the merchants and financiers, and slight attempt was made to exercise control over the internal affairs of the Empire – beneficial though such control would undoubtedly have been to British trade.[5]

Moreover, before 1860 at the earliest, world trade and investment in southern countries simply did not seem to amount to enough, either from the point of view of the weaker countries or from the standpoint of London, to constitute ties of genuine influence. It was only after 1860, with the development of the railway and under the full impact of the repeal of the Corn and Navigation Laws (1846 and 1849), that Britain – with Brazil, Argentina, Egypt, and Turkey – began to seal the links making them increasingly dependent upon the international economic system.[6] It was later still, and then less intensely, that these kinds of economic ties were created with China, as loans were not contracted there in any amount until after 1894, as the compradors of the treaty ports were never important in internal politics, and as trade with the outside world never represented more than a small fraction of the Chinese net national product.[7]

In order to illustrate this debate, let us consider the case of Argentina, where, well before the end of the century, British trade and investment were particularly well established. As I agree with the general lines of the position taken by Gallagher and Robinson and believe that the economic impact of Britain on the South merits the term imperialism (despite the import of Platt's objections), I propose to examine the case of Argentina strictly in the light of the evidence provided by H. S. Ferns, an authority in the field who is opposed to their view and who would seem more favorable to the approach indicated by Platt. In the words of Ferns:

Can the term imperialism be applied to Anglo-Argentine relations? If we accept the proposition that imperialism embraces the fact of control through the use of political power, then the verdict is unquestionably "Not Guilty" ... The Argentine Government has always possessed the power to forbid, to encourage, or to shape the economic relations of Argentina with other communities including the British community. The British Government has never had the power to oblige Argentina to pay a debt, to pay a dividend, or to export or import any commodity whatever. The only occasion when the British Government went beyond talk in dealing with Argentina, during the troubled time of General Rosas, they were defeated and they formally admitted that they were defeated. When powerful financial interests urged the use of political power to influence Argentine economic policy in 1891 the British Foreign Secretary privately and publicly repudiated such a suggestion. Every crisis in the economic and financial relations of Britain and Argentina has been resolved in economic and financial terms – by a weighing of advantages and disadvantages of both parties – and not by the intrusion of political power.[8]

Is this not, however, a decidedly narrow construction of the term imperialism? If we can maintain, for example, that the international system, run under British auspices so far as Argentina was concerned, fostered and then sustained the economic organization of this South American country, and that in turn the dominant class that emerged from this process controlled the Argentine state, then we might agree that imperialism existed despite the fact that London itself did not directly intervene to control the decisions of the Argentine government. Certainly Ferns provides evidence aplenty that precisely such a process was at work; it is rather that he prefers not to call it imperialism. Yet he writes:

One may deplore the consequences for Argentina, and likewise the consequences for Britain, of this kind of relationship worked out by the Argentine landed and commercial interests of Great Britain . . . If, over a long span of time, Argentina has possessed a weak and narrowly based industrial structure compared with that of the United States or even Canada, this has been due to the concentration of effort in Argentina upon agricultural and pastoral enterprise and upon the production of pastoral and agricultural commodities. Political power and/or decisive influence upon policy in Argentina has belonged until recent times to the interests with most to gain by such a concentration.[9]

Nor is Ferns at all ambivalent about the role Britain had in encouraging such a development. Writing of the difficult period between 1852 and 1862, during which the stability and development given to Argentina by General Rosas since 1835 had been overturned by civil strife, Ferns makes it clear that the British recognized they had a common cause with those

Argentine forces favoring a united, economically liberal future for their country:

Always at the centre and sometimes at the edge of this confusing and changing scene, we find a succession of British diplomatic agents urging moderation upon the actors in their most ferocious moods, tripping up some as they advanced and giving others a shove in the direction they conceived to be right. There was nothing haphazard or random in their tripping and pushing, however, for they obeyed that grand design of policy planned by Castlereagh.[10]

This was quite consciously a "diplomacy to end diplomacy;" a diplomacy that would let the strength and momentum of automatic economic processes conduct future Anglo-Argentine relations. The policy was "triumphant":

The determination of the British Government to ally itself politically with the Confederation and to apply pressure to Buenos Aires Province both for the purpose of altering its independent course in the direction of incorporation in the Republic and for the collection of the Loan of 1824 may be properly regarded as one of the critical events in the history of the Argentine community. Had Buenos Aires succeeded in maintaining its political independence it would have been obliged, at least in the formative stages, to undertake its own capital accumulation. The social, political, and economic consequences of this would have been profound, for it would have been the means of creating in the richest and most compact productive area of Argentina a class of financiers and entrepreneurs dominant in their own community and independent of others. On a smaller scale there would have been created a class of similar character to that which existed in the United States. . . . As it was, the eventual integration of Buenos Aires Province in the Republic placed the financial resources of the richest area at the disposal of the whole Republic, and made these resources the means of financing vast railway schemes . . . This investment was encouraged . . . by the dominant landed interests, which saw in the process advantages to themselves both in economic benefits and political power . . . A geographically more concentrated development confined to the Province of Buenos Aires and the southern pampas . . . would have been not only less burdensome but might have led to a more balanced economic and industrial development. As it was, saddled with a vast foreign investment, Argentina was obliged to export or go bankrupt, and this meant concentration upon a limited range of exportable staple products with all the social and political, not to mention moral and intellectual consequences of intense specialization in an agricultural and pastoral setting.[11]

If I have gone on at some length with respect to Ferns's book, it is because of its deserved high reputation and because of the good illustration it provides of the problems encountered in defining the term imperialism. Clearly, for Ferns (as for Platt), Britain's general policy, implemented for the most part indirectly through economic agencies and the "tripping and pushing" where possible of local politicians, should not be construed to constitute imperialism. In my opinion, by contrast, the same evidence dictates a different conclusion: Because the distribution and stability of power (economic, social, and political) in Argentina depended heavily on the structure of an international system that it could do nothing to control and that functioned in good measure (at least insofar as Argentina was concerned) in line with British will and ability, the connection may legitimately be called imperialist. Indeed, even had the effort to create such a structure failed, it might still be called imperialist. And even though Platt objects to the use of the term, he observes that from an early point in the century "the Government recognized its duty to open world markets to British trade and to protect legitimate trade in these markets once opened: British policy in China, Japan and Latin America was wholly determined by this duty and policy in the Levant and North Africa, if very much more closely tied to conventional political aims, depended to a lesser degree on an official engagement to smooth the way for British trade."[12] The important point, however, is to avoid becoming too deeply enmeshed in quarrels of definition. Whatever the preferred nomenclature the reality of the power relationship should be seen, as clearly as possible, as it actually was.

The thrust of British commercial policy after about 1820 was increasingly in the direction of free trade. In place of narrow, competitive mercantilism with its practices of colonial annexation and protectionist tariffs, Free Trade Britain proclaimed the doctrine of prosperity with peace through an international economic division of labor based on comparative advantage in production. Adam Smith had laid out the logic of the plan in 1776 in *The Wealth of Nations* and his successors in Britain (and later in the United States) refined and expanded it thereafter. Economic superiority and the ideology of laissez-faire

Table 1. *British commerce by destination/provenance as a percentage of total British trade*

	1860		1913	
	Imports	Exports	Imports	Exports
Latin America	9	9	10	11
Africa (total)	8	4	6	10
South Africa	1	1	2	4
Asia (total)	14	17	12	24
India	8	11	6	13

were not of themselves, of course, enough to ensure the British order of things. The other essential ingredient was the unquestioned naval supremacy of the country: the knowledge of nations weak and strong that Britain commanded the oceans. British products, British ideas, and the British navy: From the defeat of Napoleon until at least the 1880s, these were to stand as the pillars of the world order known as the Pax Britannica and to define the basic aspects of what became, as the century progressed, an increasingly complex structure of relations between the rapidly industrializing states of Europe and North America and the preindustrial lands of Asia, Africa, and Latin America. Yet of these three ingredients of British power, the most crucial with respect to these southern lands was the impact of British commerce.

"The cheap prices of its commodities are the heavy artillery with which [European capitalism] batters down all Chinese walls, with which it forces the barbarians' intensely obstinate hatred of foreigners to capitulate," as Marx put it in his famous lines of 1847. So between 1840 and 1913, world trade grew from some $2.8 billion to $38.2 billion (American billion), with Britain as the world's largest trader.[13] The relative place of the preindustrial world in this process is suggested by the data shown in Table 1.[14] The figures for overseas investment are equally important. Although it has recently been questioned whether indeed the amounts were so great, it has been estimated that in 1825, just under $1 billion were invested abroad (almost all of this by the British or the Dutch). By 1870, this sum had grown to just under $8 billion, and by World War I it had reached nearly $39 billion (American billion).[15] British investments represented approximately half of these totals throughout this period. By 1914, some 20 percent of British investments were in Latin America, 5 percent in the Middle East and Asia, and 23 percent within the empire (excluding Canada and Australia).[16]

Although, as we shall see below, it is possible to maintain that for the period under consideration this commerce was of growing importance to the European states, it would seem reasonable to conclude that it was also of great significance to the lives of Africa, Asia, and Latin America. In Asia, for example, the great port cities of Bombay, Madras, Calcutta, Manila, Batavia, Colombo, Rangoon, Singapore, and Saigon, all of which in large measure had been created by the stimulus of contact with European traders, came as the nineteenth century progressed to have a growing effect on their hinterlands as magnets for economic development. Even where this was less the case, as in China, where the treaty ports had relatively little impact on the rest of the country, the change could be startling: Shanghai is estimated to have had, by 1832, a volume of shipping equal to or greater than that of London.[17] In the Middle East, Charles Issawi reports, "foreign enterprise dug the Suez Canal; developed the ports of Port Said, Beirut, Haider Pasha, Mersin, and Alexandretta; built the Berlin-Baghdad and Syrian railways, as well as the light railways in Egypt; and provided gas, electricity, and water in Istanbul, Alexandria, Cairo, Beirut, Damascus, Baghdad, and other cities."[18] As Herbert Feis concludes:

In 1870, the eyes of China watched only the slow movement of native junks down inland rivers; the tired traveler was jounced in stagecoaches from the fever-stricken coast to the plateau on which Mexico City stands; the rushlights or candles of antiquity still burned in the houses along the Bosphorus Straits. In 1914, the locomotive speeded on heavy rails to the Siberian coast and into the heart of China; four railways entered Mexico City; power plants sent the electric light that was reflected in the Straits; all had been provided by foreign capital.[19]

Compared with the rate at which the discoveries of the agricultural revolution, or those of the age of bronze and iron, spread through human society, the influence of the industrial revolution was as lightning: Within little more than a century – some four generations – it had profoundly affected virtually every economic, social, and political organization on earth. Old economic and social relations had disappeared or had been transformed as new ones arose, and the political face of the globe (in domestic as well as international terms) changed more quickly and inalterably than ever before. Little wonder, then, that from the perspective of the South the economic expansion of the North would appear to be the critical element in modern imperialism.

As was earlier indicated, this commerce did not move in a political or power vacuum. The supremacy of the British navy was not for a moment in doubt, and this knowledge could be used to gain or to guarantee commercial agreements in the South of definite and growing importance to all the parties involved. For over two hundred years before Napoleon's defeat, Britain had been engaged in a series of contests with the Continental powers for paramount influence with respect to commerce in these regions and now it had completely triumphed. The first area in which the new policy was applied was Spanish America, where the newly independent republics were seeking to make good their separation from Madrid. "Only England, mistress of the seas, can protect us against the united force of European reaction," declared Simón Bolívar, and it was precisely this that Foreign Secretary Canning proceeded to do when he warned the French that Great Britain would not tolerate an effort to extend their occupation of Spain in 1823 (to restore the monarchy of Ferdinand VII) to a reimposition of European rule in South America.[20] British recognition of the independent republics typically took the form of commercial agreements binding the Latin American states to free trade. Although Britain did not question the right of these sovereign states to impose such taxes and tariffs as they saw fit, it did encourage them to keep such levies low lest the advantages of free trade be lost. What Britain did insist upon in the name of free trade was that British commerce gain entry to these countries on an equal footing with the trade of other countries, and that once established, British traders be treated in a nondiscriminatory fashion relative to domestically owned business.[21]

By formal agreements reached with Turkey in 1838 and with China in 1842 and 1858, Britain infringed upon local sovereignty substantially more than it had in Latin America. In both instances, tariff levels were set by international conventions, to be modified only with the consent of all the contracting parties. And tariff levels were low: Most items imported into Turkey under the Convention of 1838 and into China under the Treaties of 1842 and 1858 paid a duty of only 5 percent, on which no additional excise taxes could be levied. Other concessions of an economic nature were made to Britain as well. Thus, the Sublime Porte agreed to disband its rather elaborate system of state monopolies in favor of free trade, and the Chinese were made to cede Hong Kong and open an expanding number of treaty ports to foreign commerce. At the same time, the Capitulations in Turkey and the grants of extraterritoriality in China gave Europeans in these countries special privileges that especially rankled local pride.[22] (In Latin America, by contrast, the only privilege generally accorded foreigners was religious freedom.) Of course, the British expectation was that local economic growth would be accelerated and political stability enhanced. So Foreign Secretary Palmerston could hope that "commerce may go freely forth, leading civilization with one hand and peace with the other, to render mankind happier, wiser, better."[23] But the result in the Ottoman Empire and China (as well as along the west coast of Africa) was that this commerce tended to dislocate the established social structure. Eugene Staley provides a series of illustrations of this process in the case of China, for example. In one instance:

The first railway, for example, was laid between Shanghai and Woosung (twelve miles) in 1875. The permit issued by Chinese authorities made plain that only animals were to be used as motive power, but Messrs. Jardine and Company, ignoring the protests of the natives, soon installed a steam locomotive. All the prejudices of the conservative Chinese culture were aroused. The populace feared for the graves of ancestors . . . No sooner was the road in operation than the porters, carters, wheel-barrow men, and others dependent upon the old carrying service between Shanghai and Woosung found their occupation gone. With starvation staring them in the face they rose in desperation.[24]

Similarly, David Landes recounts Egypt's experience in dealing with the influx of foreign loans and investments in the mid-nineteenth century:

Some of these enterprises were legitimate ventures . . . Some were frauds. Some enterprises were large and more or less permanent . . . But all were designed to exploit the needs of Egypt and the weakness and ignorance of the Egyptian government. All aimed at making the most of a good thing, imposing one-sided conditions and charging exorbitant fees. All were intended to yield exceptional, even fabulous, profits, although it must be admitted that results did not always meet expectations . . . Egyptian society did not contain the entrepreneurs, investors, or engineers to effect an economic revolution . . . Only Europeans could supply the capital and skill to implant the techniques and structures of Western civilization. The Europeans knew it too, and they demanded and received every farthing the traffic could bear.[25]

Between the onset of the Crimean War and 1875, Turkey contracted an external public debt of some 200 million Turkish pounds, only 10 percent of which went to economic development. The rest went into military expenditures, private extravagances of the sovereign, and the service of loans earlier engaged. At the same time, the country was in balance-of-trade deficit. Egypt, for its part, saw its external public debt rise from 3.3 million Egyptian pounds in 1863 to 91 million in 1875, although its balance of trade was strongly positive (from 1873 to 1874, it ran a 9.5 million pound surplus). When these states defaulted, the Europeans moved in. Turkey's case was complicated by its recent defeat by Russia and the Russian demand for indemnities. As we have seen, the Congress of Berlin of 1878 provided for the partial dismemberment of the Ottoman Empire. In 1881, as a consequence of the financial imbroglio, the creditor powers took further action. Foreigners were placed in charge of certain Turkish state monopolies, excise taxes, and customs, as well as put in receivership of the annual tribute of Bulgaria (which was never paid). In the case of Egypt, local resistance to European demands brought a confrontation that ultimately produced the British occupation of that country.[26] It was none other than President Woodrow Wilson who recognized the extent to which loans of this sort amounted to imperialism. Commenting on his refusal to allow American participation in a banking consortium that was lending to China, he declared in 1913:

The conditions of the loan seem to us to touch very nearly the administrative independence of China itself, and this administration does not feel that it ought, even by implication, to be a party to those conditions. The responsibility on its part which would be implied in requesting the bankers to undertake the loan might conceivably go to the length in some unhappy contingency of forcible interference in the financial, and even the political, affairs of that great oriental State, just now awakening to a consciousness of its power and of its obligations to its people. The conditions include not only the pledging of particular taxes, some of them antiquated and burdensome, to secure the loan, but also the administration of those taxes by foreign agents. The responsibility on the part of the Government implied in the encouragement of a loan thus secured and administered is plain enough and is obnoxious to the principles upon which the government of our people rests.[27]

Commerce was, in short, backed by the flag. It is true that British naval appropriations fell in the years between Waterloo and the Crimean War, and that naval commanders themselves did not like to consider their mission to be that of servants to commercial interests. It is also the case that to some states the power of the navy was an inducement to enter into business – not from the threat of coercion so much as from the hope for additional gain. Thus, most Latin Americans saw the British navy as a protector of their sovereignty, and the Sublime Porte had reason to appreciate British assistance in warding off the Russians and disciplining insurgent vassals such as Mehemet Ali. But as Foreign Secretary Palmerston put it in a private note in 1850 (the year he embargoed and then seized Greek ships in the port of Piraeus after a British subject, Don Pacifico, could not get satisfaction for his claims against the Greek government):

These half civilized Governments such as those of China, Portugal, and Spanish America, all require a dressing every eight or ten years to keep them in order. Their morals are too shallow to receive an impression that will last longer than some such period and warning is of little use. They care little for words and they must not only see the stick but actually feel it on their shoulders before they yield to that only argument which to them brings conviction, the *Argumentum Baculinum*.[28]

Indeed, despite the mid-Victorian bias against annexations, they certainly could occur, as the political leaders of Latin America, Asia, and Africa were well aware. Although it was in the last quarter of the century that the great "scrambles" for territory occurred, the years between 1815 and 1878 (the Congress of Berlin) saw their share of European expansion. France entered Turkey's tribute state of Algeria in 1830, Senegal in 1854, China's sphere of influence in Cochin China in 1858, and Mexico from 1861 to 1863. Russian expansion carved away at the possessions of Turkey, Persia, and China. And antiimperialist Britain itself took over Singapore, Aden, Hong Kong and Kowloon, Lower Burma, and Lagos (not to speak of expansion from Australia, India, and South Africa). To be sure, London was determined to have its way in the cheapest and most effortless manner possible. But usually the knowledge that Britain had the force and would use it if necessary for the defense of its citizens and their commerce was alone sufficient to induce restraint, as C. K. Bartlett has detailed in a survey of the threat of force in these areas during this period.[29] Or, as Landes reports in the case of midcentury Egypt:

Once the representatives of the Western nations learned that the [Egyptian] Viceroy was incapable of resisting threats of force, that the mere lowering of a consular flag was enough to bring him to his knees, the gates of corruption were opened wide . . . Nothing was too far-fetched to serve as an excuse for a raid on the Viceroy's purse. If a man was robbed because of his own negligence, the government was at fault for not maintaining law and order. Indemnity. If a man sailed his boat poorly and caused it to founder, the government was at fault for leaving the sandbar there. Indemnity. One litigant, an Austrian noble named Castellani, succeeded with the help of his government in extorting 700,000 francs on the grounds manifestly falsified, that twenty-eight cases of silk cocoons had been ruined by exposure to the sun when a train from Suez to Cairo started late.[30]

The foregoing analysis thus indicates that there are solid grounds on which to categorize as imperialist the economic expansion backed by military force of Britain in the decades after 1815. This is not to say that the impact in Africa, Asia, and Latin America was everywhere the same. Nowhere in China or the Ottoman Empire was there to be found a political leader like Brazil's Joaquim Nabuco, who could declare: "When I enter the Chamber [of Deputies] I am entirely under the influence of English liberalism, as if I were working under the orders of Gladstone . . . I am an English liberal . . . in the Brazilian Parliament."[31] But whether it contributed to the creation of a new order (as in Brazil) or to the destruction of an old one (as in China), the intensity of this economic expansion was such that it basically affected the social and political organization of virtually all parts of the preindustrial world.

It will remain for the following chapter to examine in closer detail the consequences to the South of British expansion. It should be reiterated here, however, that economic expansion became imperialism as much as a result of the character of southern societies as of aggressive designs formulated in Britain. The significance of liberal economic imperialism therefore seems to be of a different magnitude depending on whether it is viewed from Britain or from the periphery: To the former, economic issues could be handled in a relatively routine fashion and seldom presented themselves as the basic problem for political leaders to address; but to the latter it clearly and immediately involved the very structure of social life. (This may help explain as well the difference in the literature on the period – the contrast between, say, Platt on the one hand and Gallagher and Robinson on the other.) Certainly London could define its interests in these regions as economic and decide to back them by force. But political leaders were not the playthings of economic interests, nor did they ever judge strictly economic questions with respect to Africa, Asia, and Latin America as high-priority matters for the sake of which a forward policy would be pursued.[32] Thus, although the expansion of mid-Victorian Britain occurred under the auspices of capitalist business and finance backed by the state, we must look not so much to the force of capitalism as to that of industrialism, not so much to the character of European governments as to those in the South, if we would understand the basic features of the process. We must therefore be cautious not to define imperialism too narrowly, but to be able to see it on occasion more as a function of "indirect" economic than of "direct" political forces, of southern rather than strictly northern social and political structures. In short, imperialism was as much a consequence as a motive of British foreign economic policy – or at least so it appears in the years before 1875.

In the final quarter of the nineteenth century, however, the character of imperialism underwent a decided change. It was certainly not that economic factors or the political capabilities of southern governments ceased to be relevant to imperialism's development, but rather that the course of events came to be determined more by deliberate political calculations made in northern capitals. As increasingly sharp problems of great power rivalries came to dominate European chancelleries, questions of imperialism became the stuff of "high" politics. If we would understand the logic of these changes we should therefore turn our attention more to political than to economic processes, more to northern than to southern governments. In the last quarter of the century, the preceding period of liberal, economic imperialism increasingly gave way to the impetus of what might be termed political imperialism. So far as Great Britain was concerned this new era would be characterized by deliberately preemptive annexations on its part – actions that were quite different in intention from its policy of the preceding half century.

The logic of political imperialism

It is commonly agreed that sometime in the 1870s a new phase of European imperialism opened. In the four decades prior to World War I, Britain's imperial holdings grew from 9.1 to 12.6 million square miles; those of France from 0.2 million to 4.35 million square miles; those of Germany to 1.2 million square miles; and Russia's holdings expanded to over more than 1 million square miles in Asia. At the same time, Japan defeated both China (in 1894–5) and Russia (in 1904–5) to win a paramount position in Korea and Manchuria; Austria-Hungary gained mandates in the Balkans; and the United States took the Philippines and Puerto Rico after war with Spain and intervened repeatedly in Central America and the Caribbean thereafter. In short, the period of uncontested British international hegemony had ended, and London found that to protect its far-flung interests it was obliged to leave its "splendid isolation" and move into alliances with regionally dominant powers. In the process, the principal tenets of the Pax Britannica were overturned. In the place of the open door and free trade in commerce and the noninterference of government with economic affairs came a period typified by annexations and spheres of influence of an increasingly protectionist, neomercantilist sort.

The earliest and at one time most widely accepted explanation for this phenomenon locates the cause of the sudden outburst of great power imperialist rivalry in changes in the structure of late nineteenth-century capitalism. According to this school of interpretation, of which Hobson and Lenin are the best-known exponents, the vertical and horizontal integration of the means of production occurring in the last quarter of the century allowed trust (or monopoly or cartel) capitalism to increase the volume of its output by the same force with which it increased the inequality of income distribution in society at large. These economic and social realities created a mighty push for imperialist expansion, as the growing volume of goods and capital generated by the trusts could not be absorbed domestically and so created the conditions for a business downturn and depression. To sustain their economic strength and their political stability, capitalist states perforce became imperialist, moving abroad in competition with one another to place the surplus goods and capital they could not absorb at home.

It is not proposed to recapitulate in detail here the telling criticisms of Hobson and Lenin, except to point out that these critiques stress that cartels were not important in the late nineteenth century in any capitalist countries but Germany and the United States; that neither trade nor investment particularly favored the newly acquired areas; and that countries such as Japan, Russia, and Austria-Hungary were concerned by the imperialist scrambles every bit as much as Britain and Germany, although the former were quite lacking in the economic characteristics reputedly necessary to stimulate expansion. When chronological considerations and studies of the foreign policy perspectives of government leaders are brought up as well, the case that economic considerations dictated late nineteenth-century imperialism in the manner supposed by Hobson and Lenin is impossible to maintain.[33]

At the same time, the shortcomings of Hobson's and Lenin's theses do not warrant a wholesale disregard of economic factors in European imperialism in the four decades preceding World War I. The most obvious role economic developments played in this respect was that as other nations industrialized, they began to look to Britain as their competitor in international economic relations. The problems were born not simply of the fact that large industrial processes involved increased raw materials supplies (competition for mineral and agricultural resources abroad), or that larger levels of output needed to be reached in order to provide economies of scale (competition for markets), or that handsome profits made in business were scouting the globe as surplus capital for the best investment opportunities (competition for political influence in foreign loans). All these tensions were substantially exacerbated by the particular problems of late nineteenth-century capitalist production, which in 1873 fell into a long-term depression lasting (despite several brief recoveries) until 1896. This downturn in the business cycle made foreign ventures all the more attractive and encouraged business and finance to rely more and more on their governments to promote their interests. For nearly two decades preceding the depression there had been a heyday of free trade with commercial and financial transactions among the European powers markedly expanding. But as the level of prices fell, business turned to government for protection. And, with the exception of London, these governments responded. In 1879, Germany passed a new tariff law, and the tariff it put into effect was raised in 1890 and 1902. France raised its tariffs in 1881 and again in 1902. Russian tariffs rose in 1882 and 1891, and the United States, where tariffs were already relatively high, raised them again in 1890 and 1897. As a consequence, the direction of trade began to change. The industrial states exported relatively less to one another while the importance of the southern areas of the globe grew. Thus, Britain, which had sent 20 percent of its exports to the United States in the 1850s, sent only 6 percent there by the turn of the century, and German trade with the rest of Europe fell by 30 percent in relative terms between 1880 and 1914, largely as a result of increased commerce with southern countries, especially in Latin America.[34] Nor did these shifts in trade occur without political oversight. H. A. Turner and H. U. Wehler have documented that Bismarck was well aware of Germany's growing reliance on foreign trade, and that he reluctantly concluded after 1882 that colonial possessions were part of the protection Germany needed.[35] In such circumstances, even the firmly noninterventionist British state changed its approach. No later than 1886, D. C. M. Platt concludes, "The evidence for finance and trade as determining factors in extra-European diplomacy and imperial expansion ('formal' and 'informal') becomes overwhelming."[36]

Doubtless, then, a part of the tensions bedeviling European relations toward the end of the century reflected problems born of their capitalist economic structures. But one may legitimately speculate whether affairs would have been so different even had there been a transition to socialism here during this same period. Given the small resource and population bases of Western European countries relative to the kinds of raw materials and to the size of markets needed for modern economic production, foreign trade and investment were becoming indispensable elements to their existence. With the possible exception of "land empires" such as Russia, the United States, or China, it is difficult to conceive how an industrial revolution could come about in a small country *without* profound consequences for its foreign policy. "To accuse a British Secretary of State of indifference to the commercial interests of the country (is) to accuse him of being deficient in common sense," Palmerston is reported to have declared to the Commons in 1834, and one can suppose he would have said no differently had he been a socialist.[37] A Europe divided into a plurality of states would needs have been competitive in international economic relations even had socialism proved triumphant there.

Certainly one of Lenin's more dubious assumptions was that in some fashion government planning might end European rivalries. Hobson was equally naive in his belief that income redistribution within Britain would decisively alter the course of events:

If the consuming public in this country raised its standard of consumption to keep pace with every rise of productive powers, there could be no excess of goods or capital clamorous to use Imperialism in order to find markets: foreign trade would indeed exist, but there would be no difficulty in exchanging a small surplus of our manufactures for the food and raw material we annually absorbed, and all the savings that we made could find employment, if we chose, in home industries . . . The only safety of nations lies in removing the unearned increments of income from the possessing classes, and adding them to the wage-income of the working classes or to the public income, in order that they may be spent in raising the standard of consumption . . . It is idle to attack Imperialism or Militarism as political expedients or policies unless the axe is laid at the economic root of the tree, and the classes for whose interest Imperialism works are shorn of the surplus revenues which seek this outlet.[38]

But unless Britain wanted to return to the conditions of the seventeenth century, or to those of an even earlier time, this is precisely what it could *not* do. To have a modern economy, Britain needed access to the trade and investment opportunities of the world. Thus, many of the investments abroad – such as railways in Argentina and the United States – stimulated both the export of British steel for the completion of such projects, and the import of wheat and meat into Britain in greater quantities at lower prices once they were successful. Britain had become heavily and irreversibly integrated into a world division of labor. These involvements raised serious political problems in regard to world affairs which Hobson's advocacy of a "little England" went nowhere to address. As a powerful, early industrializer, Britain was perforce economically expansionist. Socialism (Lenin) or liberalism (Hobson) surely might have modified certain aspects of this world role – curtailing the import of luxury goods from China, or managing the terrible trade cycles that excited competitive nationalism – but only a political faith bordering on the religious would conclude that a world of general peace and prosperity would emerge from a transformation of economic relations alone.

Indeed, in its own way, a Socialist Britain at the turn of the century (if only one we imagine to ourselves) might have been a more powerful imperialist country than was the case under capitalism. For the most telling charge against the character of British overseas investments is that only a fraction of them were of direct benefit to the home economy in terms of long-range British development. Under Socialist planning, probably not so much of the money sent abroad would have been wasted by ill-conceived schemes or insolvent foreign governments, and not so much would have gone to build up the economic plants of eventual rivals to Great Britain. The result might have been a more enduring, powerful world imperialist presence than was the case. Of course, the most extreme case is that of France, whose investors managed to lose an astonishing two-thirds of their foreign investments by 1918. As A. K. Cairncross remarks:

The French rentier – the most cautious of capitalists and the most credulous – was content with a gilt-edged return on securities in which no self-respecting gambler would have dabbled. He was financing the warmongers for a mere pittance. He was starving French industry of capital. And he was doing little or nothing to promote French commerce or to reduce the cost of imported products.[39]

Although the British record may have been substantially better, there were instances aplenty of defaults by Latin American and Mediterranean governments on loans floated in London as well.[40]

Money lost was not the most serious shortcoming of British lending abroad, however. The fact was that for a variety of reasons Britons were not investing at home. Thus, just before World War I, German capital formation was nearly 16 percent of the net national product, compared with only 8 percent in

Britain; but the British were sending 53 percent of this abroad, as opposed to 6 percent for Germany.[41] Apparently by 1911, the situation had become so critical that domestic investment was not even high enough to keep what productive apparatus there was from running down.[42] According to W. Arthur Lewis,

Britain was caught in a set of ideological traps. All the strategies available to her were blocked off in one way or another. She could not lower costs by cutting wages because of the unions, or switch to American-type technology because of the slower pace of British workers. She could not reduce her propensity to import by imposing a tariff or by devaluing her currency, or increase her propensity to export by devaluing or by paying export subsidies. She could not pioneer in developing new commodities because this now required a scientific base which did not accord with her humanistic snobbery. So instead she invested her savings abroad; her economy decelerated, the average level of unemployment increased, and her young people emigrated.[43]

In such circumstances it is reasonable to maintain that a Socialist Britain might have broken through these "traps," whether ideological or structural. Had a government planning agency invested less abroad in favor of improving the home plant and directing such foreign investments as were made with a deliberate design to serve domestic needs thereby, the overall effect might primarily have been to make Britain a more potent force in world politics than was the case. But this is not to say that such a change would have necessarily either dampened European rivalries or softened European imperialism. (Indeed, it is ironic that even if the Soviet Union today remains a largely self-contained economy, its spokesmen repeatedly support the creation of a "world socialist system" based on an "international socialist division of labor" whose two main premises are identical to those of nineteenth-century Britain and twentieth-century America: that all will prosper equally thereby, and that peace among nations will be promoted.[44] Neither of these assumptions is self-evident.)

These observations suggest the crucial importance of the international political setting into which industrial development was introduced. For the spread of the industrial revolution in Europe occurred within a political context whose heritage was centuries of fratricidal warfare. Thus, the tensions associated

Table 2. *Volume of steel produced (in millions of tons)*

Year	Britain	Germany	United States	World
1880	1.29	0.69	1.25	4.18
1900	4.90	6.36	10.19	27.83
1913	7.66	17.32	31.30	75.15

with capitalist industrial development came to exacerbate the quarrels of a perennially rivalrous region politically. Economic developments influenced the interests of the various states and markedly affected the power at their disposal. But these economic forces could not of themselves spell out necessary political outcomes. To see how these developed, we must turn to the relatively independent realm of European politics.[45]

Politically speaking, the most important feature of the dissemination of the technics of the industrial revolution was that as this know-how spread to the Continent and to North America, it became apparent before the end of the century that Britain's physical ability to control world events was in rapid decline. The Russians, for example, were able to make themselves into formidable regional threats to Britain through the extension of their railways into Asia, bordering Persia, Afghanistan, and China. More importantly, it was recognized at the time that both Germany and the United States would surpass Great Britain economically sometime around the turn of the century. Steel production figures (Table 2) present this development graphically.[46] Nor was there much indication that these trends would be reversed, given the stagnation of the British economic system noted above. As a result, the British were being outpaced not only in established undertakings such as steel, but also (by the Germans) in new fields of technological importance such as chemicals, electronics, and optics, where foreign superiority was overwhelming.[47] At one and the same time, therefore, economic factors were creating the possibility of serious new political conflicts in international relations, just as they were undermining the ability of Great Britain, the guarantor of the world order, to manage events in its accustomed ways. In a world of rival nation states, rapid and uneven economic change had laid the groundwork for a political crisis of the first magnitude.

But it is in *political* terms that the ensuing conflicts must be finally understood, whether we are looking for the causes of the "new imperialism" or for those leading to the outbreak of World War I. In the case of the war, for example, however much economic differences contributed to the growth of Anglo–German rivalries, it would surely be difficult in the extreme to attribute the growing animosity of these nations strictly, or even largely, to such considerations. If only economic competition were at stake, why was there no struggle between Britain and the United States, and why did the United States and Germany not enter into more vigorous opposition to one another? Again, what can simple economic necessity tell us of the unification of Germany and the profound political consequences this entailed for Europe; of the conflict between Russia and Austria-Hungary over influence in the Balkans; of the German decision to ally with Austria; of the French decision to ally with Russia; of the British determination that no single power dominate Western Europe or the approaches to India?

Of course, economic developments may have rather automatic political repercussions. By 1894, German trade surpassed that of Britain in Holland and Belgium, and by 1912 had doubled in these two countries so crucial to the British scheme of things on the Continent. By 1913, German trade had surpassed that of Britain throughout the Balkans as well, and had grown from a small fraction to nearly half that of Britain in the Ottoman Empire (actually predominating in most of Turkey proper). The extent of this commerce combined with the expansion of the Baghdad Railway under German auspices (begun in 1888, with the final – and perhaps most vital – concession granted in 1899) to establish Berlin's influence in the Eastern Mediterranean along the route to India.[48] In effect, a single power was coming to exert growing strength in the two areas of the world most crucial strategically to Britain. It was not, therefore, the fact of German economic expansion alone that concerned the British so much as the geographic setting in which this occurred and the political consequences it potentially entailed, not only for the European but also for the Mediterranean balance of power. By contrast, the mounting commercial influence of the United States was taking place in regions of relatively minor concern to London: the Pacific and the Caribbean.

We should not abandon economic determinism to fall into the determinism of international systems theory, however. For the alliance system that ultimately divided Europe was in no way rigorously foreordained by balance-of-power considerations engendered by German expansion. It must be recalled that Anglo–German rivalry was not truly acute until after the turn of the century (incidents such as German support for the Boers notwithstanding), and that it grew during a sustained period of general economic prosperity. For most of the latter half of the nineteenth century, and certainly after the Franco-Russian Alliance of 1894, it was Russian moves in the international arena that most concerned London.[49] As late as 1901, there was considerable support in Britain for joining Berlin in an international condominium favorable to the interests of both parties.[50] However, by this time opinion in Britain had begun to change as the full import of the second German naval law of 1900 became apparent. As Winston Churchill stresses in his chronicle of these times, it was not at all economic thinking that determined the mood in London, but rather the clearly offensive military thrust being mounted by Germany in a geographic setting of first-rank importance to Britain.[51]

Why, then, did Germany build the fleet? The answer must be found not in the dictates of international affairs, but in the struggles of domestic German politics. With the tariff of 1879, Bismarck laid the foundations for the famous alliance of "iron and rye," the historic compromise by which German industry and the great Junker landlords (who held many of the most important posts in the imperial bureaucracy, especially in the army) agreed to work together against their domestic and foreign enemies. After Bülow became foreign secretary and Tirpitz navy secretary in 1897, this pact was reconfirmed by providing industry with large naval appropriations understood as anti-British, while agriculture received high tariffs known to hurt the Russians.[52] German militarism may therefore be attributed to the particular political outcome of class conflict in that country in the last two decades of the nineteenth century: to the ability of the Junkers to retain a decisive role economically and through the government bureaucracy; to the compliancy and expansiveness of the middle class; and to the relative weakness and nonrevolutionary reformism of the proletariat.

Thus, it was not so much balance-of-power constraints that ordained the fleet as it was the building of the fleet, which brought about crucial changes in the system of European alliances. As if in recognition of these changes, Britain conceded preeminence in Latin American affairs to Washington between 1901 and 1903 (with respect to a future isthmus canal in Central America and to the debt controversy over Venezuela), so freeing itself to concentrate better on problems in the European balance of power. In January 1902, London left "splendid isolation" by entering into alliance with Japan; in April 1904, the Anglo-French entente was announced; and in August 1907, the Anglo-Russian entente was concluded. Although this series of agreements was not premeditatedly conceived to challenge Germany, it nonetheless came to be the structure of international understandings that did so much to sweep the world into war in 1914.[53]

Yet if the structure of economic and political relations among the European states seemed to predispose them increasingly to war, a caveat is nevertheless in order. For at closer inspection, at the level of analysis of elite decision making, the course of history appears more fluid, its development more accidental. Here Fortuna seems to rule. The problem, however, is that even with sound information and a thorough understanding of the premises by which they determine policy, statesmen cannot confidently predict the outcome of their conduct: Equally plausible cases can often be made for the results of radically different actions. And yet so frequently it seems apparent (in retrospect especially) that the making of a certain easily alterable decision has set in motion a decisive train of events. In short, the art and the study of diplomacy are well worth our attention.[54]

It should by now be evident that a variety of intersecting, yet distinct, historical processes was at work feeding the great power rivalries of the four decades prior to World War I. The goal is to refrain from collapsing these different dimensions into one – as though politics may be reduced to economic forces, or domestic concerns to international interests (or vice versa) – and yet not to hold them so rigidly apart as to miss their interactions. It is necessary instead to look for the inter-connections of these various processes and to attempt to assign some ranking to them in terms of their weight on specific historical outcomes. If, for example, it is indisputable that economic developments stimulated important changes in both European domestic and international politics and bred new tensions there, key features of the "new imperialism" and the path to war nonetheless remain to be explained. Thus, the alliance system played a key role in the descent into war. The conflict began, it should be recalled, not between Germany and Britain, but between Russia and Austria-Hungary, who drew their greater allies in behind them. Given their deep and long-standing differences, it would be absurd to suggest that Russia and Austria served as proxies for British and German capital respectively. And only a politically based theory can appreciate the logic of Winston Churchill's reasoning as he explained British foreign policy in 1936 in classic balance-of-power terms:

Observe that the policy of England takes no account of which nation it is that seeks the overlordship of Europe. The question is not whether it is Spain, or the French Monarchy, or the French Empire, or the German Empire, or the Hitler regime. It has nothing to do with rulers or nations; it is concerned solely with whoever is the strongest or the potentially dominating tyrant. Therefore, we should not be afraid of being accused of being pro-French or anti-German. If the circumstances were reversed, we could equally be pro-German and anti-French. It is a law of public policy we are following and not a mere expedient dictated by accidental circumstances, or likes and dislikes, or any other sentiment.[55]

In short, although the spread of the industrial revolution to the Continent tended to upset the European balance of power while encouraging militarism in Berlin for domestic reasons, the political outcome was in no sense rigidly determined by economic forces. The centuries-old political fragmentation of Europe and the continued hegemony of the military caste within Germany (to cite two of the more important political legacies) fashioned these economic changes with a strength quite their own.

As rivalries intensified in Europe in the last quarter of the nineteenth century, they came to involve Asia, Africa, and (to a lesser extent) Latin America. Whereas during earlier years of the century imperialism was mainly (though far from solely) a matter of economic demands, now political motives came to the fore with the more deliberate weight of the imperialist capitals behind them. Where states were strong, the European capitals looked for allies; where they were weak, the Europeans looked for spheres of influence. Imperialism came increasingly to reflect not the attitudes of the Europeans toward the Africans or Asians, but the Europeans' attitudes toward each other.

As the preceding section indicated (and as the next chapter will elaborate), most of the areas in Asia and Africa into which great power rivalries projected themselves in the last part of the nineteenth century had already been destabilized by combinations of domestic turmoil and foreign penetration earlier in the century. That is, governments in most of these regions were weak – and their very weakness excited the intervention of competitive great powers into their affairs and so weakened them further. In China, for example, the Opium War of 1839–42 played a role in unsettling conditions in southern China and so had a part in the massive Taiping Rebellion of 1850–64, which did so much to sap the central authority structure of the country. The renewal of British and French hostilities between 1857 and 1860 greatly amplified these internal difficulties, as a result of which China lost substantial territory to Russia and found its sovereignty further compromised on matters of trade and extraterritoriality. After the defeat of the Taiping rebels, China essayed a conservative restoration (supported in particular by London), but defeat in war with Japan in 1894 opened up the land to a real threat of partition. The interaction of a weakening China with an increasingly competitive international state system could only worsen the prospects of the Manchu dynasty.

Similar developments had already occurred with the Ottoman Empire, when an uprising in the Balkans in 1875 (motivated in part by local taxation efforts to repay European creditors) brought in the Russians, which in turn alarmed the Austrians and the British. By the terms of the Berlin Congress of 1878, Russia, Austria-Hungary and Britain were awarded Turkish territory, France and Italy were promised future compensation at Turkish expense, and Serbia, Rumania, and Montenegro became independent. The following year "anarchy" (London's term) in Egypt resulted in British occupation for the purpose of securing the Suez Canal. Once again the pattern emerges: As Turkey weakened it incited foreign intervention – which in turn contributed to its further decline.

By the end of the 1870s an analogous process was taking place on the west coast of Africa. The effect of the changeover from the slave trade to palm oil production and the growing influence of British missionaries and consular officials combined to contribute to the development of severe internal social tensions and the weakening of political authority.[56] Moreover, the growing ability of the European traders to penetrate the hinterland (largely thanks to the steamboat and the Gatling and Maxim guns) meant that African middlemen were being cut out of business. When economic recession hit the area in the late 1870s, conflict sharpened on all sides, pitting not only Africans against Europeans but Europeans against each other. As A. G. Hopkins reports:

In the last quarter of the century the indigenous rulers were called on to make concessions over such matters as railways, internal tolls and slavery, which they judged, quite rightly, would undermine their political independence. At that point the dialogue over peaceful coexistence came to an end. Possessing fewer internal assets, and experiencing at the same time greater external pressures, the modernising aristocracies of West Africa were less able to control their future than their revolutionary counterparts in Japan after 1868.[57]

In the South too, then, imperialism had increasingly become a function of political circumstances in the last quarter of the nineteenth century. The inability of local governments to hold together domestic social forces and to defend their interests as states with respect to the international system contributed now to their occupation.

Thus, a growing political "anarchy" in parts of Asia and Africa intersected in the final years of the nineteenth century with a growing political competitiveness on the part of European powers for influence in these regions, an intersection that prompted a new era of imperialism. At the opening of this period, as Ronald Robinson, John Gallagher, and D. K. Fieldhouse have suggested, political weakness, or power vacuums, in the South was especially instrumental in provoking European intervention and thereby inciting European competition.[58] But as the century closed, the European contest gained in intensity in its own right, and into this political vortex a weakening South was swept, first in the partial dismemberment of the Ottoman Empire, then in the partition of Africa (which actually occurred in several stages, the latter being more combative), later in the scrambles over China, later still in the confrontations over Morocco, and finally in the effort to control events in the Balkans. A politically motivated imperialism had come to be the scourge of Asia and Africa, where earlier the force of economic imperialism had worked almost alone.

Imperialism thus emerges as a multiform process whose pattern was determined in the course of the years of British hegemony largely (though not exclusively) by the agents of capitalist industrial expansion, by the momentum of great power political rivalries, and by the capacity of southern governments to deal with these forces. The experience of this century, from 1815 to 1914, is especially interesting because it divides into periods in which the relative predominance of political and economic factors can be seen on the part of Britain. The historical account thus permits a useful comparative analysis. At the same time, this chapter has left in relative neglect the study of what was occurring within southern regions as European power expanded outward. It is to this matter that we now turn.

2

The impact of imperialism: the perspective of a century, 1815–1914

The preceding chapter dwelt chiefly on the forces behind the European penetration of the preindustrial lands of the periphery in Asia, Africa, and Latin America. It sought to situate the economic, social, and political development of these lands within a historical framework defined by European (and later by Japanese and North American) imperialism. Yet if European power played a crucial role in the historical change of these lands and peoples, it in no sense strictly determined how their economic, social, and political development would proceed. The familiar contemporary charge that the logic of imperialism consigned these areas to backwardness and "underdevelopment" is a myth of giant proportions. The equally fashionable (and related) assertion that these regions can be comprehended only by analyzing them in their "totality," that is, as products of an imperialist international order, runs the serious risk of failing to identify local factors of fundamental importance in any effort to understand their development. One example makes the point: The effect of British trade and investment varied so greatly among countries on the periphery – it contributed to Egypt's collapse, to Argentina's agricultural-pastoral orientation, and to Australia's relatively rapid industrialization – that it seems clear that local development can be better explained by *local* circumstances than by any great variation in behavior on the part of London.

This chapter falls into two parts. The first discusses the variety of state organizations on the periphery by identifying those general domestic characteristics most responsible for the wide variety of responses to imperialism. The point is not to dismiss the importance of imperialism – the preceding chapter should be evidence enough of that – but to ask, once it has been accounted for, what local factors stand out as determinants of the subsequent course of events.

The second part of the chapter restates the argument of the first part in terms of an extended critique of those students of nineteenth- and twentieth-century imperialism who give the molding power of the international system on the periphery more weight than it warrants. Ultimately, of course, the problem is not to choose between internal and external variables but rather to see how they work together, now the one predominating, then the other, in an interaction in which all play their roles. Just as Chapter 1 stressed the importance of seeing economic and political forces at once as separate and yet as interdependent, so this chapter makes much the same point with reference to the respective influence of local and international forces. The first part of the chapter deals especially with the three-quarters of a century prior to 1914; the second part includes discussion of development on the periphery in more recent times as well. Chapter 5 returns to some of the questions raised here.

The peripheral state and imperialism

The primary single structure the student of imperialism should study in order to understand the impact the international system has on the periphery is the organization of the state there. As the following chapter will recount, even in colonial settings, where the state apparatus was under foreign control at the highest levels, natives invariably wielded significant power at lower levels of the government and in a variety of informal ways. Indeed, it was precisely the fate of these constellations of interests accommodating or opposing foreign rule that made for many of the significant differences in the pattern of postwar decolonization. For the colonial regimes themselves had never amounted to more than a thin crust of

European officials and officers atop complex networks of local collaborating groups. In India, for example, Mahatma Gandhi tirelessly pointed out to his fellow countrymen that (in the 1930s) a mere 4,000 British civil servants assisted by 60,000 soldiers and 90,000 civilians (businessmen and clergy for the most part) had billeted themselves upon a country of 300 million persons. The British had achieved this success by constructing a delicately balanced network through which they gained the support of certain favored economic groups (the Zamindars acting as landed tax collectors in areas such as Bengal, for example), different traditional power holders (especially, after the Great Mutiny of 1857, the native princes), warrior tribes (such as the Sikhs of the Punjab), and aroused minority groups like the Muslims. In every colonial territory such a brokerage system was to be found. In some there was a foreign economic presence: the Chinese in Vietnam, Malaya, and Indonesia; the Asians in East Africa; the Levantines in West Africa; the settlers in Kenya and Algeria. Or again, there were alliances with traditional ruling groups: the Native Authorities in Nigeria, the Princely States in Malaya, the imperial bureaucracies in Tunisia and Morocco, the Hashemite family in the Fertile Crescent, the ruling cliques in Cochin China and Tonkin interested in acting independently of Hue. Still another source of support came from the oppressed groups who found their rights protected and their interests secured by foreigners: Muslim sects in the Levant, Jews in Algeria, Christians in many parts of Asia and Africa. Simple rivalries also played their part, as in the "politique des races" practiced by Gallieni in Madagascar, or the support of competing religious brotherhoods in the British Sudan or French North Africa. And there were the agents of Western ways: caids in North Africa, native schoolteachers in West Africa, and economic middlemen (the compradors). The latter entered early into important collaboration with European overseas expansion when a rich Hindu merchant failed to bring his army to the support of his Muslim overlord, the nabob of Bengal, and so assured Robert Clive's great victory at Plassey in 1757. Not that this description should give the illusion of a system of permanent alliances:

Old friends could become new enemies and old enemies new friends on the shifting bed of political competition until ultimately the collaborative networks found themselves superseded by indigenous forces determined to achieve independence. In short, even when they failed to control the heights of the state, native political forces were very much present in the colonies and it was their character and structure that profoundly influenced the process of decolonization. Therefore, to say that it is *the state* on the periphery that should be investigated in order to make sense of the impact of imperialism there is to understand that term in the broad sense of the organization of political life there. It is the historically specific political structure of class and community groups struggling or allying with one another so as to give themselves identity in terms of political institutions, practices, and beliefs that best reveals the fate of a country faced with the challenge of European imperialism.

Just as the variety of local political structures working for or against colonial rule must be understood in order to make sense of the intricate decolonization pattern, so in a parallel fashion the range of state structures in the South in the nineteenth and twentieth centuries is surely the best general organizational feature available with which to sort through the wide number of cases involved and to make sense of their experience. Quite obviously, a spectrum of state structures may be said to exist, from those that clearly are the paramount power within their society – monopolizing the means of violence and so enforcing a complete set of rules ranging from property ownership relations to the way political participation is permitted – to those that are states in little more than name, lacking both the party and bureaucratic structures that alone would give them the scope of local control properly incumbent to a state. Yet today, as yesterday, even in these latter cases (except perhaps for a few extreme examples such as we currently see among the sheikdoms of the Arabian peninsula or in the poorest parts of Africa), the existence of an indigenously controlled state does insulate the local society from the international system more effectively than was the case under direct colonial rule. On the one hand, short of military intervention the leverage of the outside is significantly reduced, as foreign ties with local groups are in general restricted to certain economic interests and occasional religious bodies. However powerful these local groups may be, foreigners have neither the scope nor the intensity of ties within the independent southern country that they had under colonialism. On the other hand, the power capacity of local interests and the state grows as bureaucrats in the government and army, jealous of their positions, show themselves likely to act on behalf of foreigners only when such behavior coincides with their own interests. Thus, however great the diversity among southern countries, they almost all have in common a state apparatus that depends on the aggregation of at least some local interests and that is possessed of the ability to take at least some initiatives in regard to domestic and international issues. In this respect, the use of the word "neocolonial" is misleading to the extent it suggests, as apparently it does to many, that the political distinctions between independent status and colonial status are trivial. Surely Kwame Nkrumah overstated the case when he wrote in 1965, "The essence of neo-colonialism is that the State which is subject to it is, in theory, independent and has all the outward trappings of international sovereignty. In reality its economic system and thus its political policy is directed from outside."[1]

Nevertheless, such an overstatement should serve as no license to rally to the opposite extreme, to assume the unquestioned dominance of political over economic forces, or of local factors over those of foreign origin. We should recall that during the nineteenth century, world trade and investment grew tremendously under the impetus of the industrial revolution. From 1840 to 1913, world trade increased from about $2.8 billion $38.2 billion, and international investment (from 1825 to 1913) from some $1 billion to $39 billion (American billion). In both respects, the periphery was well represented (particularly as the century advanced). The annual rate of export growth for Western Europe and the United States from 1883 to 1913 was actually somewhat less than that of the preindustrial world, and investments on the periphery accounted for perhaps more than 40 percent of money invested abroad by 1913.[2] How could this dramatic expansion have failed to have repercussions in the preindustrial world, especially in circumstances such as were discussed in the preceding chapter where the imperialist nations took a political interest in the conduct of the regimes in Asia, Africa, and Latin America? As John Gallagher and Ronald Robinson put it with respect to the concerns of the British early in the century:

Ideally, the British merchant and investor would take into partnership the porteños of Argentina, the planters of Alabama, the railway builders of Belgium, as well as the bankers of Montreal and the shippers of Sydney ... At the same time, the trader and missionary would liberate the producers of Africa and Asia. The pull of the industrial economy, the prestige of British ideas and technology would draw them also in the Great Commercial Republic of the world. In time the "progressive" native groups within the decaying societies of the Orient would burst the feudal shackles and liberalise their political and economic life. Thus the earlier Victorians hoped to help the Oriental, the African and the Aborigine to help themselves. Many would be called and all would be chosen: the reforming Turkish pasha and the enlightened mandarin, babus who had read Mill, samurai who understood Bentham, and the slaving kings of Africa who would respond to the Gospel and turn to legitimate trade.[3]

Nineteenth-century Asian and West African history is, of course, largely that of the failure of this dream. The disintegration of their political regimes, the occupation of their lands, the humiliation of their cultures – these were the fruits of internal factors abetted by the corrosive influence of European power. In the case of Latin America, however, the possibilities afforded the region by contact with the international system after the middle of the century encouraged relatively rapid economic growth based on the export of livestock, agricultural produce, and minerals, and tended to confirm the power of the state against internal divisions. By contrast, whatever the differences in their social and political paths of development, both Australia and Japan responded to the international spread of the industrial revolution by industrializing themselves and evolving forms of relatively stable government. An observer interested in proving the all-pervasive power of the international system over the preindustrial world might cite any one of these cases to establish the point. But when the range of countries on the periphery is set side by side, what emerges is the variety of local responses and the importance of local circumstances. Not so much designs formulated at the center, but rather conditions affecting the state's authority on the periphery were the fundamental factors determining the impact of European economic power abroad. A simple comparison illustrates the point: By 1880, Egypt and Argentina had each received British investments totaling between 20 and 25 million pounds sterling, and each was permeated with foreign influence. Egypt was on the verge of collapse, however, while Argentina was moving into position to become Britain's most important trading partner in Latin America. To understand the difference we must investigate domestic factors.

If we would attribute the variety of the response on the periphery to the global spread of the industrial revolution and the political pressures emanating from Europe (and later from Japan and the United States) that accompanied it in the roughly seventy-five-year period between 1840 and 1914, we should keep in mind the most salient features of the economic, social, and political characteristics of these different lands. The most important economic factors concern a range of issues including natural resource endowment, climate, population pressures, the availability of capital, the existence of a large local market, and the skill base of the native peoples. According to W. Arthur Lewis, for example, specific combinations of overpopulation and bad climates for the production of certain crops may have, virtually alone, precluded many tropical countries from easy access to industrial development through interaction with the world economy. Overpopulation depressed agricultural wages (so restricting the market for the production of certain goods), and poor climatic conditions inhibited progress in the production of food grains. In combination these two problems created a tremendous obstacle to the agricultural revolution that was needed as a precursor, or at least as a concomitant, of an industrial revolution. It is important to stress that these obstacles were *local*, not international:

There was never any attempt to prevent tropical countries from increasing their food production. The British were just as willing to import food as to

import raw materials, and encouraged Indian wheat production to the extent
of financing irrigation works. Moreover the plantations everywhere – in
Dutch, French or other territories – needed food for their Indian and Chinese
labourers . . . It is simply not true that the industrial nations stood in the way
of developing food production in the tropics.[4]

Lewis stresses the importance of other ecological factors as
well: "The principal reason why India developed more slowly
than almost any other country [between 1870 and 1913] was
simply lack of water . . . If Brazil had had the right kind of coal,
it would by 1913 probably have been well on the way to becoming a major industrial power."[5] D. C. M. Platt makes a similar observation when he points out that in comparison to Britain and Japan, nineteenth-century Latin America lacked iron,
industrial fuels, abundant capital, skilled labor, or the kind of
communication routes that would have made for more effective regional markets.[6] Of course, the international economic
system may have had some retarding effect on local industrialization efforts by controlling the world market for manufactured goods and by enlisting the support of local interest
groups to press for low tariffs on manufactures imported into
Africa, Asia, and Latin America. Moreover, in situations of direct colonial control (as in India and Egypt), the colonial government at times enacted legislation that deliberately curtailed
the development of local industrial processes such as textile
manufacture. These admittedly negative factors must nevertheless be weighed against the transfer of technology and capital that association with the world market brought these lands
and that there is no reason to think they would have developed
on their own (with the possible exception of Japan). In fact,
one of the most persistent myths propagated by southern nationalists and Marxists is that European and North American
economic expansion inevitably occurred in a fashion detrimental to the economic well-being of the peoples on the periphery.[7]

   Except in certain atypical cases, however, economic conditions do not alone explain the pace or the form of change on
the periphery. New technologies may obviate disadvantages in
climate or raw material endowment. Government policies may
aid in the mobilization of capital, the creation of demand, or

the education of the population. For a more complete picture of how different societies responded to the pressures of the international system in the period from about 1840 to 1914, some understanding of the variety of social and political structures on the periphery is needed. The most important question in this respect is how well the state is able to handle the realignment of social groups, be they class or ethnic, in the transformations of their relations that must inevitably occur over time as adjustments take place in response to contact with the international system. New sources of wealth and power appear while others are threatened with extinction or forced to transform themselves. New kinds of social contracts are entered into while old ties are broken or refashioned. New techniques, new beliefs, new practices, new organizations: All must somehow be accommodated or elaborated. Only the agricultural and metallurgical revolutions of thousands of years ago can match in their impact on the quality of social life the influence of the industrial revolution as it now spreads around the globe.

Hence there were understandably vast differences on the periphery with respect to how the global expansion of the industrial revolution backed by European power would be accepted. Whatever their differences, Australia and Japan industrialized successfully. By contrast, nineteenth-century Latin America was less dynamic economically and less stable politically, although it appeared more able than China, the Ottoman Empire, or the city-states of West Africa to deal with the international system. Thus, three general types of development may be suggested: that where industrial development occurred with political stability; that where raw materials development coexisted with political rigidity and the recurrent threat of civil war; and that where political collapse took place complete with the risk of foreign occupation.

A good part of the secret of Australia's success was simply that it inherited from Britain a set of skills, attitudes, social organization, and political institutions that facilitated movement into the modern world. By contrast, although Latin America shared with Australia a geographic distance from the regions of European rivalry, its dominant elites in the nineteenth century came, as Claudio Véliz has insisted, from Euro-

pean cultures that had not experienced the fruits of either the
industrial or the French revolution and who were thus decidedly preindustrial in outlook and practice.[8] Moreover, these
elites in many instances ruled over subject populations (for
example, the Indians in Peru and Mexico, and the Africans in
Brazil) in a manner that favored economic as well as social
rigidity. But even in Argentina, where the population was almost wholly European, severe civil disturbances have remained a hallmark of more than a century and a half of independence. Endemic class and ethnic conflict would thus seem
to create rigidities unfavorable to rapid economic change.

A closer comparison of Argentina with Australia may make
this point even more sharply. Although both were countries of
European settlement and began their economic development
with the export of agricultural and pastoral staples, the Australian advantage was clear before World War I. By 1913, Australian per capita output in manufacturing was 75 percent that of
the United States, with a per capita consumption of such goods
of $330, whereas Argentine production stood at 23 percent and
consumption at $175.[9] Moreover, the trend has continued. By
the mid-1960s, Australian national income was nearly three
times that of Argentina and came from a much more advanced
and diversified industrial base.[10] Two basic conditions appear
to have favored the Australians. First, they were far more involved in the international economic system than were the
Argentines: As early as 1885, foreign investment was about
five times greater in Australia (and on a per capita basis was
perhaps eight times larger), while Australian exports were
greater on a per capita basis by about 20 percent.[11] Secondly,
the virtual absence of violent turmoil within Australia and that
country's relatively egalitarian and mobile population contrasted vividly with Argentina, where what amounted to a
landed aristocracy ruled over a country with a long history of
civil disorder. The first of these factors suggests the positive
advantages to growth and stability brought by the international
system through its economic agencies so long as the second
condition is met: an internal order able to adapt economically,
socially, and politically.

By contrast, Spanish America emerged economically impoverished and politically divided from the struggle for independence from Madrid. Although Foreign Secretary Canning is widely quoted for his remark at the time that "Latin America is independent, and unless we mismanage our affairs she is English," the economic record suggests that this prize amounted to very little indeed until after the middle of the century.[12] By that time a symbiotic relationship was establishing itself, in which political stability in Latin America increased foreign economic interest in the continent in the form of loans and commerce at the same time that these links to the outside provided assistance to the various national governments intent on solidifying their power locally. As Richard Graham describes the situation in Brazil during the period from 1860 to 1865, for example:

> Whereas up to that point the landed aristocrats had viewed the central government with suspicion – first as foreign and then as radical – they now saw it wedded to their own interests. They therefore submitted to the control of the central government and, by allowing the tradition of a centralized national administration to arise, unwittingly contributed to the weakening of their own position once the central government became more responsive to the pressures of rising urban groups.[13]

The fortunes of the state in nineteenth-century Latin America were therefore characterized not only by its Iberian heritage and by its contemporary need to control a population geographically and, especially, ethnically quite heterogeneous (ranging from the Indian, mestizo, and Creole populations in Mexico to the large number of slaves in Brazil), but also by its ability to create an economic basis for rule through sales to the international system. (It is interesting to recall in this respect that the American Confederacy initially believed that Britain would intervene on its behalf once the Union blockade of cotton exports was felt in Lancashire, and indeed Prime Minister Palmerston and Foreign Secretary Russell at first hoped for a Southern victory.)

It is a favorite charge against British imperialism that it "delayed" and "distorted" Latin American economic development by fostering a "dependent" form of economic growth. By encouraging economies based on the export of raw materials, so the argument runs, those groups benefiting locally from such commerce were enabled to take political power and so enforce a system of social relations that discouraged industrialization. To be sure, there is no reason to question that Britain promoted precisely such developments; the case of Argentina was discussed in Chapter 1. But in the balance of forces that brought about this kind of development for Latin America, the weight of internal forces appears preponderant. Consider the continent in the aftermath of the wars of independence against Spain. The mix of natural resources necessary for industrialization (including coal, iron, and later, oil) was lacking.[14] Capital was scarce, markets were few, communications were poor, national populations were small, the agrarian structures of the countries were rigid, and political instability was rampant. In such circumstances, it would appear more reasonable to conclude that working with the international system provided far greater economic stimulus to Latin America than would otherwise have been conceivable. Carlos Díaz Alejandro writes that the growth of Argentina from 1860 to 1930 was so rapid that it "has few parallels in economic history," and he points out the compelling logic of reliance on the international system:

Pre-1930 growth can be said to have been "export-led" [because] . . . exports and capital inflows led to an allocation of resources far more efficient than the one which would have resulted from autarkic policies. In particular, the domestic cost of capital goods, which would have been astronomical under autarky, say in 1880, was reduced to a low level by exports of commodities produced by the generous use of an input – land – whose economic value under autarky would have been quite small.[15]

Indeed, it may well be that closer analysis will reveal that what many have accepted as an article of faith – that it took the Great Depression to stimulate industrial production on the continent by throwing it on its own – is a serious exaggeration. Carlos Manuel Pelaez reports that in the case of Brazil the conventional economic wisdom, which holds that limited industrialization will follow in the wake of staples export, appears confirmed:

The valid historical fact is that Brazil effected its first stage of modernization and industrialization in a form that was not significantly different from that of other areas of recent settlement. Coffee trade constituted the engine of growth, providing the social overhead capital, the foreign exchange for the purchase of industrial equipment, the market for new manufactures, and the supply of skilled immigrant labor that flowed into Brazil in response to the high returns available in coffee plantations.[16]

Moreover, it should be recalled that tariffs were the chief source of revenue for these states in the nineteenth century and that they could act, in effect, as protection for national infant industries. In Argentina in 1870, for example, at least $14 million of the $14.8 million state budget came from trade duties. As D. C. M. Platt writes:

> It is clear that by the last decades of the nineteenth century there were no serious institutional obstacles to the development of manufacturing. In Mexico, at least, import substitution had become a prime element in government tariff policy, and to a lesser extent the same was true of the other Latin American nations with industrial pretensions – Brazil, Argentina, Chile, Peru.[17]

Far from inhibiting growth, the international system surely accelerated it and might have done so even more in some settings had barriers been lower. Thus Díaz writes of twentieth-century Argentina:

> The most ironic lesson of postwar Argentine experience is that if there had been less discrimination against exports, manufacturing expansion would have been greater. Indeed, the annual growth rate of manufacturing during 1900–1929 (5.6%) was higher than during 1929–1965 (3.7%). The ratio of imported to total consumption of manufactured goods probably would have been higher, but there is little to be said on economic grounds for minimizing this ratio.[18]

Whatever the political obstacles to certain forms of economic change in Latin America, they would appear altogether greater in such traditional regimes as those of China, West Africa, and the Ottoman Empire. Take the issue of railway construction, for example. The first railway was not opened in China until 1875 and was shortly thereafter dismantled in the face of violent popular opposition to its use. By 1900, Argentina – where the political elite encouraged such construction – had fully seven times the railway mileage of China.[19]

Whereas in Argentina, the railways worked to confirm certain groups in political power, in China the opposite occurred: Both the Boxer Rebellion in 1900 and the overthrow of the Manchu dynasty in 1911 had as their proximate causes disputes over the introduction of the rail. It was not, of course, the railway itself that managed to destabilize China politically, but the social tensions already at work that this issue served to exacerbate. By the opening of the nineteenth century, signs of crisis for the dynasty were already beginning to appear.[20] Then in 1839 came the First Opium War, followed by the terrible Taiping Rebellion (1854–62) and the Second Opium War. Britain tried thereafter to support earnestly the efforts at restoration of the conservative order in China, but the challenges proved too great and the deficiencies too acute. As Mary Wright observes, the system simply lacked the ability (though not the will) to reform itself: "The obstacles to successful adaptation to the modern world were not imperialist aggression, Manchu rule, mandarin stupidity, or the accidents of history, but nothing less than the constituent elements of the Confucian system itself."[21]

Like China, the Ottoman state in the early decades of the nineteenth century was a complex, long-lived bureaucratic institution. But as the pressures of Western expansion began to mount, Constantinople proved unable to reverse a decline of some two hundred years, the consequence of internecine warfare and economic decay. To be sure, the Anglo-Turkish Commercial Convention of 1838 and the large debts run up by the sultan in later years turned out to be part of the solvent corroding the empire. But was this influence more the cause or the effect of a deficient state authority? Surely it is the latter that deserves the emphasis.

There seems to be no disagreement among historians that, by the seventeenth century at the latest, the state left by Suleiman at his death in 1566 was in decline. An attempt by Selim III to imitate Peter the Great and to modernize defensively to protect his realm against Russia and the West met with defeat when the Janissaries (backed by religious authorities) assassinated him in 1808 to obstruct his reforms. The state's next ambitious attempt at reform, the Tanzimat proclaimed in 1839 under Abdul Medjdid, achieved some notable results, but it proved quite unable to live up to the expectations of its authors – not because of foreign opposition (indeed, Britain and France were eager that the reforms succeed in order to build up Turkey against Russian expansion) but because the Ottoman government could not overcome *internal* obstacles to its proposals. It was not until Mustafa Kemal took charge of the Turkish government after World War I that the state gained the strength to define its objectives and attain them as the result of a concerted effort at internal reform.[22]

What a powerful state might have accomplished in the Middle East is suggested by the history of the amazing Albanian adventurer Mehemet Ali, who became pasha, then viceroy of Egypt. Arriving in Egypt in 1801 with the Ottoman forces sent to reclaim the land after Napoleon's withdrawal, Mehemet Ali managed to gather a following around himself, and in 1811 completed the work of internal reform of the local elite structure by smashing the Mameluke ruling class and emerging as the undisputed leader of the land. Ali was thereupon free to begin an effort that can best be described as nothing other than the forced industrialization of Egypt. His state created marketing monopolies in agriculture and dramatically increased the production of export crops, particularly cotton. With the substantial revenues gained from these sales abroad, the state created protected industrial monopolies within Egypt. By the 1830s, there was a work force of at least 30,000 in modern iron foundries, cotton mills, ammunition works, and a shipyard. Industrial employment was not to reach this peak again for nearly a century.[23]

The obstacles Ali faced were tremendous. Egypt in 1800 was a very backward land. Its population of between 6 and 7 million in Roman times now numbered no more than 2.5 million. Wheeled vehicles were unknown, transportation unsafe, and the formerly great city of Alexandria had a population of only 8,000 living in its ruins. But if these internal factors did not provide reason enough to ensure Ali's fall, his overweening ambitions to claim for himself the entire Ottoman Empire finally did. In 1831, under the pretext of pursuing 6,000 escapees from forced labor in Egypt into Syria, Ali began the first of two campaigns whose ultimate goal was to take Constantinople. The result was consternation in Europe as Britain and France saw Russia offer its aid in defense of the sultan. A second campaign begun at the end of the decade finally prompted London's intervention, and in 1842 Ali was obliged to reduce substantially the size of his army (the chief market for his factory production) and to dismantle his industrial monopolies, permitting the import of cheap European goods.

Now the stage was set for the "underdevelopment" of Egypt. Ali's successors converted Egypt into a single crop export economy based on cotton and contracted larger debts than they could repay. Ultimately, as is well known, the nationalist reaction to these foreign pressures alarmed the British to such an extent that they saw no choice but to occupy Egypt in order to assure the security of the Suez Canal. "It would be detrimental to both English and Egyptian interests to afford any encouragement to the growth of a protected cotton industry in Egypt," wrote Lord Cromer, consul general of Egypt in 1891. During his tenure in office (1883–1907), Cromer refused to protect any Egyptian manufacturers, going so far as to levy an excise tax on those products made within Egypt so that they should have no protection behind a revenue-raising import duty.[24] It was not until 1920, with the founding of the Bank Misr by Egyptian capital, that a stable foundation was finally provided for the growth of an Egyptian entrepreneurial class. Tariff autonomy (1930) and fiscal autonomy (1936) followed, permitting the Egyptian state to take a more forceful hand in the country's economic development. Thereafter, as Charles Issawi reports, there were shifts of economic power in three primary directions: of business over landed interests; of national over foreign investment; of state over private initiative. Especially since Nasser came to power and since the Suez Invasion of 1956, the role of the state has emerged as the decisive element in Egypt's economic development.[25] One can, to be sure, mark the principal periods of Egyptian economic activity in terms of the movements of the international system. But I would suggest that a better way to understand the Egyptian experience is by reference to the vicissitudes of the Egyptian state.

Although the political institutions of West African city-

states had precious little in common with those of China or the
Ottoman Empire in the nineteenth century, their character
played an equally important role in the conduct of European
imperialism in the region in the last quarter of the century.
Indigenous African institutions had managed to adapt first to
slavery in the sixteenth century, and then to trade in palm oil
and groundnuts in the early part of the nineteenth, drawing
strength for themselves in the process. But as the nineteenth
century wore on, political disintegration began to set in. On
the one hand, there were no effective political structures linking the various African communities to each other, so that
Europeans achieved a powerful position by acting as regional
intermediaries between groups.[26] On the other hand, the city-
states themselves came to be rent by internal conflicts – the
product of slave revolts, the spread of Christian missions, and
the long-term evolution of clan antagonisms.[27] With the coming of economic recession in the late 1870s and the heightened
rivalries between Germany, France, and Britain discussed in
the preceding chapter, the fate of these city-states was sealed.

The cases of China, the Ottoman Empire, and West Africa
contrast vividly with the experience of Japan. And certainly
Japan's ability to industrialize and to become in its turn a leading member of the international community cannot be understood apart from the actions of the state. For, in the aftermath
of the Meiji Restoration (1868), it was the state, acting on behalf
of the nation and not at the behest (although in the interests) of
any particular group or class, that undertook a fundamental
reordering of the Japanese government and economy. It was the
state that insisted on agrarian reform in order to accelerate industrial development; it was the state that invested in a whole
range of industrial enterprises that merchant capital at first
feared to undertake; it was the state that absorbed those samurai it could into its bureaucracies, then broke the resistance of
the rest; it was the state that began modern systems of banking,
taxation, and education in Japan.[28] Obviously these dramatic
developments cannot be isolated from the international system, or from the advantages given the state in its social and
economic heritage from the Tokugawa period. But to under-

state the independent role of the state – to see developments in Japan either as the product of international factors alone or as the reflection of no more than domestic class interests – is to miss the central feature of Japan's exceptional record.

We have seen that for a variety of reasons that depended on local circumstances, non-Western societies that might be called traditional had great difficulty adapting politically to their environments in the decades prior to World War I. Although different elements of traditional society were able to adapt themselves to the changing order and so be a source of regeneration for future years, only in Japan was an indigenous political order able to devise a functional alternative to the Western paths of modern economic development in the period that concerns us.[29] Elsewhere, adaptations were partial or incomplete because they did not take hold politically (and it should be recalled that the Tokugawa shogunate was overthrown in 1868 in Japan itself). However, the state does not exist alone, in a world apart from the rest of society; it is not as if the Japanese option might have been adopted in China, Argentina, or Old Calabar. From its history prior to 1868, the Japanese state inherited a blend of economic, social, and political advantages that contributed mightily to the success of its ambitions. We may nevertheless focus on the history of Japan in terms of its state activities, as ultimately this was the vehicle most central to determining the collective fate of the Japanese people.

Given the multitude of economic, social, and political factors involved in the efforts of states on the periphery to maintain their authority and expand it in the seventy-five years before World War I, it is difficult to establish useful profiles of what success or failure entailed. Yet even if each case must be finally understood in its own terms, certain general observations are in order. One element determining the fate of the southern lands was their raw economic potential. Conduct here depended on the mix of natural resources, climate, the skill structure of society, and the availability of capital for investment. Assuming these factors were not inimical to development, sociopolitical variables must then be evaluated. The key issue here appears to be whether the unity of the country could be preserved while old orders of right were ended and new sources of power and privilege came into being. The success of such a venture depended invariably on the power of the state to rewrite and enforce a new social contract. The state, therefore, had to emerge as triumphant over society. Theda Skocpol has analyzed the problem in the following manner with respect to China, France, and Russia:

> The adaptiveness of the earlier modernizing agrarian bureaucracies was significantly determined by the degree to which the upper and middle ranks of the state administrative bureaucracies were staffed by large landholders. Only state machineries significantly differentiated from traditional landed upper classes could undertake modernizing reforms which almost invariably had to encroach upon the property or privileges of the landed upper class.[30]

Once the power of the state as such was assured, its form of action varied, depending on time and place. Thus Alexander Gerschenkron has not only laid out what is common to "late industrializers" during this period – the speed of industrial growth and its concentration in large enterprises favoring capital goods production, for example – but has also indicated how different countries used different structures to the same functional end of growth: So England used accumulated capital, Germany the investment banks, and Russia the state budget.[31] In terms of forms of the state that have brought about these ends, the range is more limited. As Barrington Moore has maintained, only two basic forms of the state have successfully matched the economic accomplishments of Western democracies: a state born of revolution from below under communism, or one born of revolution from above under fascism.[32] In either case, the state stood supreme.

Reiterating the identity of the peripheral state

In order to clarify more sharply the argument presented in the foregoing pages, let us set it against what is today perhaps the dominant mode of analysis for studying the impact of imperialism on the periphery since the early decades of the nineteenth century. The most distinctive feature of this tendency is its insistence that social developments in Africa, Asia, and Latin America be seen within a historical and global context dominated by the force of imperialism. Political collapse or authoritarianism, social conflict or civil war, economic backwardness or mass poverty: All these are assigned to the responsibility of the workings of an international system dominated first by Britain, then by the United States. One might not take such writing too seriously except that it constitutes much more than simply a movement in the intellectual history of our day: It is an ideology as well, joining southern nationalists and Marxists within the confines of a generally agreed-upon form of historical analysis able to motivate significant political activity on the part of two of the most important political forces of our century. My purpose is to investigate what I consider to be a serious historiographic failure in this writing with the hope of helping to save what is possible of the study of imperialism from what are today the ravages of the ideologues.

Although it is obviously oversimplifying to reduce a complex and variously interpreted approach to a few propositions, a summary presentation of the general tenets of the "dependency" or "neocolonial" form of historical analysis will be attempted here, although the discussion will later show that there are substantial disagreements among its different proponents. According to the best-known advocates of this perspective (many of whose names will appear in the following pages), sovereign states of the South have long been dependent on the international economic system dominated by the northern capitalist powers (including Japan) for an evolving mixture of technology, financing, markets, and basic imports – dependent to such an extent that these less developed lands may be called "hooked": They cannot do with their dependence, but, just as certainly, they cannot do without it.

They cannot do with their dependence, so the thesis runs, because their form of incorporation into the international system has tended to inhibit their industrialization, relegating them instead to the less dynamic forms of growth associated with agriculture or the extractive industries. A surprising number of these writers – until quite recently the great majority of them – maintained that these countries would simply be unable to move beyond industrialization associated with limited import substitution. As we shall see, such a basic error in analysis is typical of this group's way of thinking, of its preference for conclusions dictated by theoretically logical, if empirically unsubstantiated, concepts drawn on the grand scale. No wonder, then, that a number of statistically minded political economists have sought to test these propositions and been unable to confirm them. It appears as a general rule that those countries most integrated into the world economy have tended to grow more quickly over a longer period than those countries that are not so integrated.[33] For those like Fernando Henrique Cardoso, however, who see the clear evidence that the manufacturing sector *is* expanding dramatically in many Third World countries, the process remains nonetheless neocolonial, as the leading sectors are inevitably controlled by multinational corporations with their headquarters in the North[34] As a result, for whatever benefits they may bring in the form of managerial and technological know-how, these corporations take more than they give and – what is more important – make it virtually impossible for local, self-sustaining industrialization to occur. This form of analysis, it should be noted, has affinities with Marxism, for it is the economic process that is seen as the dynamic of history. Thus the stages of economic development of the international system (from mercantilism to free trade to finance capital to the multinational corporation, to take one possible way of marking its development through time) come to interact with the various preindustrial economies in ways that may vary but that in every case soon establish the dominance of the world order over the form of growth followed locally. Over time, imperialism changes in form but not in fact.[35] Nor is it argued that the process is sowing the seeds of its own destruction in any dialectically recognizable fashion. For the present at least, the system is still expanding and consolidating its gains.[36]

But if the Third World cannot do with its dependent status, neither can it do without it. For what has occurred is that the local political elites in these areas have almost invariably structured their domestic rule on a coalition of internal interests favorable to the international connection. That is, it is not the sheer economic might of the outside that dictates the dependent status of the South, but the sociological consequences of this power. The result, as most writers of this persuasion see it, is that the basic needs of the international order must be respected by the South if this system is to continue to provide the services that the local elites need, in their turn, in order to perpetuate their rule. In other words, a symbiotic relationship has grown up over time – a relationship in which the system has created its servants, whose need is precisely to ensure the system's survival, whatever the short-term conflicts of interest may be. In the case of decolonization, for example, those nationalists leading the drive against colonialism in Africa and Asia potentially faced two foes in addition to their colonial rulers: rivalrous local class or ethnic groups whose loyalty these nationalists had not managed to secure, and neighboring peoples hostilely anxious to ensure the service of their interests in the wake of the departing northerners (see Chapter 3). In no significant way is the situation altered once independence is obtained: Civil war and jealous neighbors – in each case potentially abetted by the diffusion of the East–West confrontation – continue to jeopardize these independent regimes. Thus the system has at its disposal sanctions for transgressing its basic rules that are all the more powerful because their greatest force comes *not from an active threat of intervention so much as from a threat of withdrawal*, a withdrawal that would leave these dependent regimes to the fate of civil and regional conflict, which a great many of them would be quite unprepared to face. And once again there are affinities with Marxism, as it is understood that economic forces do not act in any sense alone but must be grasped sociologically as modes or relations of production creating specific configurations of political conflict over time.

Certain of these observations are persuasive and serve as a useful antidote to the claims of those who see in decolonization's "transfer of power" more of a watershed in world history than was actually the case. But at the same time, these insights exist alongside a number of arguments of dubious validity which I will try to link to a single yet fundamental theoretical shortcoming common to this style of thinking. In a word, too many of these writers make the mistake of assuming that because the whole (in this case the international system) is greater than the sum of its parts (the constituent states), the parts lead no significant existence separate from the whole but operate simply in functionally specific manners as a result of their place in the greater system. As a result, these writers suggest, it is sufficient to know the properties of the system as a whole to grasp the logic of its parts; no special attention need be paid specific cases insofar as one seeks to understand the movement of the whole. "Apart from a few 'ethnographic reserves,' all contemporary societies are integrated into a world system," writes Samir Amin, an Egyptian working in Africa and known in Europe as a leading dependency theorist. "Not a single concrete socio-economic formation of our time can be understood except as part of this world system."[37] As a consequence, in the words of André Gunder Frank, one of the more influential members of this school who is working on Latin America, "Underdevelopment was and still is generated by the very same historical process which also generated economic development: the development of capitalism itself."[38] In myriad forms, the argument appears again and again. A writer on contemporary African politics asserts that underdevelopment "expresses a particular relationship of *exploitation*: namely, the exploitation of one country by another. All the countries named as 'underdeveloped' in the world are exploited by others and the underdevelopment with which the world is now preoccupied is a product of capitalist, imperialist and colonialist exploitation."[39] A book comparing China's and Japan's economic growth after their contact with the West goes so far as to maintain that Ch'ing China and Tokugawa Japan were similar enough up to the early 1800s, and that any later difference in their economic performances should be explained chiefly by the character of their contact with the West:

This study argues that the paramount influence in the rise of industrial capitalism in Japan was . . . [that Japan] occupied a position of relative autonomy within the nineteenth-century world political economy. For a variety of reasons other societies were more strongly incorporated as economic and political satellites of one or more of the Western capitalist powers, which thwarted their ability to industrialize . . . in contrast . . . China's location in the world political economy dominated by the Western capitalist nations, must be considered of prime importance in China's failure to develop industrial capitalism during the nineteenth and twentieth centuries. China was more strongly incorporated than Japan and thus lacked the autonomy to develop the same way.[40]

Similarly, two writers maintain that they "view Latin America as a continent of inadequate and disappointing fulfillment and seek to pinpoint the co-ordinates of sustained backwardness in examining the process of economic change in a dependent, peripheral, or colonial area."[41] And a book on the Middle East concludes: "The products of Turkish craftsmen, well known and in great demand in Europe during tbe seventeenth and eighteenth centuries, declined along with the products of the rest of the Middle East when Turkey failed to keep pace with the industrial development of the West. Machine production swept craftsmanship off the markets not only in Europe, but also in Turkey. The latter fell back on agriculture, but in 1908, under the Young Turk movement, she began to take an interest in industrial development."[42]

In the United States, this general argument has reached its fullest expression in the work of Immanuel Wallerstein, who has published only the first book in a four-volume series under the instructive title *The Modern World-System: Capitalist Agriculture and the Origins of the European World-Economy in the Sixteenth-Century*.[43] In a companion essay written after the book's completion, Wallerstein approvingly cites Georg Lukács and says that a central tenet of Marxist historiography is that the study of society should "totalize," or begin with an understanding of the whole. The passage from Lukács is worth quoting:

It is not the predominance of economic themes in the explanation of history which distinguishes Marxism from bourgeois science in a decisive fashion, it is the point of view of the totality. The category of the totality, the domination determining in all domains of the whole over the parts, constitutes the essence of the method Marx borrowed from Hegel and that he transformed in

an original manner to make it the foundation of an entirely new science . . .
The reign of the category of the totality is the carrier of the revolutionary
principle in science.[44]

Working from this perspective, Wallerstein declares: "The only
kind of social system is a world-system, which we define quite
simply as a unit with a single division of labor and multiple
cultural systems." And he explains:

But if there is no such thing as "national development" . . . the proper entity
of comparison is the world system . . . If we are to talk of stages, then – and
we should talk of stages – it must be stages of social systems, that is, of
totalities. And the only totalities that exist or have existed historically are
mini-systems ["simple agricultural or hunting and gathering societies"] and
world systems, and in the nineteenth and twentieth centuries there has been
only one world-system in existence, the capitalist world economy.[45]

Although Wallerstein's position (to which we will return
later) is the most detailed yet to appear, the American writer
still most frequently cited by those who favor this approach is
probably Paul Baran. Appropriately enough, Baran chose as
the epigraph for his book *Monopoly Capital* (written with Paul
Sweezy) Hegel's dictum "The truth is the whole." And fortu-
nately for our purposes, Baran's writing is a particularly egre-
gious example of this form of reductionist historiography.
   Taking the case of Indian economic development, Baran portrays the country under the pressure of British imperialism as
a tabula rasa, so that all the land's problems, past or present,
supposedly spring directly from this foreign presence. In a passage extraordinary in its exaggeration, he writes:

Thus, the British administration of India systematically destroyed all the
fibres and foundations of Indian society. Its land and taxation policy ruined
India's village economy and substituted for it the parasitic landowner and
moneylender. Its commercial policy destroyed the Indian artisan and created
the infamous slums of the Indian cities filled with millions of starved and
diseased paupers. Its economic policy broke down whatever beginnings
there were of an indigenous industrial development and promoted the pro-
liferations of speculators, petty businessmen, agents, and sharks of all de-
scriptions.[46]

And he speculates on what India's fate might have been without the British: "Indeed, there can be no doubt that had the

amount of economic surplus that Britain has torn from India been invested in India, India's economic development to date would have borne little similarity to the actual somber record ... India, if left to herself, might have found in the course of time a shorter and surely less tortuous road toward a better and richer society."[47]

But surely this account – which, it should be noted, is based on virtually no hard evidence – imputes far too much power (for evil or otherwise) to the British. Thus, despite his allegation that India without the British might have found its own autonomous way to industrial development complete with less human suffering, Baran makes no effort to assess the probability that Mogul India could have accomplished such a transformation or to evaluate what price the pre-British system exacted from its subjects. Life was surely not easy under the Mogul in Delhi (warfare was constant, particularly in the years preceding the British takeover, and the taxation levels were quite high), and the most serious accounts of which I am aware dismiss out of hand the likelihood that pre-British India had any capacity in its contemporary form for sustained economic change. As M. D. Morris writes:

The British did not take over a society that was "ripe" for an industrial revolution and then frustrate that development. They imposed themselves on a society for which every index of performance suggests the level of technical, economic and administrative performance of Europe five hundred years earlier.[48]

Nor is it at all accurate to suggest, as Baran so adamantly does, either that pre-British India was without original sin or that the British were the authors of unmitigated evil. "Parasitic landowners and moneylenders" were not unknown before the British set foot on the subcontinent; British "commercial policy" is now thought by some to have "destroyed" far fewer artisans than was previously believed; British economic policy surely did more to create the foundations for industrial society in India than to "break down whatever beginnings there were" (however much the effort fails by comparison with Meiji Japan); British "land and taxation policy," far from "ruining" the village economy, was surely less exploitive than that of the

Great Mogul and probably provided for a modest per capita increase during the nineteenth century; and British "administration," far from destroying "all the fibres and foundations of Indian society," actually accommodated itself rather well to indigenous ways in the manner of most conquerors of large populations.[49] Of course there is no particular reason to sing hosannas about the British presence. For example, British rule clearly inhibited industrialization in the late nineteenth century: The efforts of Lancashire especially were successful in keeping Indian custom duties low until World War I and so stunted the growth of Indian manufactures.[50] But as the Great Mutiny of 1857 demonstrated, India herself possessed strong forces resisting change. In what seems to me to be a balanced judgment of the forces guiding India's development, Barrington Moore puts the effects of British policy within the context of the persisting strength of indigenous practices and institutions:

In addition to law and order, the British introduced into Indian society during the nineteenth century railroads and a substantial amount of irrigation. The most important prerequisites for commercial agricultural and industrial growth would seem to have been present. Yet what growth there was turned out to be abortive and sickly. Why? A decisive part of the answer, I think, is that *Pax Britannica* simply enabled the landlord and now also the moneylender to pocket the surplus generated in the countryside that in Japan paid for the first painful stages of industrialization. As foreign conquerors, the English were not in India to make an industrial revolution. They were not the ones to tax the countryside in either the Japanese or the Soviet fashion. Hence, beneath the protective umbrella of Anglo-Saxon justice-under-law, parasitic landlordism became much worse than in Japan. To lay all the blame on British shoulders is obviously absurd. There is much evidence . . . to demonstrate that this blight was inherent in India's own social structure and traditions. Two centuries of British occupation merely allowed it to spread and root more deeply throughout Indian society.[51]

In a parallel fashion, when he takes up the question of the reasons for the success of Japanese industrialization, Baran advances the same reductionist formula: Once again the part (Japan) disappears into the momentum of the whole (the dynamism of expansionist capitalistic imperialism):

What was it that enabled Japan to take a course so radically different from

that of all the other countries in the now underdeveloped world? . . . reduced
to its core, it comes down to the fact that Japan is the only country in Asia
(and in Africa or in Latin America) that escaped being turned into a colony
or dependency of Western European or American capitalism, that had a
chance of independent national development.[52]

And then, in explaining why Japan was not so incorporated,
Baran refers once more to the properties of the international
system: its preoccupation with other parts of Asia, its conviction that Japan was poor in markets and resources, its internal
rivalries. That Japan may have escaped colonial rule and initiated the single successful attempt to industrialize outside of
North America and Europe in the nineteenth century for reasons having to do with forces internal to the country is not an
idea to which Baran pays the slightest heed. Indeed he so ignores conditions in late Tokugawa Japan that he actually calls
the Meiji Restoration a bourgeois revolution!

The point of this discussion is not to doubt that the international system under the expansionist force of European and
American capitalism had an impact on the internal development of technologically backward areas of the world over the
last two centuries. These writers have served a purpose in making us aware of how intense and complex these interactions
were (and remain), and there is substance to their criticism that
development literature as it is currently written in the United
States tends to mask these linkages for its own ideological reasons.[53] Nor is the objection to the simple omission of evidence
relevant to the construction of a historical argument. Selective
judgment in the presentation of material is an inevitable part
of the study of history. Rather, the objection is to a certain style
of thinking that, to use two of this school's favorite words, is
biased and ideological, distorting evidence as much in its fashion as does the "bourgeois science" it claims to debunk.

As I suggested earlier, the chief methodological error of this
kind of writing is to deprive local histories of their integrity
and specificity, making local actors little more than the pawns
of outside forces. Feudalism as a force in Latin America? Non-
sense, says Frank (to be applauded by Wallerstein); because
capitalism has penetrated every nook and cranny of the world

system, the concept of feudal relations of production cannot be validly used.[54] Destroy the particular, exalt the general in order to explain everything. Cite Hegel: "The truth is the whole." Tribalism as a force in Africa? Colin Leys cannot bring himself to use the word without putting it in quotation marks, asserting that "among Africanists [this] point . . . perhaps no longer needs arguing." " 'Tribalism,' " Leys maintains, "is a creation of colonialism. It has little or nothing to do with pre-colonial relations between tribes . . . In neo-colonial Africa class formation and the development of tribalism accompany each other."[55] Why? Because the logic of the whole (capitalist colonialism) has found it expedient to work its will in the part (Africa) through creating, virtually ex nihilo, the divisive force of "tribalism." By such reckoning, all the social structures in history after a certain low level of development in the division of labor could be dissolved – feudal and bureaucratic estates, castes and clans as well as tribes – in favor of class analysis, the only "real" social formation.

Because this approach is formulistic and reductionist it is bad historiography. It is formulistic in the sense that it seeks to specify universal laws or processes in blatant disregard of the singular or the idiosyncratic. And by the same token it is re-ductionist, because it forces the particular case to express its identity solely in the terms provided by the general category. The error here, it should be repeated, is not that the approach draws attention to the interconnectedness of economic and po-litical processes and events in a global manner, that it refuses to grant the part *any* autonomy, *any* specificity, *any* particular-ity independent of its membership in the whole.

The problem of the relationship of the whole to the parts (like that of politics to economics, or of psychology to sociol-ogy) is a recurrent one in the social sciences. The only success-ful resolution of the problem of understanding their interac-tion, so far as I am aware, is to recognize that although the whole does have a logic indiscernible from analysis of the parts considered separately, the parts too have their identities – identities that no amount of understanding of the whole will adequately reveal. In his monumental *Critique de la raison dialectique*, Jean-Paul Sartre makes a telling criticism of Marxists who make "a fetish of totalizing," and illustrates it with an example of the problem of relating an individual biography to a social milieu:

"Valéry is a petit bourgeois intellectual, no doubt about it. But not every petit bourgeois intellectual is Valéry. The heuristic inadequacy of contemporary Marxism is contained in these two sentences."[56]

Thus part and whole must be comprehended at once as aspects of each other and yet as analytically autonomous – although the degree of relative independence will obviously be more or less complete depending on the historical moment. The theoretical consequences are clear: Systems composed of complex parts may expect change to come not only from the evolution of the whole (considered dialectically or otherwise), or from influences without in the form of the impingement of other systems, but also from developments *within the parts*, whose movements are endogenously determined. Therefore, in studying the patterns of relations between countries on the periphery and the core lands of Western Europe and the United States, we must be aware not only of the way the system as such is changing (for example, in terms of balance-of-power relations among the great powers, or with respect to changes in the international division of labor), but also of the manner in which parts of this whole (such as the form of state organization on the periphery) may transform themselves for local reasons but with important repercussions for the entire system of relations between strong and weak. Historical analyses that hold to these premises may be difficult to write, as lines of movement become more numerous and more difficult to see synthetically. But only this form of writing can hope to portray at all adequately the complexity that history actually is.

In line with the analysis presented in the first part of this chapter, the political organization of social life on the periphery emerges as the single most important variable to grasp if we would understand the historical identity of these peoples. For political organization represents the ability of these groups seen in class or communal terms to act historically, to lead their collective lives. The state thus focuses the coalitions and conflicts of present social forces within an organizational entity whose administrative and coercive capacities are the legacy of the past as well as the creation of current generations. Its story is that of the individuality of the people it encompasses in relation to global history. And it is the abrupt dismissal of the importance of analyzing political life on the periphery in other than a reductionist manner that is the cardinal error of the approach we have been reviewing.

Thus, although Immanuel Wallerstein promotes the study of the "world-system," as we saw earlier, the reverse side of the coin is his disinterest in political life on the periphery:

> The world-economy develops a pattern where state structures are relatively strong in the core areas and relatively weak in the periphery . . . What is necessary is that in some areas the state machinery be far stronger than in others. What do we mean by a strong state machinery? We mean strength vis-à-vis other states within the world-economy including other core-states, and strong vis-à-vis local political units within the boundaries of the state.[57]

Bereft of significant political activity, the periphery is then understood to operate in terms of social groups organized around economic interests. It is therefore international ties of cooperation and conflict based on class that permit a unified analysis of world politics:

> We must maintain our eye on the central ball. The capitalist world economy as a totality – its structure, its historic evolution, its contradictions – is the arena of social action. The fundamental political reality of that world-economy is a class struggle which, however, takes constantly changing forms: class-consciousness versus ethno-nationalist consciousness, classes within nations versus classes across nations.[58]

Although there may be instances aplenty when state action is unimportant, Wallerstein's hasty disregard of its potential significance is in error. Even on his home ground of the sixteenth century, Wallerstein overstates his case. As Theda Skocpol has pointed out, the strong states of that era were not at the core in England and Holland, but on the periphery in Spain and Sweden. Holland was ruled by a federation of merchant oligarchs whereas the English crown, deficient in terms of a bureaucracy or a standing army, was beholden to merchants and local notables.[59] Later history substantiates his position no better. As Alexander Gerschenkron has demonstrated, the "late industrializers" in every case were successful because of exceptionally strong state structures that were determined to modernize. One-time peripheral countries like Russia, Prussia, and Japan could not possibly have developed as they did without the vigorous leadership of the state.[60] Nor is the contemporary governmental structure of the United States the Leviathan one might expect of the "core country of the world-economy" any more than are many governments on the periphery today the weak structures one might anticipate on the basis of Wallerstein's writing.

Having created a historical arena in which the only actors are social groups responding to economic interests, Wallerstein is free to weave a tight net of interdependence among the actors in question. As he puts it in an anthology on Africa edited with Peter Gutkind:

All the authors in this volume stress that there was an asymmetrical and unequal economic relationship between Africa and the industrially highly developed world and that the "change process on the periphery of the world capitalist system is not an endogenous path through stages but a process subject to powerful exogenous factors." [The authors therefore propose] the idea of the world-system and Africa's place in and relationship to this system, "whose fundamental dynamic largely controlled the actors located in both sectors of one united arena."[61]

Arguing from this perspective, Wallerstein and Gutkind arrive at the following startling conclusion:

Underdevelopment, then, is the product of the operations and contradictions *within* the capitalist system . . . and it is just as clearly revealed in the relations between England and Scotland as between Great Britain and Nigeria . . . Why is Africa (or for that matter Latin America and much of Asia) so poor? . . . the answer is very brief: we have made it poor.[62]

The problem with this approach is that it accounts only with relative difficulty for the wide variety of differences that occurs within this allegedly unified world system. Wallerstein can allude to an international division of labor, to be sure, to explain the diversity he encounters. But his failure to acknowledge a political dynamic proper to these lands and peoples results in the exclusion from his analysis of an extremely significant historical force, which thereby impoverishes his discussion and nullifies many of his conclusions. By reducing the political to the economic, and the local to the international, Wallerstein has created a caricature of the historical process whose shortcomings outweigh its insights.

It is not difficult to anticipate the line of argument to be taken by apologists for the dependency literature. They will claim that at its best this approach is more complex than the foregoing analysis recognizes, that it sees a role for the state on the periphery and for the influence of local forces on developments there that I have altogether failed to appreciate.[63] Of course, some of this writing is of high quality and has produced new insights into the character of historical change in the South. (One thinks, for example, of the work of Fernando Henrique Cardoso.) But what these apologists do not see is that dependency theory serves a historically conditioned ideological function of bringing together Marxists and southern nationalists around certain categories of analysis that serve their respective interests. As a consequence, dependency theory is wedded to its bias of seeing local problems of development in terms of international forces in order to satisfy nationalist sentiments, just as it is committed to downplaying the realm of the political by virtue of its allegiance to Marxism. The limitations of this school are therefore not peculiar to its writers of lesser talent, but are rather more of a family disease. It is ironic that these writers who delight (often with good cause) in exposing the idoleogically based assumptions of mainstream North American work on Third World development should fail to see the historical roots of their own efforts in terms of the groups they represent.

To conclude, let us turn to an interesting example of the issues raised here that occurs in a current debate over the coming to power of "bureaucratic-authoritarian" governments headed by the military in a number of Latin American states (the most important being Brazil, Peru, Chile, Uruguay, and Argentina) since 1964. Among Latin Americanists who have tried to understand this phenomenon, there seems to be general agreement that Guillermo O'Donnell has advanced the most challenging and comprehensive of explanations.[64] While O'Donnell is well aware of the wide variety of factors that might have conspired to produce these bureaucratic-authoritarian governments, his central theoretical arguments make him akin to the writers criticized in the preceding pages. Put too briefly, his core thesis is that a regional economic crisis connected to a specific stage in such an area's economic development provoked a political crisis whose resolution dictated a specific form of political outcome. Thus, in his analysis, economic forces clearly predominate over political developments in the fashion we have seen to be indicative of the approach to the study of the periphery discussed in the preceding pages. But the argument that most closely links O'Donnell to this general perspective is his insistence that both the origin of the crisis (the inability of these countries to generate internally the capital and organization needed at a certain stage to move ahead economically) and the form of its resolution (with the help offered by multinational corporations who were ready and eager to move into the situation) must be understood at their most basic levels in terms of the development of the world capitalist order. Indeed, as a similar train of events may be expected to manifest itself in other parts of the world, O'Donnell declares that the focus of his work is on Latin America "only in a trivial sense; the pertinent historical context is provided by the political economy of nations that were originally exporters of primary materials and were industrialized late, but extensively, in a position of dependency upon the great centers of world capitalism."[65]

As Albert Hirschman notes with respect to O'Donnell's work, "Considerable intellectual excitement is . . . apt to be generated – quite legitimately so – when a *specific* turn of the political tide is shown or alleged to originate in a *precise* feature of the underlying economic terrain."[66] Nevertheless, as Hirschman and a number of other scholars who contributed to a volume that reviews O'Donnell's work conclude, the evidence now available makes it difficult to accept the core thesis summarized in these lines without significant reservations.

Thus, if O'Donnell seems convincing in tying the advent of authoritarian governments on the continent to the demand of certain social groups to end the civil discord attendant upon economic upheavals typified by high rates of inflation, balance-of-payments problems, and the like, he has nonetheless not successfully demonstrated (except perhaps in the case of Argentina) the accuracy of his far more crucial proposition that this basic economic disturbance constituted an epochal crisis in the transition from one economic stage of development to another (the "deepening" of industrialization).[67] Furthermore, relatively less important issues are also open to question, especially whether authoritarian governments need be the inevitable response to such problems (however conceptualized), and whether multinational corporations are particularly keen to work with such regimes (given their equal success in democratic environments).

Yet despite the apparent problems with the central thesis of O'Donnell's work, the richness of its presentation – in particular, its sense of regional history and its recognition of the significance of the role of the state – has allowed it to serve as the basis for alternative formulations designed to explain the rise of authoritarian governments on the continent. The resulting dialogue is a salutary development. In these analyses, political events may be shown to engender economic consequences, local events to have international repercussions, and long-term cultural factors to possess amazing powers of regeneration – at the same time that the political weight of imperialism and the economic strength of the international system are recognized as the forces they are. There is, to be sure, the danger of rampant eclecticism in analyses based on such open-ended premises. Some explanations are obviously superior to others and it should be an essential academic concern to lay out the reasons for this. Nevertheless, eclecticism at least permits a climate for serious intellectual pursuit. This is more than can be said for the stifling narrowness of vision of the reductionist universe, where the political is explained in terms of the economic, where local events are interpreted in terms of external occurrences, and where truth becomes the preserve of those who have mastered the mysteries of the "totality."[68]

3

Decolonization

As the preceding chapter suggests, imperialism was particularly apt to become colonialism in those areas where the native political organization was unable for local reasons to exercise its authority effectively. At times, of course, there was a decided will on the part of the Europeans (or the Japanese or Americans) to occupy these lands. But what frequently occurred (especially with respect to the British) was that the spectacle of a government unable "satisfactorily" to manage local affairs provoked the intervention of a foreign power fearful that some advantage it sought there could not be promised by the regime in place. In a real sense, then, however much imperialism was the product of an assertive Europe, it must also be seen as a function of the incapacity of governments in the preindustrial world to maintain their stability as they faced new and intense demands from without that compounded internal problems.

If this premise is accepted, it permits us to see decolonization not simply as an act of European withdrawal, but equally as a new form of political assertion in Africa, Asia, and Latin America. Thus, two calendars must be kept in mind: the one that charts the place of southern countries within great power perspectives and so dates most crucial events around World War II with the rise of the United States and the Soviet Union; and the other (less familiar to most) that locates developments of particular significance to the rebirth of political strength in the South, where many of the cardinal dates precede 1939, and indeed in some cases even 1914. If the two world wars and the depression put their mark on southern nationalism, they were by no means its exclusive determinants.

This is apparent not only in the Mexican Revolution of 1910 with its pronounced bias against the United States, but also in the fact that the strongest early reactions to European imperialism came before World War I from the two great traditional states Europe had done so much to humiliate: Turkey and China. Thus, by 1896, the exiled intellectuals in Western Europe known as the Young Turks had begun to enter into contact with reformist military officers in Turkey and with disgruntled subject populations throughout the empire to bring about Sultan Abdul Hamid's overthrow. A British proposition that Macedonia be granted autonomy moved these various forces into action in June 1908. By December, a new parliment had its first meeting with a clear Young Turk majority, and the following April, after an attempt at counterrevolution, the sultan was deposed. In the case of China, a revolutionary coalition of equally varied elements succeeded in overthrowing the Manchu dynasty early in 1912. Although civil war soon broke out, the one feeling shared by virtually all Chinese was hostility to the ceaseless interventions of foreigners since the 1830s.

World War I gave added stimulus to political activism in the South. In some cases this was the result of imperialism intensifying its pressures, as in Japan's Twenty-One Demands on China, presented in January 1915. In colonial circumstances, by contrast, the effect of the war was generally to liberalize regimes. So in 1916, France moved fully to assimilate the Four Communes of Senegal into the French Republic and offered a series of overdue reforms (including an end to special native taxes, a relaxation of the provisions of the native penal code, and a token increase in the political voice of the Muslim community at the local level) to the Muslim Algerians. Similarly, Great Britain found itself obliged to declare that the eventual goal in India was self-government, and entered into negotiations with the local political leadership in Egypt that led to a form of semiindependent status for this country in 1922 (although it was not until the Anglo-Egyptian Treaty of 1936 that the Egyptians themselves recognized a relaxation of London's grip). In Latin America, by contrast, the major effect of the war was to restructure the links connecting the continent to the international economic system, as industrial goods previously imported now had to be produced domestically; there was, too, a sharp rise in foreign demand for raw materials. Politically, the general effect of this development was to encourage the rise of populist governments directed against the landowning elite (often seen as in league with foreign powers). Certainly the war did not single-handedly produce these events: The great Mexican Revolution had begun in 1910 with a similar populist appeal directed against the narrow circle surrounding Porfirio Díaz and the enormous inflow of capital from the United States. But the rise of populist governments and the economic reorganization of much of the continent might be said to constitute a sort of "decolonization" of Latin America and might be viewed as a process the war accelerated but did not create.

The war also greatly abetted the Russian Revolution of 1917, which in turn had repercussions in much of Asia and some of Africa. Lenin was able not only to formulate a theoretical attack on colonialism that was ideological dynamite, but also to back it up with an organizational method that had proved its effectiveness and with the resources of the Soviet state. His new government immediately renounced czarist designs on Constantinople, the northern part of Persia, and Manchuria. Instead, Lenin offered material aid to Ataturk, Reza Khan Pahlevi, the emir of Afghanistan, the Wafd party in Egypt, and the Kuomintang in China in their respective efforts to diminish outside influence in their national affairs. The subsequent growth of local Communist parties, the actions of Comintern, and the conduct of other national Communist parties – most notably the French – played an undeniably important role in the later ground swell of opposition to colonialism (although Communist influence fell far short of being the "international menace" that Western statesmen began to decry in their concern over southern nationalism immediately after 1921).

In the years following World War I, the pace of colonial nationalism quickened. The slow spread of Western education, the increasing economic development of areas related to European capitalism, and the accumulating know-how acquired from discussion and agitation were serving to create the necessary bases for strong nationalist movements after 1945. During the interwar period a hallmark of modernity, political parties, began to form for the first time in many of these areas. The National Congress party of India had been founded in 1885, substantially earlier than an organized, Westernized local elite arose in most of the imperial domains, but its functional equivalent could be discerned clearly throughout the lands of European rule by the early thirties (with the exception of certain parts of black Africa), while the Congress party's own stance became substantially more antagonistic to continued British rule as a consequence of Gandhi's agitation.

Outside the colonial order, other challenges to European imperialism were to be heard in these years. The most striking defiance was surely that of Turkish nationalist Mustafa Kemal, or Ataturk. Reacting to the wartime designs of France, Britain, Italy, Greece, and (until 1917) Russia to reduce his nation to an area of some 20,000 square miles, Ataturk in 1919 stirred his countrymen to a resistance effort that by 1923 had established the boundaries of a state of 300,000 square miles, boundaries that would endure.

So too in China nationalist forces were on the move. May 4, 1919, saw the first student-worker protests against the decision at Versailles to turn German concessions in Shantung over to Japan, and in 1921 the Chinese Communist party was born, to take its place in 1924 alongside Sun Yat-sen's Kuomintang (founded in 1912). The success of this combination against local military dictators throughout China gave way in 1927 (after Sun's death) to civil war between Communists and Nationalists. This strife encouraged Japanese ambitions. The invasion of Manchuria by Japan in 1931, and of China proper in 1937, decisively changed the course of the Civil War, preparing the terrain for the eventual Communist victory of 1949.

The growth of nationalist sentiment in Asia and the Middle East, and the challenge of the Russian Revolution, did not go unnoticed in those European capitals most directly concerned, Paris and London. Nor did these capitals fail to recognize how gravely the terrible toll of the war – the millions dead, the material destruction, the pretensions of cultural superiority debunked – crippled their own ability to maintain their international dominion. They looked, however, to the map, where large gains had been registered. Not only had these countries claimed Germany's African colonies (leaving to Japan Berlin's Pacific holdings north of the equator, and to Australia and New Zealand those to the south), but they had proceeded to the final dismemberment of the Ottoman Empire (after the occupation of Algiers in 1830, and of Egypt in 1882, and machinations in the Balkans over the preceding several decades). The League of Nations duly sanctioned these arrangements, and the evident powerlessness of the Arabs suggested that European might had no serious contestants overseas.

Furthermore, World War I had amply demonstrated to the public and to the leadership of both France and Great Britain the practical advantages of empire, for there was general agreement that the hundreds of thousands of workers, the vast stores of supplies, and the million and a half fighting men furnished by the two empires had given these countries a decisive edge in the struggle against Germany. At the same time, the increasing participation of Socialist parties in their respective national governments meant that except for the nascent Communist parties and a scattering of intellectuals, fundamental opposition to imperial possessions ceased in the Western democracies. Leftist critics no longer directed their attacks against colonialism as a system, but instead called for remedies to specific abuses, and this in the interests of the mother country as well as the foreign subjects. In short, just at the moment when powerful forces were beginning to put an end to European rule overseas, many Europeans were for the first time coming to the conclusion that their national survival might depend on the preservation of empire. Faced with the growing power of the United States, Japan, and the Soviet Union, the proposition that local nationalisms would be the wave of the future appeared a bit absurd. It was easy, then, to predict the international role of a European nation bereft of empire. The example of Spain was there for all to ponder.

Whatever the European will, the increase in the strength of

nationalist organization in most areas of European domination proceeded apace, with World War II providing the decisive blow. The fall of Singapore in February 1942, and the surrender of Rangoon a month later, climaxed the expansion of Japan's Greater East Asian Co-Prosperity Sphere and encouraged (as in the case of the Dutch East Indies), or permitted by default (as in the case of French Indochina), the mobilization of such strong nationalist forces that it seemed highly improbable that the old colonial regimes could reinstate themselves without being severely contested. Similarly, World War II exacerbated tensions in the most important of imperial possessions – India – sharply intensifying the demands for independence at the same time that it placed the British in a more unfavorable position either to refuse or to stall. In Africa, although its influence was less direct, the war strained colonial relations as well. The northern part of the continent was an important theater of military action (with the conspicuous absence of the dominant colonial authority, France, noted by all), and southern Africa suffered harsh requisitions in order to further the Allied war effort.

Despite the established pedigree of local nationalism in most imperial domains by 1945, and despite the apparent decline of European power internationally, virtually no one foresaw the scope of the decolonization process – much less its speed – in the immediate aftermath of the war. Part of the reason is undoubtedly that changes of such magnitude are very seldom predicted. More specifically, however, the Europeans professed pride in the solidarity of their empires during the conflict, while interpreting the emerging postwar international order as one to be marked by the increasing interdependence of nations – not by their fragmentation at the hands of nationalism. National independence seemed a vain, anachronistic goal.

The forecast of the character of the new international order was to turn out to be correct; the forecast of which units would join in association proved mistaken. For in the two decades after the end of World War II, London and Paris came to recognize that their best safeguards lay not in revitalized empire but in a united Europe within an Atlantic Alliance. Not the Commonwealth or the French Union, but such vehicles as the General Agreement on Tariffs and Trade, the International Monetary Fund, the World Bank, and later the Organization for Economic Cooperation and Development proved to be the arena for supranational integration. It was coordination among the states of the North, and not the character of their connection with the South, that would establish the most original and important structures of international relations after 1945. This did not seem to imply, however, that the South would be forgotten. To the contrary, after 1945 France and Britain made a greater financial effort than ever before to provide for the economic interdependence of Europe with its overseas possessions. At the time, it was not anticipated that the South would unsettle the international system to the extent that was ultimately to be the case.

Perhaps the major reason for discounting the significance of southern matters after 1945 was that the major menace to the North seemed to come from the Soviet Union. Outright opposition to the fate of Poland began in 1945, and the Cold War was officially inaugurated so far as Washington was concerned with the announcement of "containment" in the Truman Doctrine of March 1947. Strategic thinking at this time was preoccupied with such problems as calculating the damage a nuclear attack would inflict on the Soviets as against the number of hours it would take Russian divisions to occupy Western Europe. It remained unanticipated that the major theater of conflict in the postwar period would be in the South.

Yet in short order the first violence to wrack these politically unstable areas of the world made its appearance. On May 8, 1945, the very day Paris was celebrating the defeat of Germany, Muslim riots around the town of Sétif in Eastern Algeria claimed over a hundred European lives. Reaction was swift. French planes strafed forty-four Muslim hamlets, an offshore cruiser bombarded more, and groups of settler vigilantes summarily executed hundreds of natives. Testimony to the ferocity of the repression is the fact that the number of Muslims who died in these events has never been determined, though estimates range from 6,000 to 45,000. The following year war broke out in Indochina, in a struggle that would eventually kill 100,000 French (including mercenary auxiliaries) and cost the lives of untold thousands of Vietnamese. Again, in 1947, an uprising in Madagascar killed some 100 Europeans, provoking a French repression that by official estimates took 86,000 native lives. By the time the Algerian conflict ended in 1962, another 750,000 deaths had been added to the rolls of decolonization.

"Police action" that mushroomed into armed repression occurred in the British Empire as well, most notably in Malaya (1948–54) and in Kenya (1952–5). But the British possessions came more to be noted – as the Conservatives especially had warned – for the violence the subject peoples inflicted on each other rather than for nationalist confrontations with London. Thus, it was Greek against Turk on Cyprus, Jew against Arab in Palestine, and Hindu against Muslim on the Indian subcontinent. Struggles between blacks and Asians in East Africa, between Africans and Arabs in the Sudan and Zanzibar, between Nigeria and Biafra, and within Northern Ireland have been later, indirect consequences of this same decolonization process.

With the beginning of independence in Algeria in the summer of 1962, the critical phase of European decolonization came to an end except in the Portuguese holdings in Angola and Mozambique. Thereafter the United States inherited such legacies of these empires as would continue to trouble international affairs: Vietnam in Asia, Israel in the Middle East, South Africa and Rhodesia in Africa. But the concern of the present chapter is solely with French and British decolonization (although a comparison is drawn at one point with Dutch Indonesia), mainly over the years between 1939 and 1962.

Despite the historical significance of European decolonization after World War II, there has been no serious interpretive account of it as an overall process. A number of excellent case studies exist that analyze specific policies or periods in the imperial capitals or in the colonial territories, and there are several chronologically complete surveys of the decline of European rule overseas. These have been neither directed nor followed, however, by studies attempting to conceptualize synthetically the entire period. In default of a wide-ranging debate over the character of decolonization as a historical movement – an effort to see some pattern in events – a kind of conventional wisdom has grown up that attributes the differences in the British and French experiences to a combination of their respective imperial traditions and the governing abilities of their domestic political institutions. As yet, there has been no systematic attempt to separate carefully the chief variables to be analyzed, to assign them weights of relative importance, and to coordinate them in a historical and comparative manner. This chapter hopes to open discussion of these questions.

Although there were definite political options in imperial policy open to Britain and France after 1945, the historically conditioned realm of the possible precluded the adoption of certain courses of action. The material hardships following the havoc of the war combined with the clear ascendance of the two "antiimperial" powers, the United States and the Soviet Union, and with the increased maturity of nationalist elites throughout Africa and Asia to force a decided retrenchment of Europe overseas. In retrospect, we can see that the truly important political decisions to be made by Paris and London after 1945 concerned not whether the colonies would be free, but rather which local nationalist factions they would favor with their support and over what piece of territory these new political elites would be permitted to rule. What would be federated, and what partitioned? Who should govern, and according to what procedures? These were decisive issues over which the Europeans continued to exercise a significant degree of control. When the Europeans did not respect the historically imposed limits of their power, however, their policies were to meet with defeat. Thus, although the Suez Invasion of October–November 1956 constituted a political crisis of the first order in Britain, it was the only occasion when colonial matters occupied such a position. In France, by contrast, the interminable wars in Indochina and Algeria not only cost the lives of hundreds of thousands of Asians and Africans but eventually brought the collapse of the Fourth Republic as well.

A comparative analysis of British and French abilities to

withdraw from their empires after 1945 suggests four respects in which the British were favored. First, there was the legacy of the past in terms of ideas and procedures on imperial matters, precedents built up over the decades before the Second World War that served to orient European leaders and organize their responses to the pressures for decolonization. On this score, the British proved temperamentally, and especially institutionally, more fit than the French to cope with overseas challenges to their rule. Second, there were the international "places" of Britain and France and especially the different relations maintained by the two countries with the United States. Third, there was the question of the domestic political institutions of France and Britain with their very unequal capacities to deal with a problem of the magnitude of decolonization. The French multiparty system with its weak governing consensus clearly was not the equivalent of the two-party system in Britain. Even had the French system been stronger, however, it is not evident that it would have dealt more effectively with decolonization, for national opinion, especially the "collective conscience" of the political elite in France, was significantly different from that in Britain.

The fourth variable to be analyzed directs attention from Paris and London to the character of the nationalist elites with whom the Europeans had to deal. It will be maintained here that the conflicts in Algeria and Indochina were full-fledged peasant rebellions and so presented France with a kind of nationalist united front that Britain was simply fortunate enough to escape (at least until Suez). Thus, the comparative study of European decolonization depends in important measure on the comparative study of colonial nationalism. Such an argument is in line with the proposition, advanced in the preceding chapter, that imperialism was to a certain extent the function of southern political capacities. The same is true of the character of decolonization. Partly because of the importance of this theme, partly because it is almost always neglected in favor of explaining decolonization by reference to Paris and London, nearly half of the chapter will deal with the character of colonial nationalism as a key variable determining the pattern of this process.

Decolonization in Paris and London

In terms of colonial ideology and institutions, the British experience prepared London remarkably well for the liquidation of empire after 1945. In a sense, one may mark the first phase of British decolonization as stretching from the Durham Report of 1839 (relative to Canada) to the Statute of Westminster of 1931. By this series of measures, Britain created the dominion system and institutionalized a procedure for gradually loosening control over her possessions. For a time, to be sure, the final character of the commonwealth (as it came to be called after the turn of the century) remained in doubt. During the interwar years, however, it became clear that the sometime dream of "imperial federation" whereby London would control the economic, defense, and foreign policies of the several allied Anglo-Saxon peoples would never come to fruition. Instead the measured progress from representative to responsible government and from there to commonwealth status would culminate in the establishment of fully sovereign states. However grand in theory the ideas of a stronger federal structure may have sounded when proposed by men like Joseph Chamberlain, the experience of World War I served instead to weaken the alliance. It was British entanglements, after all, that had involved the dominions in warfare far from home and at a cost of over 200,000 lives. It was wiser, perhaps, for them to imitate the United States and delay involvement in these "foreign" affairs. Or better yet, the dominions might make common cause with Washington, which emerged from the war appearing both militarily and economically better suited than London to lead the Anglo-Saxon world. Thus, the Balfour Declaration of 1926 only stated what had already been decided in fact: the sovereignty of the dominions in all respects. The Statute of Westminster of 1931 served as a final confirmation of the declaration. Although the Ottawa Agreements inaugurating an imperial preference system were signed the following year, they failed to provide economic unity where political unity was lacking. The British Commonwealth of Nations was not to be a federal organization.

In these circumstances, the Government of India Act of 1935

must appear as the first major step in the decolonization process that began in earnest after 1945. For although the act itself fell far short indeed of according independence to India, it was now undeniable that the "white" dominions would eventually be joined in their informal alliance by peoples of other racial stocks. To the Indians, of course, this was scant satisfaction because not only the time of their independence, but more importantly, the politically most crucial features of their emerging state seemed to be outside their ability to control. But in London the act was in many ways decisive. It largely reconciled popular and elite opinion to the eventual independence of this "crowning jewel" of empire, considered along with the British Isles themselves to be one of the "twin pillars" of Britain's international rank. Of course there is the mistake, encountered in the works of Britons especially, of seeing in retrospect a grand design for decolonization which in fact did not exist. Closer inspection commonly reveals the British to have been following Burke's sage counsel to reform in order to preserve: London made concessions more often to subvert opposition to British rule than to prepare for its demise. So, for example, to see Indian independence in 1947 as necessarily following from the Government of India Act of 1935, and that act as unerring confirmation of the intentions of the Government of India Act of 1919 (itself supposedly the natural product of the Morley-Minto reforms of 1909), assumes a British gift for foresight that a detailed examination of the historical record makes difficult to sustain. What is lacking in these accounts is a sense of the conflicts, hesitations, and uncertainties of the past and of the attempts to reinterpret or renege on the promise of eventual independence for India.

Nonetheless, the British *did* establish a tradition of meeting colonial discontent by reforms that associated the subject peoples more closely with their own governing. The prior evolution of the dominion system *did* exert an important influence on the style of British policy toward India. And the ultimate decision to grant India independence and to permit it to withdraw from the commonwealth if it wished *did* constitute a momentous precedent for British policy toward the rest of the colonies.

How limited, by contrast, was the experience of the French in handling political change within their empire. In January and February of 1944, a group of colonial civil servants met in Brazzaville, capital of the French Congo, to draw up proposals for imperial reorganization in the aftermath of the war, but the many worthwhile recommendations they made – the end of forced labor and special native legal codes, the creation of territorial assemblies and their coordination in a "French Federation," the representation of colonial peoples at the future French Constituent Assembly – failed to deal with the truly central problem, the possibility of a colonial evolution toward independence.[1] That is, the French are not to be criticized for failing to provide complete and immediate independence to their colonies, but rather for their steadfast refusal to consider even eventual separation a viable political option. As the conference report preamble put it: "The goals of the civilizing work accomplished by France in the colonies exclude any idea of autonomy, all possibility of evolution outside the French bloc of the Empire; the eventual constitution, even in the future of self-government in the colonies, is denied."[2]

Nor were matters to improve with time. Despite the rapid enactment of a host of unprecedented reforms proposed by the conference over the next two years, there was no thought of conceding to colonial nationalists political advantages that might lead to independence. By the summer of 1947, this had been made clear on successive occasions to the Indochinese, to the Tunisians and Moroccans, to the Malagasies, to the blacks of West and Equatorial Africa, and to the Algerians. Indeed, the matter had been fixed by the Fourth Republic's Constitution in the terms providing for the "French Union" in its Title VIII.[3]

Experts in jurisprudence have convincingly pointed out the ambiguity and contradictions with which the final text establishing the French Union abounds. Its one central feature stands out clearly enough, however: The authority of France over the union was beyond dispute. Neither in the immediate nor in the far future would there be a partnership among equals within this "federation." The only significant power whatsoever conferred on the union was that of pooling members' resources for the common defense (Article 62). But it was "the

Government of the [French] Republic [which] shall undertake the coordination of these resources and the direction of the policy appropriate to prepare and ensure this defense." In legislative matters, the union was totally subordinate to the National Assembly (Articles 71–92). Nor could foreign nationalists convert the union into a platform from which to dislodge France from her overseas possessions, for its key institutions (the presidency, the high council, and the assembly) were safely under metropolitan control (Articles 62–6 and Article 77). What the union assured, in essence, was that the peoples of the empire would be neither French nor free.

Compared with the British case, the French position is especially striking. For what Paris seemed intent on doing was to form an equivalent to the Imperial Federation, which the British, working with people similar to themselves racially, economically, and culturally, had abandoned some twenty years earlier. How are we to understand, then, this historically outdated institution, the French Union?

Scarcely a book appears on the modern French Empire that does not give special attention to the ideology of "assimilation" as legitimizing colonial rule. Thus, whereas the French had aspirations of making fellow citizens out of their colonial subjects ("the Greater France of 100 million Frenchmen"), the British had typically spoken of self-government. In part, this stems from a difference in philosophic temperament. When the French were declaring the universal rights of man, Burke was moved to say that he knew only of the rights of Englishmen. In other words, leaving aside such important exceptions as Lyautey and Jules Harmand, who championed "association" rather than "assimilation" as a goal for national policy, the French claimed a general relevance for their national values that the British never assumed, believing instead in the basic distinctness of different social patterns. In each case, of course, the dominant culture was asserting its superiority over the natives, but the British version of future developments proved more amenable to fulfillment in the light of the course of history (however much it, like the French policy of assimilation, would have been content to attach its promise to an infinitely receding historical horizon).

I am skeptical of the importance of this doctrine as a basic cause of French shortsightedness after World War II. First, the doctrine of association, which was quite close to the British notion of things, had in fact come to achieve wide acceptance during the interwar period and so might have provided a guide for decolonization after 1945. Certainly the Brazzaville Conference respected its basic tenets. Secondly, not many colonial specialists could have been taken in by the rhetoric of assimilation. For what it achieved in application was a division of colonial peoples into the few who might achieve the status of French citizen and the many who could not hope to qualify for such rights and immunities. The great bulk of the colonial subjects were thereby denied the protections associated with Western liberal and democratic traditions. In practice, assimilation served not as a bridge but as a barrier to political liberty. This was so patently true that it is difficult to believe many colonial experts could have been deceived. Finally, it is not doctrinal utterances but established institutional procedures for handling political issues that play the major role in preparing governments for action. Here one might be tempted to contrast British indirect rule with French direct rule, except more recent scholarship has tended to doubt the significance of this distinction.[4] In any case, it was not the agencies of indirect rule (the Native Authorities in Africa, the Princely States in India and Malaya) that served the British as institutional frameworks for decolonization, but instead the more centralized executive councils that developed, as we have seen, from procedures evolved over the hundred years before the Second World War with the Anglo-Saxon dominions.

Past experience has given the British still another, but less frequently noted, advantage over the French in reacting to the pressures for decolonization after 1945. By the middle of the nineteenth century at the latest, London had come to appreciate the convenience of "informal empire," of supporting a dependable local elite in order to assure a stable environment for trade and investment. Thus, British "antiimperialism" of the nineteenth century came to be predicated on the assumption that free trade could harmonize interests among nations, ridding the world of war through a growing and mutually profitable economic interdependence. However illusory such ideas, they appeared to work especially well in Latin America, where, after an interlude of anarchy following the Napoleonic Wars and the struggle for independence from Spain, national regimes emerged whose stability depended to a significant degree on financial connections with Britain. In the opinion of the British, working with such national import-export elites seemed far more sensible than attempting to exercise direct political control over faraway peoples of different ethnic stocks. Similar arrangements were contemplated for the Ottoman Empire and Persia at the same time, and for China and parts of Africa thereafter. Only the inability of native regimes to maintain themselves in the face of mounting domestic and foreign pressures prompted Britain's direct (and generally begrudging) intervention. With the exception of India, the British far preferred the sort of arrangement they had worked out in Latin America to that they felt obliged to undertake in Egypt and East and West Africa. Although they had finally undertaken to experiment with a protectionist empire during the interwar period, this style never suited the free trade imperialists nearly as well as it had the French. (For a more extended discussion, see Chapter 1.)

The reasons are obvious. As a much weaker power in the international arena, France simply could not maintain the kind of informal control the British enjoyed. However much some may like to explain direct rule by reference to "national character" (that is, the French "habit" of centralized administration), this constraint of international politics emerges as a decisive determinant of national policy: In order to be imperialists the French had to be protectionists. This very reliance of the French on an economically protected empire meant that those interests involved overseas were usually more intensely committed than their British counterparts, who, obliged to calculate the value of colonial possessions without such large advantages being conferred by London's rule, were correspondingly less insistent that colonial nationalism be opposed. The difference between the French and the British was as true in West Africa in the 1870s as in the Middle East half a century later, when the French were obliged to stake out their claims against those protégés of the British, the Hashemite family. Thus, from colonial ideology to colonial practice, from the realm of the economic to that of the political, the differences in imperial traditions must be furnished their role in determining the pattern of postwar British and French decolonization.

Prewar theory and practice did not alone decide postwar imperial policy, however. That the United States emerged after 1945 as the world's dominant power clearly helped the British to accept their decline in international affairs more than it did the French. Thus, Britain's wartime cooperation in the development of the atom bomb had extended into an important place for it within NATO, where they held five of the thirteen principal command posts, with seven reserved for the Americans and one for the French. But the most salient aspect of the difference in Washington's relations with Paris and London emerges perhaps from an analysis of the quality of the bonds linking Franklin Roosevelt to Winston Churchill and to Charles de Gaulle. Although Roosevelt held Churchill in high esteem, "he hate[d] de Gaulle with such fierce feeling that he ramble[d] almost into incoherence whenever we talk[ed] about him," Cordell Hull reported in the summer of 1944.[5] With the North African landing of November 1942, and the assassination of Darlan a month later, the Americans moved to make General Henri Giraud, and not de Gaulle, head of civilian administration there and commander in chief of the surrendered French army of several hundred thousand men. Despite de Gaulle's ability in 1943 to rally behind him the National Liberation Committee (CFLN) and certain resistance groups operating inside France, the Americans continued to oppose his leadership. Even at the moment of the Liberation of France, Roosevelt refused to recognize the General's authority, insisting instead that a military administration run the country until the wishes of the population were made known by elections. It was the end of October 1944 before the United States finally recognized de Gaulle's Provisional Government.[6]

Certainly more than personality factors were at play. For the features of de Gaulle's personality that the Americans and sometimes the British found so antipathetic had to do with his determination not to let France be absorbed by her allies during the war and be relegated to a satellite role deprived of all initiative thereafter. So, early in the struggle, he had protested the manner in which the British occupied Diego Suarez on Madagascar and conducted operations against the Vichy troops in Syria. Similarly, the General had intimations of Roosevelt's plans for the French Empire: that Indochina or Morocco might be made a trusteeship of other powers; that British or American bases might be permanently established on New Caledonia or at Bizerte and Dakar; even that a new buffer state might be created between France and Germany, to be called Wallonia and to run from Switzerland to the Channel. De Gaulle's sharp reaction to such considerations was in perfect accord with his ambition to regenerate France as a nation. As he told Roosevelt:

I know that you are preparing to aid France materially, and that aid will be invaluable to her. But it is in the political realm that she must recover her vigor, her self-reliance and, consequently, her role. How can she do this if she is excluded from the organization of the great world powers and their decisions, if she loses her African and Asian territories – in short, if the settlement of the War definitively imposes upon her the psychology of the vanquished?[7]

This wartime experience was to leave a permanent mark on French attitudes toward the United States whenever colonial questions arose. All shades of French political opinion suspected American moves in North Africa after the Allied landing there in November 1942, as it was believed that Washington wished to expel the French in order to move in itself. Similarly, British efforts to pry the French out of the Levant at the end of the war were believed to depend on American support. And the jealousy with which the French tried to protect their monopoly over affairs in Indochina after 1946, despite their reliance on ever increasing American aid, serves as yet another instance of their suspicion of American designs.[8] One need only reflect on the welcome London gave to American involvement in British spheres of influence in Greece and Turkey in 1947, and in Iran in 1953, to appreciate the importance of the difference relations with Washington made in the overall process of European decolonization.

Certainly, at times, the British had reason to find the relationship most frustrating. To many, it appeared that the United States would have its own way at every turn, insistent on its rights but reluctant to honor its obligations. America's power, geographic isolation, and (as the sentimental liked to feel) immaturity in foreign affairs combined to produce this mixture of righteousness and irresponsibility the British found so taxing. But it was only a minority who argued, as some radical American historians do today, that Washington's moves were in fact premeditated efforts to sap British power in a design to replace that nation in internal affairs. These observers could point, however, to American carping during the interwar period at imperial and commonwealth arrangements that favored the United Kingdom economically as the prelude to a move after 1945 to replace the British in the Mediterranean and the Middle and Far East. Max Beloff nonetheless portrays the dominant mood when he writes: "The degree to which British statesmen and diplomats expected a natural sympathy for British policy to exist in the United States and equated any hostility to or criticism of Britain with treason to America and not merely to Britain can be abundantly illustrated."[9] Surely the confidence with which Britain relied on American power to fill the vacuum left by the disintegration of its formal and informal spheres of control around the globe is remarkable, especially when contrasted with the French experience. So, to cite but one example, Gabriel Kolko may characterize Anglo-American relations over Middle East issues as marked by unrelieved antagonism. But Anthony Eden's own account of how he wooed Washington's intervention in Iran to topple Prime Minister Mossadegh and his evident relief that a consortium arrangement could be worked out that preserved British interests in the area (however much it may have furthered the ambitions of the Americans in the process) makes it difficult to agree that all was cynical maneuvering for advantage between the two Anglo-Saxon powers.[10] As we shall see in Chapter 4, on the other hand, there was no doubt of the aggressive American intention that European overseas empire be terminated after World War II. For a combination of easily understood political and economic reasons, Washington had sought since the late nineteenth century to deny spheres of influence in the South to its northern rivals by supporting nationalist movements in these regions, and during as well as in the aftermath of the war, the United States decisively reaffirmed this traditional policy – only now expanding it in scope to include Eastern Europe, the Balkans, and the areas of formal and informal empire from the Near East to the Orient.

The third of the major differences in the respective abilities of the British and the French to decolonize takes us from international considerations to an analysis of their domestic political institutions. Britain had a "loyal opposition," a stable two-party system, and a strong executive. France, however, was plagued by disloyal opposition from both the Right and the Left, by a multiparty system, and by a notoriously weak executive. Hence the French were not so able as the British to process a problem of the magnitude of decolonization.

To an observer with a background in French domestic politics, surely the most striking thing about the British political system during this period is the manner in which its institutions seemed to function more effectively during crisis. Faced with a challenge to its authority from abroad, the system organized its responses as ranks closed and hierarchies of command asserted themselves. This resilience of British institutions was highlighted especially at the time of the invasion of the Suez Canal Zone, the single occasion on which matters related to empire drew the concerned attention of the British public and its leaders. It is not a question here of whether the policy was a colossal blunder, or whether the fault for its failure lay with Eisenhower and Dulles. The point is simply, as Leon Epstein demonstrates in his careful study of British politics during this period, that the system performed remarkably well.[11]

Not that there was always unanimity. As the most thorough study of party politics during decolonization suggests, imperial issues were perhaps as much a matter of serious bipartisan dispute during the 1950s as at any time in modern British history.[12] But the discipline of the parties, the institutional strength of government leadership, and the way partisan conflict tended to increase party solidarity (rather than create centrifugal struggles, as was so often the case in France) meant that from the mid-1940s until the mid-1960s British imperial policy was characterized by coherence, consistency, and strength.

The most delicate balance point at this time in British politics was the Conservatives' effort not to let these issues tear them apart after they came to power in 1951.[13] As David Goldsworthy documents, the Conservatives were the party of empire. They were tied to it emotionally in perhaps their most vital collective myth, the pride in empire, and connected to it concretely through settlers, business interests, and the Colonial Service, all of which sought their place in its ranks.[14] Yet despite Churchill's return to power, the single serious misstep under their leadership was Suez. A part of the reason for their success was surely that Labour had shown the way by granting independence to the several territories of South Asia and by preparing the road for the future independence of the Gold Coast. In addition, there was luck: Churchill was out of office after the spring of 1955 and so was not able to maintain the mistaken policies he was drawn to, paramount of which was the creation of the Central African Federation in 1953.[15] Harold Macmillan (from 1957) and Iain Macleod (from 1959) proved themselves more realistic leaders. They were substantially aided in the pursuit of their policies by the logic of the British political system, which made it quite difficult for the recalcitrant reactionaries in the party – who represented probably no more than 10–15 percent of its strength, but who could rally greater support on specific issues – to create enough instability in the system for concessions to be made to them. Try as they might, first over Egypt, then over Cyprus, and finally over Central Africa and Katanga, they remained isolated and impotent.[16]

In contrast, if there is one point on which French Socialist politicians, academic observers, and right-wing military officers are in agreement, it is that the manifold structural shortcomings of the governmental system under the Fourth Republic (pejoratively referred to as "le système") were responsible for the terrible trials of French decolonization. Charles de Gaulle expressed with characteristic bluntness the sentiments of many when he replied in 1948 to an interviewer who inquired how he would "significantly modify the foreign policy of France" should he return to power:

> I will not have to change the foreign policy of France since at present France has no foreign policy. Her regime does not permit it any more than it permits her to have an economic policy worthy of the name, a social policy, or a financial policy, etc. The truth is there is nothing. Thus I will not change this policy which does not exist, but I will make the policy of France.[17]

A general theory of the Republic's weakness could readily amalgamate the various criticisms of le système into a unified explanation of its difficulties.[18] Under both the Third and Fourth republics, the root cause of political weakness was political division, which, although not so serious as to prevent a governing-center coalition for France, nonetheless habitually precluded the unity indispensable for effective government. We are told that this political division was the product of the simultaneous playing out of several historical conflicts wracking French society at large (Williams, Hoffmann), of the difficulty of governing against the cynical opposition of those who denied the entire system legitimacy (Aron), and of French attitudes toward power which hindered the growth of effective authority relations (Crozier) – all aggravated by a form of constitutional government that, with its multiple parties and weak executive, exacerbated these conflicts in the very seat of power (Wahl, MacRae, Barale), and so encouraged the irresponsibility of elected officials (Leites). Inability fed upon inability until the default of government authority reached such proportions that, at the first serious threat of military insubordination, the regime totally collapsed.[19]

At first reading this seems to make good sense of the French experience and to contrast meaningfully with the case of British domestic institutions. But on closer analysis this account shows serious problems, as it neglects to point up the stubborn colonial consensus that reigned from the Socialists to the Right and that contributed as much to the ineffectiveness of the political system as this regime, in turn, made a sound policy impossible to agree upon or implement. For as a review of the Indochinese policy of the Blum and Ramadier governments in 1946–7 and of the Algerian policy of the Mollet government of 1956–7 demonstrates, it was unity, resolution, and action that at these critical junctures of Socialist national leadership emerge as the hallmarks of the regime. What typified these truly decisive periods of Socialist leadership were not so much the shortcomings of the political system through which the Socialists had to govern as their own unrealistic, tenaciously held positions on colonial matters. Admittedly the French political system was a weak one, and its divisions clearly complicated the reaction to colonial nationalism. But it is all too tempting to use the system as a scapegoat and so to forget the dedication of the Fourth Republic to an image of France that found its highest expression with de Gaulle: To be internally stable, France required international greatness, and to obtain this rank it had to count on its empire, as in this enterprise it had no certain friends.

Time and again throughout the history of the Fourth Republic, beneath the invective of political division, one finds a shared anguish at the passing of national greatness, a shared humiliation at three generations of defeat, a shared nationalistic determination that France retain her independence in a hostile world – all brought to rest on the conviction that in the empire they would "maintenir." Thus the Socialists shared with most of their fellow countrymen an image of France, a kind of collective conscience, born of the political paralysis of the thirties, the shame of the Occupation, the stern prophecies of General de Gaulle, the fear of domestic communism, and the initial expectations and ensuing disappointments of the Resistance. With most of their fellow countrymen, they too experienced the loss of Indochina as the failure not of a historically absurd colonial policy first launched by de Gaulle, but as the failure of a regime. They feared, then, that the decline of France to second-power status marked not so much an inevitable phase of world history, but the inner failing of a people. The

charges of being a "bradeur d'empire" raised much more profound self-doubt in the National Assembly than did charges of
"scuttle" at Westminister.

It was, therefore, not only the political institutions of France
and Great Britain that were dissimilar, but perhaps more importantly, the national moods or psychologies of the political
elites in these two countries. Where, for example, does one
find in the annals of French leaders anything equivalent to the
entry in the journal of then Chancellor of the Exchequer Hugh
Dalton, dated February 24, 1947, commenting on Lord Mountbatten's negotiations for the independence of India?

> If you are in a place where you are not wanted and where you have not got
> the force, or perhaps the will, to squash those who don't want you, the only
> thing to do is to come out. This very simple truth will have to be applied to
> other places too, e.g., Palestine.[20]

One may object that this analysis fails to disaggregate sufficiently the constituent forces in each country. How important
was it, for example, that Labour was in power immediately
after the war and so could set an example in Britain of how to
deal with colonial nationalism? Doubtlessly the influence of
the Fabian colonial bureau and the work of Arthur Creech
Jones as colonial secretary from late 1946 until 1950 had their
positive impact. But it should be recalled that Socialists led
the government in France as well in the crucial years 1946–7,
when the decision to fight nationalism in Southeast Asia was
made. Thus, at the very time the British Socialists were deciding to hasten the withdrawal from India, the French Socialists
were staging emotional appeals in the National Assembly in
favor of supporting military action in Indochina.[21] The leaders
of both parties bore Socialist labels, but they were to be recognized more clearly by their national than by their party mem-
berships.

There was in France one place a sensible colonial policy was
held. Despite the usually prejudiced attacks on the French
Communist party's colonial stand, of the major parties in
France it was the PCF alone that respected the historical limits
of the moment and recognized very early the kind of flexibility

a successful postwar imperial policy must possess. Thus, although the party tended to discourage independence movements in the empire, it chose to work with them instead of repressing them, seeking to ensure that, should separation become inevitable, it would occur under the auspices of a nationalist elite best able to represent the interests of the local population and preserve the area from the encroachments of foreign powers other than France. In these respects, the PCF compares well with the Labourites.[22]

Similarly, it is difficult to argue that economic interests offer more than a partial explanation of the different patterns of decolonization, although Miles Kahler has shown that French interests were more basically concerned than were the British, and that they found ways to vent their fears.[23] Kahler's evidence suggests that in several respects the comparably more mature British economic interests found the transfer of power easier to accommodate than did the French: From the beginning British business and finance had been relatively more exposed to the strains of free trade and so were less likely to need a protectionist harbor guaranteed by direct colonial control; the large, diversified international firms and banks headquartered in Europe understood that they could cooperate better with moderate nationalists than could smaller European economic interests, and these firms and banks were more likely to be British; and the more advanced colonial economies under British rule threatened to compete with home industries so that their independence was actually welcomed by an important part of the economic community. Of course, it is possible to find the hand of business wherever one wishes in theoretically, if not historically, logical terms. So economic interests are damned if there is federation (in Nigeria, it is sometimes alleged, this allowed for more rational exploitation by outside groups) and equally condemned if there is decentralization (in French West Africa, so one hears, these same interests would balkanize in order to divide and rule). But so long as nationalists were not avowed Communists, or, unlike Mossadegh in Iran and Nasser in Egypt, did not appear to represent threats to basic European overseas interests, leaders in Paris and London could realistically hope to count on the pressures of economic development to create a strong working arrangement with European business. Indeed, in some instances a strong leftist nationalist was to be preferred to a compliant but incompetent collaborator.

In short, disaggregation of the "nation" into its constituent political forces offers insights into specific periods or cases, but does not appear to have conditioned the overall pattern of French or British decolonization. Just as military insubordination in France was more a reflection of the national crisis than it was the cause of it, so other political forces at work are better understood in terms of their national context rather than with respect to their own powers of initiative.

Imperial traditions and practices, international rank and ambitions, domestic political structure and psychology – in each of these respects the British were favored over the French. But such an analysis is not enough to account for the significant differences in the experiences of these two countries. Rather than compare only Paris with London, let us consider what may be learned from comparing the different colonial situations.

A comparative study of colonial nationalism

However thorough a comparison might be made of the policies of Paris and London, such an approach focuses the study of decolonization too narrowly on the imperial capitals, neglecting the decisive role played by the peoples of Asia and Africa in their own liberation. For it is possible to trace the history of decolonization not in terms of European, but of Asian and African developments. The victory of Japan over Russia in 1904; Lenin's rise to power in 1917 and his subsequent aid to national elites striving to reduce European influence in their countries; the triumph of Mustafa Kemal in Turkey after World War I; the rise of Gandhi to leadership of the National Congress party of India in 1920; the increasing importance of Cairo in Arab affairs following the defeat of efforts at Arab unity in World War I and the emergence of modern Egyptian nationalism under Saad Zaghlul Pasha; the rapid growth of colonial economies during the interwar period with the corresponding shifts in local social and political structures; the Japanese conquest of European colonies east of India and the hardships suffered by colonial peoples in all other parts of the globe during World War II; Kwame Nkrumah's return to the Gold Coast in December 1947; Mao Tse-tung's entry into Peking in January 1949 – all these developments offer an alternative way of charting the course of history and analyzing its decisive movements. From this perspective, concentration on the formal boundaries of empire or on events deemed significant at the time in European capitals risks obstructing our vision of those determining processes of history that occurred silently within colonial territories and that gave a local pedigree to nationalism; or that took place regionally without respect for imperial frontiers on the basis of communication among Asians or Africans. Looked at from this angle, history ran by other clocks whose timing mechanisms synchronized only occasionally with the pacing of events in Europe. In order to form a just appreciation of the colonial problem facing Paris and London, our attention must turn from these capitals to Hanoi and Delhi, to Cairo and Algiers, to Accra and Abidjan.

Where comparative analyses of colonial nationalism have been undertaken, they generally tend to advance typologies of nationalist leadership ("liberal separationist," "traditional-nativist," "extremist-radical," and the like), compare them to those of their local opponents ("liberal-assimilationists" and "traditional-collaborationists"), and then analyze the content of the various ideologies of nationalist mobilization (indigenous, religious, or socialist). Unfortunately for comparative purposes, such constructs show serious problems on closer inspection. Any effort to propose ineluctable stages or types of nationalist development must fail given the variety on historical record. Thus the drive for national liberation may be preceded (Tunisia), accompanied (Morocco), or followed (Nigeria) by the political predominance of traditionalist leaders and ideas. Or again, the same man (Ferhat Abbas) or the same movement (the Indian Congress party) may be successively an advocate of assimilation, separation, and revolution, whereas in other cases these various positions may be assumed instead by rival men and groups (Algeria). Or again, the same movement may contain quite heterogeneous members who span the liberal-traditionalist-radical spectrum (the Congress party), or the same individual may alone espouse the whole gamut of ideological appeals (Sukarno with his mixture of nationalism, Islam, and communism, officially proclaimed as NASAKOM). Such typologies, in other words, give us only a false sense of security which even casual reference to the historical record must easily disrupt.

We are on surer ground when we turn from a study of values and the penchant for ahistorical categories to an analysis of structure, and see that the decisive question in the comparative investigation of colonial nationalism has to do with the character of the rural–urban alliance. For whatever their values, what Bourguiba, Ataturk, Sukarno, Nkrumah, Nyerere, Ho Chi Minh, Gandhi, and Houphouet-Boigny all shared was their leadership at the moment of national independence over groupings both traditional and modern in values and structure, groupings with a scope so broad that the split between the countryside and the city was overcome. Obviously such nationalist alliances varied enormously among themselves depending on the interests represented, the solidity of the party apparatus aggregating anticolonial forces, the relative power of local groups outside the nationalist fold, and the international dangers that a young independence movement had to face. But it is, I believe, through an analysis of these forces that we can best elaborate a typology of colonial nationalism and so understand the contribution of the peoples of Asia and Africa to the character of the decolonization process. In short, *who mobilized, or could claim to mobilize, the peasantry?*

A comparison of reactions in Black Africa and Madagascar to postwar French colonial policy with those of nationalists in Algeria and Indochina offers a good illustration of the importance of local conditions in determining this historical movement. For it is important to emphasize that *French policy was essentially the same throughout the empire:* Political reforms were granted only so long as they could be seen as tending to preserve French rule. Demands for change that might ultimately destroy the French presence were to be squelched immediately. De Gaulle was the chief architect of this plan and he made its terms clear to the Vietnamese by his Declaration of March 25, 1945, which his successors in power reaffirmed in their negotiations with Ho Chi Minh at Fontainebleau in the summer of 1946. The Second Constituent Assembly adopted the same stand with the Algerians, and the first legislature of the Fourth Republic confirmed it in the terms of the Statute of Algeria, voted in the summer of 1947. General Juin took the message to Morocco after having delivered it in Tunis. Marius Moutet, the Socialist colonial minister, was relying on the same view when he called for a boycott of the extraordinary congress called at Bamako, Soudan, by the black Africans under French rule in October 1946.

The French subsequently demonstrated the seriousness of their resolve. In November 1946, they shelled the port of Haiphong, taking the lives of several thousand Vietnamese in their determination to rid the city of the Vietminh. In March and April 1947, they responded to a nationalist raid on an army base on Madagascar with a repression that by official estimates killed 86,000 natives. As the Sétif repression of May 1945 had momentarily cowed the Algerians, rigged elections commencing in the spring of 1948 kept the peace in North Africa. But shortly thereafter, the French felt obliged to launch a concerted repression south of the Sahara against the Africans of the Rassemblement Démocratique Africain (RDA).

If the policy was the same, the results were not. Within a month of the French attack on Haiphong, the Vietminh had replied with a coup attempt in Hanoi. Although the Sétif repression effectively fragmented the Algerian political elite for a time, a revolution willing to give no quarter finally broke out in 1954. But in Black Africa the policy succeeded. We may discover why by making a closer analysis of the situation, using the variables mentioned earlier: the ability of a nationalist party to buckle together the alliances of the forces it represents; the relative strength (actual or potential) of this party's local opponents; and the need of such a party for aid from the international system to maintain its local predominance. Thus, to understand the process of European decolonization means to put some order into the variety of colonial situations with which it was concerned, as a French policy anachronistic in certain areas proved well suited to master the events in others. Why did French policy succeed so well in Africa when it failed so totally elsewhere?

Immediately after World War II, African nationalism in the French territories found its most advanced expression in Senegal and the Ivory Coast. But as we shall see, it was the Ivory Coast that was quickly to emerge as the key territory in French policy south of the Sahara. Here the leading political formation was Félix Houphouet-Boigny's Parti Démocratique du Côte d'Ivoire (PDCI), which was founded on the basis of the support of the coffee and cocoa planters' voluntary association, the Syndicat Agricole Africaine (SAA). As president of the SAA, Houphouet had been elected to the French Constituent National Assembly, and there, in the spring of 1946, had proved instrumental in passing the legislation that ended the bitterly hated forced-labor regulations that were in effect throughout French Africa under the Third Republic and that had been intensified under Vichy. By this legislation, Houphouet was able in one stroke to secure a decisive blow for his own class against the European planters in coffee and cocoa (who could not compete with the Africans without the help of cheap, requisitioned labor) and to enlist the support of the great mass of the territory's inhabitants who were subject to these terrible regulations. So Houphouet-Boigny, owner of the largest coffee and cocoa plantation in the Ivory Coast, became, in the words of Ruth Morgenthau, "a hero and liberator. This achievement was the beginning of a myth around Houphouet, the first truly national Ivory Coast tradition."[24] By October 1946, the PDCI had 65,000 members and was the largest party in French tropical Africa.

At the very time the Ivory Coast was securing an initial measure of national unity behind Houphouet, the country was finding itself in increasing turmoil with the French administration. The economic aspect of the problem was familiar throughout the postwar world: shortages and inflation. But it was aggravated in the Ivory Coast by the sharp decline in world market prices for coffee and cocoa, which together constituted 75–92% of the country's exports between 1947 and 1957.[25] In the Territorial Assembly, at the same time, a number of political issues served to divide the PDCI seriously from the settler delegates and the colonial administration. What brought these local issues to the intense concern of Paris, however, were the alliance that had grown up between the PDCI and the French Communist party, and the increasingly dominant role the PDCI was playing throughout the Federation of French West Africa (AOF).

In the first French Constituent Assembly (October 1945–May 1946), the African deputies had recognized both the Socialist and Communist parties as their allies in the effort to secure liberal reforms in colonial rule. Although the leaders of the provisional government assured the Africans these reforms would not be modified whatever the fate of the first draft of the constitution, the promise was not kept. The combined pressures of settler lobbying, de Gaulle's warning that firmness must be displayed, and the need to come to some unequivocal stand in the negotiations with the Vietminh during the summer of 1946 worked together to produce a text in which the second Constituent Assembly (June–October 1946) defined the French Union in terms distinctly less liberal than those earlier proposed.[26] In response, therefore, some 800 delegates from French Africa assembled at Bamako in October 1946 to coordinate their efforts to secure liberal reforms. In an effort to sabotage the congress, Colonial Minister Moutet used his influence inside the Socialist party to convince affiliated Africans, most notably the Senegalese, to boycott the meeting. In the absence of the well-organized Senegalese, the PDCI, with Houphouet at its head, emerged as the unrivaled leader of both French West and Equatorial Africa through the creation of the interterritorial party, the Rassemblement Démocratique Africain. This was to prove critically important several years later, when the issue of attaining independence as a federation arose; the unionists within the RDA found themselves cut off from their Senegalese allies outside and so were less able to thwart what came to be Houphouet's goal of breaking the federation into sovereign states. At the time, a boycott on the part of the French parties that had also been invited to the congress as observers meant that the Africans responded favorably to the one metropolitan party in attendance, the PCF. It was hardly surprising, then, that the newly formed RDA would affiliate itself (*apparentement*) with the Communists in the first legislature of the Fourth Republic elected in November 1946.

With the exclusion of the Communists from the French government the following May, and especially with the railway strikes in West Africa in the fall of 1947, Paris began to anticipate the need to deal with the same firm hand in West Africa that it had already shown in Indochina, Algeria, and Madagascar. In January 1948, Socialist deputy Paul Béchard was appointed governor general of AOF and Orselli was named governor of the Ivory Coast. Initially these men pursued a somewhat conciliatory policy, trying to woo the RDA and the PDCI away from the Communists. But when this showed no signs of progress, Orselli was replaced by Laurent Péchoux and the administration cracked down in an attempt to rid the territory of the RDA by the time of the elections to the second legislature in 1951. Naturally this repression (as it was frankly called) fell most heavily on the Ivory Coast. PDCI officials were imprisoned en masse, villages favorable to the party found their taxes raised, even pilgrims to Mecca were prohibited from leaving the country if they were members of the party. In a move familiar to all the French territories after the war, administrators reorganized electoral districts and rigged election results to favor their handpicked candidates. The repression did not go unanswered. Between February 1949 and January 1950, the party responded in kind to these measures. Hunger strikes, mass demonstrations, acts of civil disobedience, and actual street fighting took the lives of several score Africans; hundreds more were injured and thousands arrested.[27]

For our concerns, the most striking thing about these developments is that ultimately the policy achieved its aims. Unlike the situation in Algeria or Indochina, but like the case of Madagascar, force worked. From the spring of 1950, when Houphouet-Boigny met with François Mitterrand in Paris and determined to break with the Communists, until the present day, France has had no better friend in Africa. Here, then, is the signal success of French decolonization, the exemplar of the policy of reform within order designed to guarantee a continued French presence in the overseas territories. It raises the obvious question of what factors were present in the Ivory Coast that were lacking in Indochina and Algeria.

The most serious problem immediately facing Houphouet-Boigny in the period from February 1949 to January 1950 was the inadequacy of his party organization. Relative to other political formations in French Africa the PDCI may have seemed a potent force, but it simply could not tolerate the pressures put on it by the French administration. It should be recalled that the PDCI came into existence only in 1946, and that it built on the foundation of the SAA, created just two years earlier. Although it is true that the SAA associated tribal chiefs with commoners and that Houphouet had important credentials both as a planter and as the scion of a leading chiefly family, this simply did not constitute strength enough to oppose the French. The root weakness of the party seems to have been the tribal structure of the country (indeed, wherever we turn in colonial situations these "primordial divisions" – to use Clifford Geertz's term – constitute the basic obstacle to party formation regardless of whether the society is "tribal" or "peasant"). The PDCI was in fact an "indirect party" in the sense that its structure depended more on the loyalty of elites who maintained their bases independently of party control than on authority the party could muster on its own account. Beneath its upper levels, party structure mirrored rather than bridged the cleavages within society at large. Once the top split, the party, devoid of horizontal linkages at lower levels, simply fragmented into its constituent parts. As Aristide Zolberg puts it: "The structures created in 1947 helped maintain ethnic ties even when economic and social change might have diminished their importance . . . basic party units coincided with ethnic wards, and party life also reinforced ethnicity . . . Those who were particularly responsible for party organization knew that its machinery was adequate only for electoral purposes."[28] Quite simply, under French pressure this elite disaggregated as some succumbed to hopes for personal gain while others responded to fears of personal loss.

This alone, however, cannot explain Houphouet's capitulation to the French. Other parties at other times have been fractured by repression, only to arise more powerfully thereafter. Is it not conceivable that Houphouet could have appealed over the heads of his fellow party leaders to the people, retired to the bush, and begun a war of national liberation against the French? If a West African specialist may balk at the idea, certainly a student of Asian politics would not. Houphouet was, after all, widely agreed to have charismatic personal qualities, and the election results after his reconciliation with France suggest that in the eyes of the people his opposition served to heighten his prestige. But this is not the course of action Houphouet chose, and although the reasons may seem simple enough to the Africanist, they may be illuminating for a comparative study of decolonization that attempts to encompass the Middle East and Asia. In short, as the most prominent planter in the Ivory Coast, Houphouet-Boigny realized the obvious: The future of his class and thereby of his people lay with France. Mobilize the peasantry? Conduct guerrilla warfare? Nothing seems less probable. As this Catholic, this traditional chief, this leading spokesman of the African bourgeoisie put it to his compatriots at the opening of a fair in 1953: "If you don't want to vegetate in bamboo huts, concentrate your efforts on growing good cocoa and good coffee. They will fetch a good price and you will become rich."[29]

To promote these export crops, the Ivory Coast of the early 1950s needed the cooperation of France. For the country produced only 3 percent of the world's output – and this of an inferior variety, thus making it especially vulnerable to price fluctuations on the international market. Under a 1954 agreement with France, however, Ivory Coast coffee (accounting in those days for some 57 percent of total exports) received both a quota guarantee and a price floor in metropolitan markets.[30] The livelihood of the growing middle class of African planters, along with that of their upper-class colleagues on the great estates, depended on the stability of these contracts.[31]

Houphouet-Boigny and the interests he represented faced another challenge as well: the threat of incorporation into a federal West Africa. Since 1904, French practice had been to finance the entire federation from indirect taxes levied throughout the area. Wealthier territories perennially complained about this practice in the Grand Council in Dakar, but to no avail. After 1945, the Ivory Coast confirmed a trend begun earlier, so that by the mid-1950s it was the undisputed economic leader of the AOF, accounting for 45 percent of the region's exports. As a result of the federation's taxing system, the Ivory Coast received an average of only 19 percent of the money it remitted to Dakar. These taxes to the federal authority amounted, in turn, to two or three times the amount collected and retained locally, so that of the total governmental revenue levies in the Ivory Coast, well over half left, never to return. In addition, the area has traditionally been a heavy importer of labor from other territories, so that by the 1950s some one-fourth of the work force came from outside the Ivory Coast, and the percentage was growing.[32]

In order to make good its separation from French West Africa, the Ivory Coast needed the support of France, for throughout the federation in the early 1950s the mood was for union. Houphouet's preference for decentralization met with opposition from outside the RDA from Léopold Senghor, and from within the party, Sékou Touré of Guinea began to challenge the Ivory Coast leadership. As a result of French support, however, Houphouet could disregard the opinion of his fellow West Africans. The French National Assembly's framework law of March–April 1957 severely weakened the federal authority of the AOF by removing certain of its powers to Paris and by devolving others onto the reinforced territorial assemblies. Senghor complained of the "balkanization" of West Africa and most observers have agreed with him that this was the conscious intention of France.[33] At the Bamako RDA Conference held in September 1957, Touré was much more popular than Houphouet (who found his only backing from wealthy Gabon), but the Ivory Coast's Paris connections made it quite invulnerable to African objections.

Before the territorial assemblies had fully assumed their new prerogatives, however, the Fourth Republic fell. The French scheme of things for Africa was now expressed in de Gaulle's idea of the "French Community." By the terms of the Fifth Republic's constitution, Africans had a choice: "federation" in subordination to France, or independence. In other words, the policy of the Fifth Republic was essentially the same as that of the Fourth so far as African federations were concerned. They could expect no comfort from Paris, for France would not support a gradual evolution toward a federal structure for the AOF if that evolution reduced metropolitan control. (The contrast with the British in Nigeria at the same time is striking. Here the pressures for decentralization – at least after the Richard's Constitution of 1946 – came from the Africans themselves, and especially from the Northern Region.)

A comparison of the Ivory Coast with other colonial situations suggests that the key variable to analyze in order to understand the colonial response to metropolitan policy is the local power position of the predominant nationalist elite. For every war of colonial liberation carries within it a civil conflict, so that in fact the nationalist elite is fighting on two fronts: against the imperial power and against other local groups striving to replace it. Dominant elites are therefore prudent to avoid armed confrontation with the imperial authority. This is not only because it is sensible to recognize that, given the great disproportion of military means, it is especially their fellow citizens who will be killed. The elites understand as well that the initial military setbacks they can expect to suffer may well release the centrifugal forces of class and ethnic division that so profoundly mark most colonial societies. Because warfare in the colonial context will almost inevitably be a protracted, decentralized affair, the initially dominant nationalist elite may find its position assumed by rival leaders. It is, after all, a nationalist fairy tale that nationalism feeds on its own reversals, jumping up from the earth each time more powerful than before until the entire "people" is united on that great day of liberation. In fact, as closer inspection of virtually any colonial situation will warrant, there is a variety of nationalist movements behind what to the casual observer may seem like a single wave of nationalism, and these diverse groups are frequently seriously at odds.

Thus civil war lurks in the heart of every movement for national liberation. So, shortly after the signature of the Anglo-Irish Treaty of 1921, serious strife broke out within Ireland, and two years elapsed before the provisional government was able to bring it under control. The terms of the dispute continued to mark Irish life for decades thereafter. Again, in the very midst of fighting the Dutch effort to regain the Netherlands East Indies, the Communists attempted a coup against the Hatta-Sukarno government (the Madiun Rebellion of 1948) which the Indonesian Army never forgot. In the case of Tunisia, Bourguiba found his agreement to "internal autonomy" as a prelude to eventual independence hotly contested by Salah ben Youssef, secretary general of the Neo-Destour party, who secured important backing within the country as well as from the Algerians and the Egyptians. Only because his leadership of the nationalist movement was so undisputed could Kwame Nkrumah accept the 1950 constitution for the Gold Coast, which offered him a good deal less than independence. What he certainly must have feared was that his continued recalcitrance would prompt the British to support the separatist movement in Ashanti and the Northern Territories (as they might easily have done). "We have no program but independence," declared the Moroccan Istiqlal party in the early 1950s. This made good sense indeed for a party that represented landed interests in a country where 60 percent of the rural population was landless and where the nationalist movement was divided into three autonomous forces. It was the same slogan adopted in 1951 by the Wafd party in Egypt on the occasion of their unilateral abrogation of the Anglo-Egyptian Treaty of 1936. But the Wafd quickly saw things pass out of its hands with the mobilization of the Muslim Brotherhood and the Free Officers and the coup against the monarchy in 1952. More wisely than the Wafd, Ho Chi Minh avoided confrontation with the French until it was literally forced upon him, realizing that whatever the apparent strength of the Vietminh, Indochina was far from securely in its hold in 1946. In the case of the Ivory Coast, there is a slight variation in this pattern. For what Houphouet-Boigny had to fear was not so much local as federal interference with his position. That is, other forces in the AOF were the functional equivalent of an internal threat to his leadership.

Yet however reluctant virtually any nationalist elite may be to enter into war against the imperial authority, such confrontations do occur and we must investigate further to see the possibility of establishing categories of nationalist leadership, determining in each case the likelihood that such an elite would head a militant insurrection. Dominant groups *least likely* to mount a sustained challenge to the colonial order are those that recognize the fragility of their local control and the interest they well may have in a European connection. A particularly clear case of this, as we have seen, is the Ivory Coast. Here a local factor – the threat of the AOF to incorporate the territory – combined with an international consideration – the preferential treatment given in French markets to coffee and cocoa production, the economic basis of the ruling class – to dictate a policy of prudence toward Paris. Not that an elite based on export revenues is necessarily a willing collaborator with European interests – Colonel Qaddafi of Libya is evidence enough of this. But even in the case of Qaddafi, it should be recalled that petroleum products have demonstrated a special immunity to international pressures, and that even this is true only of the present period, as the experience of Prime Minister Mossadegh testifies. The royal court of Cambodia provides another instance of elite collaboration with the Europeans. The Cambodian king welcomed the French return because it promised to destroy the antimonarchical forces the Japanese had fielded before their defeat and to return to his rule the territory seized by Siam during the Second World War. Royal courts do not make the best collaborators, of course, as economic development tends to throw up classes whose attitudes undermine their legitimacy. European interests are most effectively represented instead by what may be called an import-export elite, whose capacity to develop economically – even if only within certain limits – allows it to cooperate usefully with the international system and at the same time to assure domestic stability. The history of Latin America from the mid-nineteenth century to World War I (and beyond) is evidence enough of this.[34]

What I have presented is, of course, an ideal type to which there are important historical exceptions. Thus, fragile nationalist elites will not always recognize where their interests lie in the manner of Houphouet-Boigny. Just as the czar was extremely ill advised to tangle with Japan in 1904 – and even more mistaken to back his Slavic brothers in Serbia in 1914 – so the Wafd party of Egypt unwittingly committed suicide in October 1951, when it chose to abrogate the Anglo-Egyptian Treaty of 1936 in a vain attempt to recover the Sudan and the Suez Canal. What occurred, quite simply, was that in undertaking policies that exceeded their power internationally, they fell prey to local opponents. Nor can one assume that the imperial power will always understand the needs of its foreign collaborators. Britain inadvertently threatened the Jordanian monarchy by its invitation to join the Baghdad Pact in the spring of 1955. And Britain ultimately destroyed the regime of its faithful Iraqi friend Nuri Pasha as Said as one of the prices it paid for the invasion of Suez. On the other hand, groups one might not expect to lead determined nationalist movements do succeed, as the survival of the Moroccan monarchy attests. In this case, the explanation seems to be that the king could count on the divisions among his local opponents to neutralize each other in his favor, while toward the French (and later the Americans) he was most conciliatory. These apparent exceptions to the ideal type seem on closer inspection rather to confirm the likelihood that rulers who base their power on traditional legitimacy or import-export revenues will be least ready to mobilize their peoples for wars of national liberation. These conclusions would suggest, for example, that Elliot Berg's influential analysis of the economic limits on political choice in French West Africa after 1945 is too narrow because it fails to distinguish the political and social variables of poverty. Were Berg correct, were economic need so decisive politically, Algeria would never have had its revolution.[35]

In light of the foregoing analysis, what sorts of nationalist elites may be expected to enter into violent conflict with an imperial regime? Three situations tend to produce such leaders: where a native elite dependent on foreign power has never been created; where such an elite, once created, is destroyed; where such an elite has been displaced by the rise of a rival political formation. Each of these ideal types has its historical example.

The case of Algeria is one in which a Muslim elite that depended for its position on the good favor of the French was simply never created. The role of local native elite was preempted by the settlers. As a result, the rise of an important Frenchified Muslim class failed to occur, and it became increasingly likely as the twentieth century progressed that the terrible grievances of the Muslim peasantry would be expressed directly against the French instead of mediated by a native bourgeoisie. To be sure, there were the various bourgeois movements associated with Ferhat Abbas and Doctor Bendjelloul which had a certain activity from the mid-1920s until the mid-1940s. But these never created any ties with the masses. In retrospect, they must be seen as highly visible but politically insignificant compared to the efforts of Messali Hadj and the Reformist Muslim Ulama who gave a popular base to opposition to the French. Once the revolution began in November 1954, the French sought desperately for some group with authority with which they could negotiate a settlement on better terms than those held out by the National Liberation Front (FLN). None was found, partly because the history of rigged elections served to stigmatize any Algerian who worked with the French as their puppet, but more importantly because the class of people who might have seen their future interests tied to France and who might have feared a radical peasant uprising just did not exist in any important number.[36]

In the case of Indochina, a nationalist elite that might have had an interest in cooperating with the French after 1945 was destroyed. Here the decisive factor was the Japanese Occupation. As George M. Kahin and John W. Lewis write:

Japan's role in Indochina was radically different from her occupation of any other Southeast Asian country. In the rest of the colonies there, the Japanese realized the advantage of working through the native elites, whom they regarded as more satisfactory instruments of administration than Western colonial civil servants. In order to secure the support of the educated indigenous groups in these other areas, the Japanese were obliged to grant them concessions . . . The one great exception was Indochina. There the pro-Vichy French administration was willing to come to terms with the Japanese . . . Thus, during the war the major channel open to those Vietnamese who wished to free their country from Japanese, and ultimately French, control was an underground movement where Vietnamese communists already had a strong and entrenched position.[37]

Other developments contributed to making it difficult to find a local counterweight to the Communists after 1945. Economically, the French presence in the 1930s had rested on the investments of a number of large capitalist firms like Michelin, the activities of a Chinese merchant class (with their families totaling perhaps 4 percent of the country's population), and the influence of a few thousand wealthy landowners whose property was located for the most part in the Mekong Delta.[38] In addition, between 1929 and 1932, the French had liquidated the most important non-Communist opposition to their rule when a combination of the Tan Viet and the Vietnam Quoc Dan Dang had risen against them. Despite the simultaneous suppression of Communist insurgents in Nghe-Tinh province in 1930–1, the ICP proved far more resilient than its fellow Vietnamese nationalists. Thus the economic base on which a collaborating nationalist elite might stand was exceeding narrow, and politically the French repressions of the thirties and the occupation of the early forties worked to the advantage of the Communists.

Although these considerations suggest that the French presence in Southeast Asia would have to be drastically modified after 1945, one cannot conclude immediately that a Communist-sponsored peasant revolution would necessarily triumph there ultimately. For the congeries of political forces existing in Vietnam that the Communists did not control – the Catholics, the Cao Dai, the Hoa Hao, and perhaps even the Buddhists – might have been welded together with other potentially anti-Communist forces to split the union of communism with nationalism. Thus, had the French seriously backed Bao Dai in 1947 and granted his demands for the unity and independence of Vietnam, as they apparently debated doing, Cochin China might effectively have been denied to Ho Chi Minh and in the process the Cambodian monarchy preserved. Paris could have counted on the threat from the North to persuade Bao Dai to limit his claims to sovereignty in favor of a veiled French presence. However much one may admire the Communist-led Vietnamese Liberation Movement, to assume its victory was somehow inevitable does not do justice to its achievement. In Malaya, where admittedly the Communists were in a more difficult situation for a variety of reasons than were their counterparts in Vietnam, a crucial part of the final British success was their willingness to respect the independent power base of Tengku Abdul Rahman, head of the Alliance party associating Malays with Chinese, in order to crush the insurgents. Perhaps the "Bao Dai formula" would have failed whatever the French position, for as the preceding analysis showed, the social structure there was not favorable to the French return. But one must be careful not to confuse the political predispositions of a particular structure with a necessary historical outcome.

A comparison of Indochina with Indonesia is instructive at this point as the chief differences between the two areas seem to be more political than economic or social if one is interested in evaluating the possibilities for a Communist-led revolution there. For Indonesia in the 1930s had, if anything, a greater percentage of landless peasants than Indochina, and the Dutch plantations and Chinese merchant class effectively stifled the growth of an indigenous middle class.[39] Moreover, communism had come to Indonesia earlier than to any other country of Asia or Africa, and had quickly made an important place for itself in local politics.

The obstacles to Communist success in Indonesia as compared to Indochina seem to me to have been essentially political. First, the Indonesian Communist party (PKI) showed very

terwar years combined with scattered disturbances in the military immediately after the surrender of Japan to make British minds turn once again to memories of the Great Mutiny of 1857. India would be done with the British.

Nevertheless, it is not clear that the organization of interests that ultimately brought India to independence would have maintained its hold on the country had an intense revolution of long duration been necessary. For not only was there the serious problem of minorities, especially the Muslims, but there was as well a destitute class of peasants whom revolution would doubtlessly rouse to political activity. An official study of landholding in India (exclusive of Pakistan) in 1953–4 found that 23 percent of the rural households were landless, another 24 percent owned less than 1 acre, and 14 percent owned between 1 and 2.5 acres.[45] One may legitimately speculate, given these figures, on the fate of the 3.5 percent of the population who were reported (in what was certainly an underestimate of their property, as the census was part of an effort to reduce large holdings) to own 36 percent of the land. As it was:

India has been governed since independence by a coalition consisting of the bureaucratic-military establishment, which implements policy, the big business groups, which have backed Congress financially, the rank and file politicans who mainly represent the rural squirearchy and richer peasants, and the intellectuals who articulate policy . . . [Nehru] was a leftist flanked by conservatives who know from experience that it was not worth opposing progressive resolutions or legislation which were not likely to be implemented.[46]

The case of India presents us, then, with a nationalist elite that would surely have hesitated long before launching into revolution, but that gave every indication of pursuing such a course should the British prove obstinate and refuse to grant independence. It is to the credit of their statesmanship that the British could view the changed status of such an important possession so realistically and attempt as best they could to harmonize their interests with the future of a country that for over a century had been the base for their foreign policy from the Mediterranean to China.

The foregoing case studies offer examples from a spectrum of colonial responses to the maintenance of European rule after 1945, ranging from militant revolutionary opposition to the call for independence with the framework of a continuing European presence. They are not intended to establish rigid, predictive models for colonial uprisings, but to establish instead a heuristic typology. The factor that this study suggests should be most closely analyzed is the place the momentarily predominant elite occupies in respect to the double challenge it faces: from the international system and from local rivals. Import-export elites and traditional rulers are threatened in both respects and are well advised to moderate their nationalist demands in order to assure continued foreign support for their regimes. On the other hand, a national manufacturing elite allied with rural forces representing more than a handful of great landlords is clearly more able to press its autonomous claims. But it must avoid if possible the radical suggestion to push for an all-out war of national liberation, as it should recognize that the radicals intend to take advantage of popular mobilization not only to oust the foreigners, but also to create a revolution from below and be done with them as well. By this same token, the most militant elite will be one that fears no local rivals – because none exists to any politically significant degree – and at the same time sees the outsiders with whom it must deal as the inveterate enemy of its most essential demands.

In this respect, Algeria and Indochina were idiosyncratic in the challenge they posed to France. These two colonies simply had no genuine parallels in the British experience. Kenya might be thought comparable to Algeria, but in essential respects this was not the case. For how could this relatively insignificant East African land be the equivalent to the British of what Algeria was to France: the home of more than 2 percent of the national population; the location of badly needed petroleum resources; and a strategic outpost of France whose capital, Algiers, was only 500 miles southwest of Marseilles? It was largely because Kenya was so unimportant that the British could arrange for the sale of the European farms at full value to the Africans and so create, virtually overnight, an export elite on whom they could base their postindependence relations.[47] In Algeria, to the contrary, the incomparably more powerful settler presence negated any attempt to create a politically important Muslim bourgeoisie. Nor could the French copy the example of the Republic of South Africa and cut themselves off from their North African territory. This was not because of "centralizing traditions," but because, unlike South Africa, Algeria was far too poor for a small minority of the population to maintain its rule without constant aid from the outside. For these reasons – which had to do with Algeria and not with France – withdrawal was especially difficult. Had the French had the experience and institutions of the British it is not evident they would have responded more ably to the crisis.

The comparison of Indochina and Malaya is more ambiguous. But the relatively greater strength of the non-Communists after 1945 in Malaya combined with a British willingness to work with these forces to weld them into a nationalist force capable of beating the insurgents. The British started with more advantages than the French and worked with them more skillfully.

The one celebrated instance where British policy failed was with Nasser. This is generally interpreted in the literature as a release of pent-up emotions over Britain's declining world role, but perhaps it is instead the one case where London shared the bad fortune plaguing Paris and found itself up against an anticolonial leader with whom it could not strike a bargain. Indeed Britain's major setback in decolonization occurred in relation to its "informal empire" in the Middle East. The first challenge had come when Prime Minister Mossadegh nationalized the British petroleum holdings in Iran. "He had never been very amenable to reason, and lately it had been necessary to humor him as with a fractious child," writes then Foreign Secretary Anthony Eden in his memoirs about this "megalomaniac," "Old Mossy."[48] In this confrontation, Britain had ultimately gotten its way, but not without being obliged to call the United States to its rescue and paying a certain price in the form of a condominium agreement on Iranian oil.

Nasser's seizure of the Suez Canal in 1956, three years after the fall of Mossadegh, seemed if anything more menacing to Eden, who had by then become prime minister. "A man with Colonel Nasser's record could not be allowed to 'have his thumb on our windpipe,' " Eden declared:

Some say that Nasser is not Hitler or Mussolini. Allowing for a difference in scale, I am not so sure. He has followed Hitler's pattern, even to concentration camps and the propagation of *Mein Kampf* among his officers. He has understood and used Goebbels' pattern of propaganda in all its lying ruthlessness. Egypt's strategic position increases the threat to others from any aggressive militant dictatorship there.[49]

The greatest threat Nasser represented was to undermine the weak, Western-oriented Arab elites of the Middle East – Libya, Saudia Arabia, Iraq, Jordan, and Lebanon, as well as the sheikdoms of the Persian Gulf – and so monopolize the region's petroleum reserves. Eden felt that this also permitted Russia a foothold in the area, and even endangered the British territories in East and Central Africa.[50] Whatever the reality of this belief, Suez – and indeed the decline of British fortunes in the Middle East altogether – was the most damaging of its global withdrawals.

It is, then, not enough to compare policy formulation in London and Paris in order to explain the pattern of postwar European decolonization. Whatever the advantages held by the British in terms of international rank, domestic political institutions, and the legacy of imperial traditions and procedures, in order to conceptualize this historical process adequately a comparative analysis must be made as well of the colonial situations over which the Europeans ruled after 1945. For the pattern of decolonization was decisively shaped by the character of the nationalist elites the European presence helped to produce in its overseas territories.

Conclusion

This chapter has maintained that if a host of factors conspired to force an end to European overseas empires after 1945, in most cases the Europeans could nevertheless significantly influence this process by their attention to grooming their successors. For virtually every nationalist movement harbored a civil war whose divisions allowed the colonial authority a strong voice in local affairs. By deciding with whom they would negotiate, by what procedure they would institutionalize the transfer of power, and over what territory the new regime would rule, Paris and London decisively influenced the course of decolonization.

In order to exploit the genuine power they had in these circumstances, the Europeans had to have the experience and the institutions to maneuver adroitly in the colonial setting, and the political wisdom to respect the limits of their abilities, to know what they could not hope to accomplish. In this respect, the British had substantial advantages over the French in four regards: their imperial traditions had given them a preference for "informal empire" and had furnished them with an established procedure for the devolution of power; their close links with the United States let them view the changing world order with more guarded optimism; their domestic political institutions demonstrated an ability to handle issues of this magnitude with relative dispatch; and, except for Suez (where intervention by the United States and the Soviet Union could be blamed), their use of force was restricted to situations where it could be realistically expected to achieve reasonable ends. In short, save for the Suez crisis in 1956, London did not define the challenge posed by colonial nationalism in terms of national security. To Paris, on the contrary, rebellion in Indochina and especially in Algeria seemed to represent just such a threat.

If it is possible to conceptualize separately these influences on the process of decolonization, it is nonetheless their close interrelationship that becomes apparent as soon as a specific case is studied. Consider, for example, the conflicts in French Algeria and Indochina. Even though, as we have seen, the social structures of these two countries predisposed them to a revolutionary break with France after 1945, it was surely not inevitable that local factors would preclude a peaceful devolution of power: France was not locked into conflict by some iron law of structural necessity. In regard to Indochina, the

French might have decided not to return in force to Southeast Asia, but to make arrangements with Ho Chi Minh for the orderly transfer of sovereignty with special safeguards for certain French interests in the area. Or, alternatively, Paris might have pursued the Bao Dai formula more realistically and so had a reasonable chance of preserving its influence in a new form in Cochin China and Cambodia. By way of comparison, British Malaya and especially the Netherlands East Indies had structural predispositions roughly comparable to those in Indochina, yet a combination of political factors discouraged Communist takeovers there.

A similar argument can be made for Algeria. In retrospect, it appears evident that Algeria would become independent of France sometime after 1945. The economic, social, and political histories of the country had been tending in this direction since the turn of the century, and international events served to confirm the process. But is it absurd to speculate that had the French been able to maneuver more wisely – had, for example, the Algerian Statute of 1947 been a genuine Home Rule Bill somewhat along the lines proposed *at the time* by the Muslim bourgeoisie and the French Communist party – the base might have been laid there for a ruling elite eager to work in collaboration with Paris?

In other words, it is conceivable that the Indochinese and Algerian revolutions might have been avoided. Although an analysis of the international and internal structural features of the two countries shows them to have been particularly prone to a revolutionary break with France after 1945, the room for political artistry in the immediate aftermath of the war seems to have been adequate to permit other developments. Admittedly all things were not possible: A political break with France was well-nigh inevitable. But the form this break would take, and in consequence, the nationalist elite independence would tend to confirm in power, might have been different. That these alternate paths were not taken by the French sends us back to the other factors under consideration – to their imperial traditions, to their international place after 1945, and to the logic of their political institutions and the opinions of their political elites.

The multiplicity of factors entering the course of postwar decolonization calls forth a last remark. There can be the terrible temptation to try to simplify such a multiform process, either by exalting one consideration over all others or by trying to force the particular case into what seems to be a general movement or pattern. Certainly decolonization acquired an international momentum, and it is possible to isolate certain variables that seem to have had a marked influence on its progress regardless of time or place. But the various colonial areas were not dominoes responding to some inevitable "historical tidal wave of nationalism" any more than the European governments had a set response to every colonial challenge whatever its nature. In each case nationalism had its local pedigree and its own internal tensions composed of unique constellations of class, ethnic, and regional alignments. So, too, different governments in Paris and London acted in noticeably different fashions.

As a historical process, therefore, decolonization was the consequence of a variety of factors, some general to the age, others more specific as to time and place. It reflected everywhere the shattering impact of World War II on the old structures of international order and the emergence of the United States as the dominant world power, able to provide a new definition of the character of the ties between North and South. But at the same time, there were in effect multiple decolonizations, whose discontinuities, ambiguities, and uniquenesses must be respected, however much this effort to appreciate the relatively autonomous role of "the parts" of the system may interfere with the desire to reduce history to a crystalline pattern by finding a single formula that makes sense of its complexity. The model for the analysis of the end of European overseas empire may be taken from the rich and ever-growing literature on its earlier expansion. Here particular case studies are informed by a generally recognized body of more comprehensive propositions that in turn are constantly reevaluated in light of new information. Today the historiography of decolonization lacks this fruitful exchange. Its present task is to elaborate a comparative framework for historical analysis and so to tie specific cases to the general movement of European decolonization.

For the purposes of this book, however, the point is not so much to see decolonization as *the end* of a historical period, but rather to see it as *the beginning* of a new period in North–South relations wherein both the system of power and the structures composing it have changed substantially in form. Like the distinction between part and whole in historical analysis discussed at greater length in Chapter 2, or between political and economic forces discussed in Chapter 1, so the distinction between continuity and change is a difficult one to make. If on the one hand it is a mistake to discount overly the significance of decolonization – to assume that it was no more than a flag-and-anthem ceremony signifying little real change – neither should we overestimate it, believing that henceforth relations between strong and weak were fundamentally changed, and imperialism a concept relevant only to the study of the past.

The most decisive change that decolonization signaled was the unequivocal affirmation of southern nationalism against foreign rule, even when this meant the mobilization of a broad popular movement, including the mass of the peasantry. Nationalism in the colonial areas may have varied quite widely in the interests it served and the future it sought, but its hostility to imperialism ran wide and deep. As it soon became evident, however, opposition to colonialism did not in itself constitute program enough on which to bridge the internal class and ethnic divisions in most of these areas and so ensure political stability; nor did it constitute plan enough to provide for economic development and so provide for regional security. As a result, few of these new states felt themselves either domestically or regionally secure, and virtually all of them looked to stabilize their situation through a multitude of new ties with the international system dominated by the United States and its allies, the former imperialist powers.

There is no reason to conclude from this, however, that nothing has changed, that imperialism has only metamorphosed, to remain as strong as ever. Unable to exert direct political rule, and increasingly unwilling to risk massive or prolonged military intervention that would have for its consequence a broad-based nationalist mobilization, the strong states find the means of influence at their disposal to be far more indirect and less sure. New ties have been created, of course, particularly through channels of economic contact and military aid, but it is altogether less likely that northern interests will be promoted as easily, as safely, and as cheaply as in the past.

4

"The American Century"

If the most important interactions in international affairs since 1945 have been those between the East and the West, the most volatile have been those between the North, or the twenty-four industrial market states grouped together since 1960 in the Organization for Economic Cooperation and Development, and the South, or the "Third World" of developing countries today numbering over one hundred. As we saw in the preceding chapter, during the two decades following World War II, one-third of the peoples of the earth were freed from colonial rule as everywhere the networks of local groups that had formed the political backbone of European rule abroad – the native aristocracies, the ethnic minorities, the comprador merchants, the local "évolués" – either were overthrown or became transmuted into opponents of the foreign presence. In 1945, France ended her mandate over Syria and Lebanon. In the summer of 1947, Great Britain recognized the independence of India, Pakistan, and Ceylon (Sri Lanka), thereby surrendering what for over a century and a half had been the greatest of the European imperial possessions. The following year, Palestine was partitioned and Israel created, and the first serious disorders in Tropical Africa – riots in the Gold Coast (Ghana) – heralded the spread of nationalism south of the Sahara. At the same time, millions of others once subject to European power without falling under formal colonial jurisdiction reasserted their national identities. With the entry of the Chinese Communists into Peking in January 1949, ending what they called the "century of dishonor," the outlines of a new period of world history, one that signaled the end of a long era of unquestioned European hegemony over the preindustrial areas of the globe, seemed to be emerging from the ruins of the war. The Korean War, the Suez Invasion, the Cuban and Iranian revolutions, the endless war in Vietnam, the spectacular rise in petroleum prices, the potential for serious violence in the Middle East and Southern Africa – it is the pacing, complexity, and possible repercussions of these matters that have most moved world politics foward since 1945.

Indeed, it may be said that two legacies of French and British imperialism to postwar American hegemony – Indochina and the Middle East – have been especially responsible for creating conditions that have severely shaken the international system set in place after World War II by the deliberate actions of the United States. That is, the challenge to the postwar international order largely determined by Washington has principally come not from the East, as had so long been anticipated, or from this country's economically dynamic friends, as some were beginning to speculate, but from those "night riders in black pajamas" – as Lyndon Johnson called the Viet Cong – the peoples of the Third World. Thus, if the center of world politics during the last thirty-five years has remained the relationship between Washington and Moscow, the dynamics of international affairs have in large measure been the result of the relationship between American imperialism and Third World nationalism. This may be affirmed without denying that American policy toward the South has substantially reflected Washington's perception of Moscow's international role. The point, however, is to insist on the reality of Third World nationalism as a potent force in world politics since 1945; a force that is neither the willing puppet of northern commercial interests (as a host of leftist theorists have alleged) nor the spineless pawn of the dominant parties in international affairs (as more right-wing writers, who see southern countries as mere counters in the contest between East and West, frequently suppose).

It has become commonplace today to criticize American foreign policy for its failure to respect the power of Third World nationalism. We are told that Washington, fixated on the menace of international communism and so viewing weak southern countries as pawns, or "dominoes," on the greater playing board of the East–West confrontation, or anxious to assure favorable trade and investment arrangements and so be assured of a steady flow of raw materials and profits, did not perceive the limits to its power coming from the ability of regional actors to move decisively in local affairs. Instead, the United States projected itself as the paramount power in all areas of the South save Africa (except for Kennedy's actions in the Congo in the early sixties). In the process, this country tried to constrain local forces into a mold suiting Washington's perception of a proper world order and so became the international center of counterrevolutionary activity in the South, friend to established wealth and power there, enemy to the militant organization of workers and peasants trying to redress generations-old grievances compounded by the tensions of contemporary change. From this perspective, the defeat in Vietnam was the tragic product of an unrealistic policy that exaggerated American power just as it underestimated the strength of local political forces in the South.

Whatever the justice of these criticisms, they too often forget that after as well as before World War II, the United States frequently found that the pursuit of its national interests abroad tended to encourage the growth of southern nationalism, and that in the twenty years following the war, Washington's more extended, if more conservative, policy toward the Third World proved quite successful in its own terms. In other words, present-day accounts too wedded to the calamity of Vietnam may both underrate the earlier strength of American policy and assume too readily that the "lessons of Vietnam" dictate some striking new departures in this country's conduct toward the South. Yet, if on the one hand American policy has not been so inflexible and unrealistic as some would suggest, neither is the United States so chastened by Vietnam that it is without will or ability to intervene in southern affairs if the case seems to warrant it (as illustrated by its role in the fall of the Allende government in Chile). Certainly we may agree that the Vietnamese War was no accident, but rather the outgrowth of a particular vision of world order held in Washington for some time, and that the lessons of the war will, and indeed should, mark future initiatives of this country. At the same time, we should not oversimplify: Neither was the war the inevitable outcome of American perceptions and international circumstances, as though some straight line can be drawn from the Truman Doctrine in 1947 to Johnson's escalation of the war in 1965; nor does its passing, any more than does that of the Korean War, whose apparent lessons were so very different and so widely misinterpreted, offer a clear indication of what future American policy toward the South should be.

The purpose of this chapter is to attempt to identify patterns in the motivation and conduct of American policy toward Asia, Latin America, and (to a lesser extent) Africa from the late nineteenth century until about 1980. In terms of motivation behind policy, the chapter will especially consider the relative weight of economic and political concerns; in terms of the conduct of policy, the chapter will review certain of the more salient ways the United States has sought to instrumentalize its interests in these regions of the world. The reader is referred back to Chapter 1, where an attempt was made to distinguish between these terms and processes with respect to the British experience between 1815 and 1914. Chapter 5 will take up the issues confronting American policy toward the Third World in the early 1980s.

American policy toward Asia and Latin America, 1898–1939

Before World War II, two basic policies represented the attitude of the United States toward Latin America and Asia: the Monroe Doctrine and the Open Door Policy. To those with a cynical turn of mind in regard to world affairs, it might appear that their terms permitted Washington to arrive at its preeminence in international politics in 1945 equipped with a singularly potent double standard by which to act with respect to the globe's preindustrial regions. For the Monroe Doctrine had been liberally used between 1898 and 1929 to block the pursuit of foreign interests in Latin America and to sanction direct United States invervention there, whereas the Open Door Policy was invoked where the American position was less secure and barriers erected by rival powers needed to be breached – in the Far East before 1914, in the Near East after World War I, and in the colonial areas and Eastern Europe during and after World War II.

The dominant and preferred American policy, expressed in the Open Door Policy as well as in the Monroe Doctrine before the Spanish-American War of 1898 and after the inauguration of Hoover in 1929, was to stand for a plural world order typified by the national government of peoples, a nondiscriminatory international economic system, and hostility to great power spheres of influence. However self-interested American policy in fact was in these arrangements, this objection should not disguise its essentially progressive cast. It genuinely opposed colonialism and championed the sovereignty of national governments in these regions, so associating the United States with the growing force of southern nationalism that the preceding two chapters have reviewed.[1] In one respect, however, this policy could be deliberately imperialist: When private American property rights abroad were threatened, Washington would on occasion defend them even if this meant jeopardizing the stability of the governments against which the claims were lodged. And American conduct could be imperialist in another fashion as well, although this reflected more the nature of social life in the South than it did intentions in Washington. For to the extent that host regimes and dominant classes in the South, and particularly in Latin America, began to draw strength from their connections with American business and thereby to protect their local power bases, a relationship of liberal imperialism was establishing its identity.

In contrast to this dominant liberal tradition of formal antiimperialism, a policy of direct intervention was pursued in circumstances in which a policy of accommodàtion with southern regimes appeared impossible. This occurred especially in situations in which instability in a weaker region deemed of importance to the national security of the United States seemed to open the way there to rival great power influence. From the time of the Spanish-American War of 1898 until the Hoover administration in 1929, such a policy of preemptive imperialism, based on modifications of the Monroe Doctrine, was standard fare in American behavior toward Central America. Let us consider each of these policies and the traditions they underwrote more closely.

In the Far East, where the Open Door Policy was first advanced in earnest (with Secretary of State Hay's Notes to the Powers of 1899 and Circular of 1900), the United States gave notice that it was not interested in extending the Asian territory under its control (after taking the Philippines), but that it would seek instead to limit the competitive scramble to partition China into spheres of influence. The American proposal, strongly seconded by Great Britain, asked that all nations agree to seek no exclusive territorial or trading advantage from Peking, and that equal, nondiscriminatory treatment prevail toward all foreigners. (Shortly thereafter investment opportunities were included.) Such a position aligned American interests with the safeguarding and strengthening of Chinese sovereignty. Of course from the Chinese point of view, American support of their country's integrity might appear suspect: The United States partook of the privileges conferred by the "unequal treaties," joined at times in banking consortia that extended still more power over internal Chinese politics to outsiders, and acknowledged in accords such as the Taft-Katsura Agreed Memorandum of 1905 and the Root-Takahira Agreement of 1908 foreign spheres of influence over areas under Peking's nominal authority (in these cases, Japanese paramountcy in Korea and Southern Manchuria, respectively). And indeed there should be no suggestion that United States and Chinese interests were in every way identical. Nonetheless, it was the general purpose of American policy to limit foreign influence in favor of expanding the power of the Chinese state, with the expectation that such developments would foster the growth of American interests as well. Thus the agreements to respect informal Japanese claims to specific parts of the Asian mainland were concluded not to sanction the partition of China but to secure Tokyo's consent to limit such claims, just as during World War I, Wilson reversed his decision not to allow American bankers to participate in consortia lending to Peking once he had determined that involvement in these ventures would be more likely than continued nonparticipation to further Chinese as well as American interests at the expense of Japan. In its basic thrust, American policy supported Chinese nationalism.

During the interwar years, this same general orientation prevailed. At the Washington Naval Conference of 1921–2, the most important international agreements concerning the Far East between the wars were reached, and by the Nine-Power Treaty, all nations represented at the conference called for the respect of Chinese independence and equality of foreign economic opportunity. When Japan commenced to violate the treaty in 1931, it was Washington that objected most vociferously. And ultimately, it was American insistence that Japan end its expansion in China that led to the Japanese–American War in the Pacific in 1941.[2]

As this example of Chinese–American relations illustrates, Woodrow Wilson's call for national self-determination in his Fourteen Points of 1918 gave a specifically democratic *content* to a *form* of American foreign policy with us virtually from the birth of the Republic. Even if Wilson did not intend that his concept be applied outside Europe, Franklin Roosevelt found it natural to do so after the outbreak of World War II, thus building on tradition in the conduct of American policy.

A basic reason for this policy of liberal antiimperialism was economic. Initially, as a young country struggling against mercantilist trade restrictions abroad, and later, as a commercial power of the first magnitude, the United States found its interests best served by a nondiscriminatory international commercial system. Although there had been some debate, the United States signed a commercial treaty with Prussia in 1785 containing a reciprocal most-favored-nation clause, and by 1789 the position of Secretary of the Treasury Hamilton had triumphed over that of Jefferson and Madison in the nondiscriminatory

Tariff and Tonnage Acts of that year.[3] In short, although it was not until 1844 that the term "open door" gained currency as the result of a nonreciprocal most-favored-nation clause in a commercial treaty with China, the spirit of the open door was as old as the United States.

By the last quarter of the nineteenth century, the fast-developing economic muscle of the United States made the government ready more than ever to promote this traditional policy. The growing volume of American production, combined with the increasingly vertical and horizontal integration of its economic structure, promised it success in competitive marketing so long as equal access to trade and investment opportunities was assured. The business community felt confident that if only the spheres of influence by rival great powers could be cracked, it could win these markets.[4] United States interests thus flowed naturally into the "antiimperialist" channels established earlier in the century by Britain at a moment when it was in the analogous position of being the world's most dynamic economy. As the British had discovered, so the Americans found that their interests were best served not by hazardous colonial acquisitions but by stable governments on the periphery, governments able to manage local affairs and stand their ground against annexationist great power demands in the name of what later came to be called national self-determination.

The American doctrine of an economic open door was all the more successful because it corresponded to the interests of most states on the periphery as well. Economically speaking, the policy's promise was to assure fair market prices for exports as well as for imports – a guarantee that weaker states had every reason to appreciate. But it was in political terms that the open door held the most appeal for these regimes, as the record of preferential economic treatment granted by governments such as that of China almost invariably involved coercion on the part of these outsiders and blatant attempts by them to convert such economic advantages into direct political control. By relying on the open door to help parry the demand for special economic privileges, weak states could thereby work to protect their autonomy. In sum, the interests of the United States and those of states on the periphery might be expected to coincide in important respects.

Of course the tie between United States economic interests and support for national self-government abroad was not always so neat as the foregoing discussion might imply. At certain moments the match seemed ideal: So it was at the turn of the century with respect to China, or under Franklin Roosevelt with his Good Neighbor Policy toward Latin America and his conception of the future of the European empires and Eastern Europe after World War II (or in the mind of Woodrow Wilson, who proved unable to realize his goals). But at other times, American foreign economic interests did not mesh so smoothly with the needs of national self-government in Latin America and the Far East. The reason for this was that like other capitalist powers of the time, the United States insisted on the sanctity of contract and property rights. This proved to be the "kicker" in the Open Door Policy that was to play such havoc in the internal affairs of Latin American and Far Eastern countries. Thus, when China agreed under treaty in 1903 that it would "offer no impediment to the attraction of foreign capital," Washington joined the other powers to use this clause to protest efforts by Peking to regulate mining conditions (including safety standards) in 1908 and again in 1914.[5] Or again, in 1925, when the Kuomintang in Canton tried to levy a tax on kerosene, imported largely from the United States into Kwangtung province (in order to aid Sun Yat-sen), the United States actively intervened to block the action by helping to sponsor a petroleum boycott (which included using connections within the Maritime Authority to quintuple taxes on Soviet oil sent to break the embargo).[6] These cases serve as but two examples of the many instances in which the impact of foreign concessions worked to undermine the legitimacy of the Chinese state.[7]

In the case of Mexico as well, American economic interests jeopardized the stability of national government. The Revolution of 1910 against the regime of Porfirio Díaz was also a revolution against American economic interests. By 1914, some $600 million had been directly invested in Mexico; and another $400 million loaned to it – and this by North Americans alone. United States citizens owned over 90 percent of the mining enterprises in the country as well as some 80 percent of the land thought to have petroleum (although British concessions actually produced more there before 1914). In addition, North Americans owned over 30 million acres of land.[8] While it was the Porfirio Díaz regime that made these transactions possible, it was accomplished in many instances at the expense of the Indian peoples whose lands and labor were required for such undertakings and whose resentment ultimately contributed to the insurgency.[9] One report gives a sample of the accumulated grievances:

Labor was hard to get for a sugar plantation in Tehuantepec. The neighboring Zapotec Indians could not be interested. Thereupon the [United States] company bribed a local political boss to arrest the Indians on trumped-up charges and deliver them at so much a head to the hacienda. The victims made a few polite motions of an agricultural nature, but soon escaped to their village. Here were fine mango trees, food like manna from heaven. Why work for aliens in hot fields? In desperation, the company finally sent its men by night and cut down the mango trees, starving the village into dependence upon employment.[10]

In the aftermath of the revolution, Washington's pressures were constant in support of "full, adequate and prompt" compensation for United States citizens whose property was damaged, seized, or otherwise endangered as the result of events there. Although Mexico protested that there was no reason aliens should receive better treatment than its own nationals, the United States managed to secure many of its demands. It did this by threatening to withhold recognition of different governments there (so blocking economic credits and arms transfers), thus making potential political instability the price for economic recalcitrance. In the end, the United States significantly contributed to the deradicalization of the revolution.[11]

Given the economic basis to the American support for national self-government in the Far East and Latin America, and considering the abundant instances when Washington challenged these same regimes for the sake of American business, it is tempting to conclude that economic calculations alone influenced United States policy toward these regions.[12] Can we reduce the dynamic of American policy so easily, however, to simple economic interest? Was American "antiimperialism" just pious ideological humbug that suited capitalist economic interests? To some extent, undoubtedly, but there was much more to it.

The political ethos and structure of the United States inherently militated against any doctrine other than that of national self-government for foreign peoples. Of course, as the Europeans have demonstrated (particularly the French, with their concept of "assimilation"), such an obstacle to foreign rule is not insurmountable in the Western democracies, although writers like J. A. Hobson have excelled at showing how a democratic spirit may be corrupted through authoritarian rule abroad. Nonetheless, the democratic-republican cast of Western politics has profoundly influenced the contact of this civilization with that of the preindustrial world, favoring a form of social and political pluralism there, for example, that encouraged the growth of local nationalism even when this was not intended.[13] How differently decolonization would have proceeded, for example – had it proceeded at all – were the colonial governments issued from Moscow or Peking.

Among the Western democracies, the disinterest in foreign rule, and hence the prejudice in favor of the self-government of others, have been particularly pronounced in the United States. Thus, unlike Great Britain or France, there have been no natural constituencies favoring colonization: no idle rich who, as in Britain, set their sights on colonial service (prompting James Mill's remark that the Indian bureaucracy was a "vast system of outdoor relief for the upper class"); no aristocratic military or publicly humiliated church that, as in France, would make its peace with republican institutions at home in return for the right to treat the colonial domain as its own *chasse privée*. Of course one may cite the case of William Walker, "the grey-eyed man of destiny," who schemed to take over Nicaragua for the United States in the 1850s, or the slave states that favored the annexation of certain Caribbean Islands for the sake of their own expansion. Yet it is precisely the anti-

democratic tendencies of the slavers that best illustrate how
immune the rest of the country was to these kinds of exploits.
If for a brief period at the turn of the century things appeared
differently, the outlook quickly returned to normal, as Ernest
May has recounted.[14] Moreover, American political institutions not only failed to compensate for this social indifference
to empire but actually encouraged a positive antipathy toward
it. Ever since the war with Mexico in the 1840s, when the annexation of that entire country was mooted, the serious objection has been raised that American political institutions simply could not tolerate the burden of assimilating a people so
foreign and so numerous. The cultural, social, and especially
political structures of the American Republic thus conspired
to favor sovereign self-government for other peoples.

The structure of the international system offered other important political incentives to the United States to support self-
government in Latin America and the Far East, in addition to
those provided by the domestic environment. Thus great
power rivalries habitually encourage action in favor of the political integrity of weaker peoples – at least when these peoples
appear to be in the sphere of influence of a rival. So the kaiser
provoked the British in 1896 when he sent the so-called Kruger
Telegram congratulating the Boers on their resistance to London, just as he alarmed them in 1898 when he visited Damascus and Jerusalem proclaiming himself the defender of the
Muslim world. Or consider Lenin's tactics. Immediately following the October Revolution, Moscow entered into mutual
aid programs with nationalist movements in Turkey, Persia,
Afghanistan, and China. As Stalin put it in 1924: "The struggle
that the Emir of Afghanistan is waging for independence is
objectively a *revolutionary* struggle, despite the monarchist
views of the Emir and his associates, for it weakens, disinte-
grates and undermines imperialism."[15] United States concern
over the "slicing of the Chinese melon" was similarly motivated. By appearing as the disinterested protector of China's
autonomy as a state, Washington might hope to hold its rivals
at bay. Of course, to Japan, Washington's idealistic declarations
in favor of such matters as China's integrity were read for what

they were. But with the outbreak of World War II, Tokyo adopted the same colors, announcing with its Greater East Asian Co-Prosperity Sphere that it was the truer champion of Asian nationalism. Such a claim was most effective in Southeast Asia from the Philippines to Burma where American, British, Dutch, and French colonialism made Japan the natural ally of local liberation efforts. To the contrary, in Northeast Asia, with respect to China and Korea, it was the United States that could appear to be the genuine champion of Asian nationalism.

If we have seen that there have been domestic and international political reasons that the United States might genuinely support national self-government for Latin America and the Far East, there is an important additional economic point to consider. It is frequently overlooked that although the United States favored an open door in international commerce, it was not until the 1930s that this country became an advocate of global free trade. Unlike Great Britain, the United States was a protectionist country, unwilling to integrate its economy with the world system as fully as had the British Isles, and hence all the less susceptible to the charge of deliberately fostering an "informal empire" abroad in Asia or in Latin America. For by 1914, the United States was not only the world's greatest manufacturing nation; it was the greatest single producer of raw materials as well. As domestic pressure groups could invariably be counted on to oppose closer ties with the South for some economic reason, efforts to integrate these economies with that of the United States in the manner of Great Britain were bound to be strongly opposed. Thus, cattle interests in this country managed to restrict imports of Argentine beef for "sanitary reasons," thereby preventing the United States from developing the kinds of ties with Argentina that had made Britain so important there.[16]

The most striking illustration of America's reluctance to act in terms of the logic of informal empire is the case of the Philippines. Although American business was central in building up the area for exports to the market in the United States – and in this respect the Philippines entered into a vulnerable, subordinate relationship that it has yet to escape – there was always some protectionist opposition to these developments expressed in Washington. With the onslaught of the depression, substantial efforts were made to limit the importation of Philippine sugar and cordage and to bar immigrant labor coming from the islands. Indeed, the pressures became so intense that in 1932 the Hare-Hawes-Cutting Act, setting conditions and a timetable for Philippine independence, passed in Congress – only to be rejected by the Philippine Senate. Under the terms of the Tydings-McDuffie Act of 1934, however, it was agreed that the islands should receive their independence after an appropriate period of time and under certain circumstances. Winston Churchill regretted these actions, saying of the 1932 proposal that it reflected "the bookkeeping considerations of profit and loss" and ignored the fact that such an issue "can only be decided upon considerations of national duty, dignity and honor, and upon its international repercussions."[17] In short, "open-door" America before World War II was not organized, and did not act, in the manner of "free-trade" Britain. The difference is often obscured in the literature arguing for an economic motive to American overseas expansion, when the drive for trade and investment is made to seem more unambiguous, and therefore more powerful, than was actually the case. As dramatized by the passage of the Fordney-McCumber Tariff Act in 1922 and the Hawley-Smoot Act in 1930, which successively raised tariffs to their highest point in this country's history, protectionism was a potent force in the United States, one that did not work well with ambitions for informal empire.

To say this is not to deny the obvious outward push of the American economy since the late nineteenth century. Part of this was a concomitant of the general process of industrialization, the search for a certain mix of material inputs and a certain level of demand to achieve economies of scale characteristic of any industrial society, be it socialist or capitalist. The United States had a natural resource base and population sufficiently large, however, that its reliance on the international system for these factors of production was never terribly great prior to 1945. Specific features of American capitalism, on the other hand, encouraged a more active international role. Thus, downturns in the business cycle after 1890 (if not earlier) prompted a search for new sources of demand abroad, and the large-scale vertical and horizontal integration of American business meant not only that surplus funds were available for investment overseas, but far more importantly that competitive scrambles for raw materials and markets would increasingly take on a global character. When Wilson expanded federal subsidies to shipping; signed the Edge Act, which fostered the spread of American banking abroad; endorsed the Webb-Pomerance Act, which was designed to permit American business to engage in cartel activities outside the United States; and supported it all with a barrage of rhetoric stressing the significance of foreign commerce to the United States, he was extending the range of overseas American interests defined in economic terms.[18]

We may, nevertheless, reject the proposition that United States policy favoring national self-government abroad was nothing more than a cover for economic self-interest, easily to be disposed with should the occasion arise. On the one hand, there was a variety of political forces, both domestic and international, that stood behind such a position. On the other hand, there were solid economic reasons ranging from the competitive posture of the United States to its domestic economic alignments that made such a policy genuine. Admittedly, there were tensions and contradictions as we have seen. But where private business interests succeeded in summoning Washington to their defense, their success generally reflected the peripheral political importance of the area to Washington. Economic considerations commanded policy not because they were more important than political factors, but rather because political stakes were low. And economic factors were imperialist largely because of the political instability of the areas where such expansion occurred, not because of some master plan in Washington. As in the British experience, political factors proceeded from a different set of calculations than did the economic, and they took precedence when a conflict between them arose.[19]

What should then be said of the Monroe Doctrine, whose implementation would seem to betray far less sympathy toward national self-government than did the Open Door Policy? At its inception in 1823, the doctrine clearly favored Latin American self-governance, warning that Washington "could not view any interposition for the purpose of oppressing them, or controlling in any other manner their destiny, by any European power in any other light than as the manifestation of an unfriendly disposition toward the United States." By the turn of the century, however, Washington's guarantee that no power from without the hemisphere would be allowed to claim new colonies there had become an imperialism of its own. In 1901, under the terms of the Platt Amendment, Cuba became an American protectorate. In 1903, the state of Panama was created at Theodore Roosevelt's instigation and the isthmus canal undertaken in earnest; in 1905, by the proclamation of the Roosevelt Corollary to the Monroe Doctrine, the United States licensed itself to intervene at will in the affairs of its southern neighbors. Between 1898 and 1920, United States soldiers intervened on twenty separate occasions in the Caribbean, demonstrating to the world that the area was Washington's private preserve. And according to a report issued in 1924, fourteen of the twenty Latin American nations then had some form of direct North American presence, including control of their financial agencies.[20]

As Taft's slogan "dollar diplomacy" connotes, the Roosevelt Corollary was not invoked without numerous instances of ill-gained profit at the expense of Central America, or of force used largely because of considerations for promoting American business interests.[21] Yet, to attribute to economic motivations the sole, or even primary, inspiration for American policy is surely to load more explanatory power onto these forces than they alone can bear. To be sure, Central America was the most important overseas area for American investment prior to World War I, but this was far from the only consideration determining policy in Washington. The failure of political institutions in the region to adjudicate civil conflicts or to discharge satisfactorily international obligations freely incurred made these states standing targets for the expansionist designs of

Washington's rivals. Thus, civil war combined with default on foreign loans to encourage Maximilian's takeover of Mexico in the 1860s, while the United States was occupied with its own Civil War. Ultimately, Maximilian was defeated by the Mexicans themselves under Benito Juárez, but plans were revealed for double Hapsburg monarchies in Latin America, one over Spanish America north of Chile, the other over Brazil.[22] Or again, at the turn of the century, Germany was widely believed to desire an enclave in the Caribbean, much like it had taken Kiaochow in China. (Indeed, Kaiser Wilhelm reportedly said that he would prefer but one colony in Latin America to all of Africa.[23]) In short, American strategic concern for the safety of an isthmus canal (finally completed in 1914) surely would have dictated an active United States involvement in the region whatever the character of the economic regime in this country, much as the Baltic States may be said to be of strategic importance to the Soviet Union, or control of Korea to China or Japan.[24] By contrast with liberal antiimperialism, we may call this "preemptive imperialism" and expect that it will appear in a region of importance to the United States when a potentially hostile great power might create a sphere of influence for itself there, either as a result of its own ambitions or because local anarchy draws it into the area.

The case of American relations with Mexico between the Revolution of 1910 and World War II is especially interesting in any attempt to weigh the relative importance of political and economic factors in motivating preemptive imperialism in Washington. Mexico was the closest and strongest of the southern neighbors of the United States, and conflicts over economic matters there appeared earlier, lasted longer, and concerned stakes of far more importance than elsewhere in Latin America. There was no reason to minimize United States opposition to the revolution once it became known that by the famous Article 27 of the Constitution of 1917, Mexico expected to nationalize the large tracts of land and the mineral and oil concessions held by foreigners, most of them Americans.[25] Short of direct military intervention (called for by Theodore Roosevelt in the 1921 election campaign and supported by many others), the United States spared few efforts to resist the expropriation of American-owned properties without full, prompt and effective compensation (which, it was common knowledge, Mexico could not provide).[26] Ultimately, a sort of modus vivendi was worked out that allowed the United States to accept the economic measures of the revolution: Some compensation was forthcoming, both the scope and the pace of nationalization slowed, and North Americans were able to find alternate sectors for investment in Mexico.

Yet even before this had been achieved, President Wilson had defined the principal American concern with respect to the conflict as political, as his refusal to recognize the government of Victoriano Huerta in 1913 indicates. Huerta was favored by most American business interests in Mexico as a conservative and as a man able to give Mexico political stability. But to Wilson the man was intolerable, for he was convinced that the Mexican had come to power by murdering the chief leader of the revolution, a man considerably more liberal than himself, Francisco Madero. As Wilson put it in a letter he wrote on November 2, 1913: "I lie awake at night praying that the most terrible [outcome] may be averted. No man can tell what will happen while we deal with a desperate brute like that traitor, Huerta. God save us from the worst!"[27]

Had economic interests been foremost in his mind, Wilson might have feared Madero and welcomed Huerta. As it was, the man who ultimately came to power was Venustiano Carranza, who was willing to risk war with the United States to stop the incursion of American soldiers in pursuit of Pancho Villa, and who became first president of Mexico under the Constitution of 1917, which included the provisions unfavorable to the American economic presence in the country. However, Washington immediately recognized Carranza. It had not done so for Huerta, but had instead sent troops to Vera Cruz to help overthrow him, apparently persuaded that whatever his economic policy Carranza would provide what America most desired: the institutionalization of the rule of law so as to provide stability to Mexico and thereby assure some measure of security to the United States.[28] To be sure, this was only the prelude to a steady barrage of pressures from Washington designed to protect American economic interests in Mexico. But as Cole Blasier has insisted, political considerations remained supreme in determining American policy toward that country.[29]

It was under the Hoover administration (inaugurated in 1929) that the United States took its first important steps renouncing the right of intervention under the Monroe Doctrine in the affairs of Latin America. Franklin Roosevelt's Good Neighbor Policy continued in this approach, so that before World War II, Washington had recast the meaning of the Monroe Doctrine in effect since the turn of the century and expressed its intention to respect the sovereignty of governments in Latin America. Although this reflected the recognition that no other great power had the ability to intervene in the region as it might have before 1914, it represented as well a distinctively new step in Washington's diplomacy affirming the political autonomy of these states. Not that North American economic interests were thereby served, however. In the case of Mexico, for example, when the Cárdenas government nationalized American petroleum investments there and refused compensation for the expropriation of American-owned land in the country, Washington vigorously protested, but it ultimately accepted the decision of the Mexican government (which in the meantime had compromised a bit). Did the growing menace of Hitler tie Roosevelt's hands? One might as easily make the opposite case: that the Nazi threat would have incited intervention. It would seem that as Cárdenas was widely known for his strong anti-Nazi sentiments, Roosevelt would waive his objections to Mexico's economic initiatives in favor of maintaining a secure southern border. Political rather than economic considerations were dominant. One might speculate that Roosevelt would have been far more belligerent had he interpreted the expropriation of the American oil industry as a mark of Cárdenas's support of the Nazis. Sixteen years later, when a far less lively economic issue coincided with what was interpreted as a security threat, the United States reacted more forcibly. Then, referring to the Guatemalan expropriation of land owned by United Fruit, John Foster Dulles declared: "If the United Fruit matter were settled, if they gave a gold piece for every banana, the problem would remain just as it is today as far as the presence of Communist infiltration in Guatemala is concerned."[30]

If both the Open Door Policy and the Monroe Doctrine were vehicles for imperialism, how very different they nonetheless were in design. The Open Door was essentially an economic doctrine, responsive to international power realities but with relatively little political clout behind it before World War II. It was imperialist more by virtue of the fragility of the countries with an American economic presence than by any deliberate effort to secure effective domination of these areas on the part of the United States. In contrast, the Monroe Doctrine was a political policy consciously calculated to influence developments in regions seen as important to the security of the United States in terms of considerations of the international balance of power. Yet, although both policies professed to support sovereign self-government for the peoples of these lands, each was composed of contradictory elements that could nullify this promise: the Open Door by its insistence on the sanctity of private property; the Monroe Doctrine by its willingness to engage in preemptive imperialism should it appear that self-government were not a viable option in an area deemed important to Washington. To say that there were tensions in these policies is not to say, however, that they were without effective direction, any more than it is to entertain the belief that the tension might be resolved by dissolving them in some reductionist manner into one of their constituent aspects. We may therefore conclude that on the whole, American policy in the years before World War II was progressive. Whatever the admittedly serious limitations on the support governments in Latin America and the Far East might receive from Washington in their quest for national strength and autonomy, on the balance the force of the United States weighed in their favor.

Yet if it were progressive, American policy certainly was not radical. The goal of a radical redefinition of relations between the core industrial states and the preindustrial world fell to the Third International, which declared at its First Congress in

Moscow in 1919 its goal of "world revolution," wherein both the internal character of countries and their international relations would be thoroughly transformed: "Colonial slaves of Africa and Asia: the hour of proletarian dictatorship in Europe will also be the hour of your own liberation."[31] As the first instruction from the Executive Committee of the Communist International (ECCI) to the Third Congress of the Chinese Communist party in 1923 read: "The national revolution in China and the creation of an anti-imperialist front will necessarily coincide with the agrarian revolution of the peasantry against the survivals of feudalism."[32]

The legacy of the period prior to 1939 to a triumphant United States in the years after 1945 was a decided prejudice in favor of the right of self-government of peoples around the world. Although the character of this concept is impossible to define narrowly and although it contained features contradictory to its basic thrust, it may nevertheless be concluded that Washington had worked with enough consistency over a long enough time in a sufficiently wide number of settings that something of a tradition had taken root firmly enough to be adjudged a guide to future action. The problem was how successful such an orientation would be in a world of rapid social and political change where, as the second instruction of the ECCI to the Chinese Communists so sharply insisted, "the central question of all policy is the peasant question."

American policy toward the South, 1940–1950

To the discomfiture of its more important allies, the United States continued its by now traditional association with the forces of local nationalism during World War II. By the terms of the Atlantic Charter, Roosevelt in effect reiterated the major features of Wilson's Fourteen Points of January 1918, and called for national self-determination and the economic open door after the war. Stalin immediately suspected the American plan, grimly asking Anthony Eden when he visited Moscow in December of that year whether the charter was intended against Germany or against the Soviet Union. For Stalin insisted that after the war the Soviet Union would expect the same territorial concessions it had received from Berlin under the terms of the nonaggression pact of 1939: recovery of the Baltic States and parts of Rumania, Finland, and Poland. From these claims it might also be anticipated that Moscow would expect that the states of Eastern Europe lying adjacent to its borders, especially Poland, would lie within a Soviet sphere of influence. For his part, Churchill was equally reluctant to give his full assent to the charter. The British resented the unilateral attempt of the United States to dismantle the imperial preference system, and Churchill specifically excluded the empire from the political terms of the charter.[33]

The extent to which Roosevelt finally came to accept a postwar sphere of influence for the Soviet Union is a matter of some debate among historians. Although by the time of the Teheran Conference late in 1943, Roosevelt had apparently accepted the idea of Russian territorial gains, opinion differs on how he foresaw postwar relations between the Soviet Union and Eastern Europe. "Tension between the American principle of self-determination and Russian security needs became the single most important cause of the disunity of the Grand Alliance," writes John Gaddis. Yet, although Gaddis, like other students of the period, feels that Roosevelt would have allowed the creation of a Soviet sphere of influence in Eastern Europe to go unchallenged provided domestic opinion did not become too inflamed, he is obliged to admit that "F.D.R.'s superficial knowledge of Eastern Europe kept him from realizing the contradiction between freely elected and pro-Russian governments in that turbulent part of the world."[34] But does not such an analysis suggest more of a discontinuity between the Truman and Roosevelt administrations than can safely be assumed? Certainly Roosevelt's adamant opposition to the arrangements Churchill was trying to make with Stalin in the latter half of 1944 to divide the Balkans into spheres of influence – like his insistence at Yalta that the Big Three sign a Declaration on Liberated Europe assuring democratic elections there after the war, and the messages he sent to Stalin and Churchill in the weeks before his death protesting Soviet activ-

ities in Rumania and Poland – indicates that he might ultimately have acted much as Truman did and so have upset postwar relations with Moscow by denying the Soviets a sphere of
influence in Eastern Europe. Both publicly and privately, and
over a long period of time, Roosevelt reiterated the standard
American opposition to postwar spheres of influence. Thus,
when at one point he gave in to a British request for support for
such a sphere in Greece, Roosevelt was clear to limit it to
merely three months. As he put it to Churchill: "We must be
careful to make it clear that we are not establishing any postwar spheres of influence." So a memorandum from the State
Department to the British embassy warned on June 13, 1944,
with respect to the Balkans:

Special efforts are being made for concerted action in laying the foundations
of a broader system of general security in which all countries great and small
will have their part. Any arrangement suggestive of spheres of influence
cannot but militate against the establishment and effective functioning of
such a broader framework.[35]

In short, in the name of a general system of collective security
(that ultimately came to be embodied in the United Nations),
the United States would oppose spheres of influence in Eastern
Europe by whatever power, Great Britain or the Soviet Union.
In the process, the traditional American support for national
self-determination would be reaffirmed and updated; there is
little reason to suppose that had Roosevelt lived the course of
events would have been dramatically altered.

This conclusion is all the more compelling when the American opposition to Soviet expansion is considered alongside
Washington's reiterated concern that the British Empire be dismantled. It is true that Secretary of State Cordell Hull later
wrote: "At no time did we press Britain, France or The Netherlands for an immediate grant of self-government to their
colonies. Our thought was that it would come after an adequate
period of years, short or long, depending on the state of development of respective colonial peoples, during which these
peoples would be trained to govern themselves."[36] But if the
United States did not insist on *immediate* independence, we
have the secretary's word for it that American pressure was

quite substantial. So, according to Hull, every effort was made beginning early in the war to have the British rally India to the Allied side by guaranteeing the country's speedy independence in the aftermath of the fighting. And as we might expect, this call for Indian self-determination was accompanied by repeated demands that the United States be extended an open door in India, in disregard of the imperial preference system. In regard to Southeast Asia, Hull reports that in September 1944, the State Department sent a memorandum to Roosevelt of which the president "warmly approved." The memorandum suggested the value of

early, dramatic, and concerted announcements by the nations concerned making definite commitments as to the future of the regions of Southeast Asia ... It would be especially helpful if such concerted announcements could include 1) specific dates when independence or complete (dominion) self-government will be accorded, 2) specific steps to be taken to develop native capacity for self-rule, and 3) a pledge of economic autonomy and equality of economic treatment toward other nations ... In addition to their great value as psychological warfare [against the Japanese at the time] such announcements would appear to be directly in line with American postwar interests.[37]

Hull reports that his proposal was transmitted throughout the State Department and to the foreign governments concerned. Churchill's response, indicated by a note to Anthony Eden in December 1944, conveys the full flavor of the British reaction:

There must be no question of our being hustled or seduced into declarations affecting British sovereignty in any of the Dominions or Colonies. Pray remember my declaration against liquidating the British Empire. If the Americans want to take Japanese islands which they have conquered, let them do so with our blessing and any form of words that may be agreeable to them. But "hands off the British Empire" is our maxim and it must not be weakened or smirched to please sob-stuff merchants at home or foreigners of any hue.[38]

In Iran, the United States was successful in exploding British and Soviet spheres of influence simultaneously, as Teheran had every reason to invite this third party in order to reduce the long-standing claims Moscow and London each had to influence in the region. "I was rather thrilled with the idea of using Iran as an example of what we could do by an unselfish American policy," wrote General Patrick Hurley to Hull in January 1944. In the secretary's words, the American mission to this country took over "finance, internal revenue, customs, price stabilization, rationing, distribution, collection of harvests, public domains, and road transport."[39] Important American interests, paramount of which was Washington's control over the projected Anglo-American petroleum agreement, were thereby assured. Under the terms of this agreement, the United States, with British assistance, would use its private oil companies to control world production and distribution of petroleum. Production and marketing schedules designed to shift consumption away from the Western Hemisphere, as well as prices, would be determined in a planned, global manner in order to ensure adequate supply at a stable cost.[40] Once again, the American practice of working with southern governments in a mutually beneficial fashion had apparently demonstrated its worth.

Of course there had always been limits to the extent to which American interests synchronized with those of governments in Asia and Latin America. But the decisive question of the period after 1945 was whether Washington would find that it could accommodate its interests to nationalism of Communist inspiration that was at the leadership of a peasant-based revolution. In the years before 1939, Communist movements had demonstrated relatively little power in these regions, and in any case the United States did not feel itself directly concerned by the matter in any area but Central America. Following the war, however, all this had changed. Communist-led resistance groups had the strength to make a serious bid for power in countries as diverse as France, Yugoslavia, Greece, Indochina, the Philippines, and China, and in most instances it was Washington that had primary responsibility for determining what the international response would be.

The contrast between American policy toward nationalism in French Indochina and Dutch Indonesia is an interesting case in point. After the war, the United States was well aware that in both areas there was serious nationalist resistance to the reimposition of European rule. A secret State Department policy statement issued in the fall of 1948 with respect to Indochina expressed no reservations: "The majority people of the area, the Vietnamese, have stubbornly resisted the reestablishment of French authority."[41] Never was there any serious question but that this opposition was genuinely nationalistic. As Secretary of State Marshall wrote in the summer of 1948: "Ho seems quite capable of retaining and even strengthening his grip on Indochina with no outside assistance other than a continuing procession of French puppet governments. . . .[In regard to Moscow] we have the impression Ho must be given or is retaining large degree latitude."[42] Six years later, when President Eisenhower was deciding whether to intervene militarily in Vietnam, he reported that he had no doubt that in a free election Ho Chi Minh would gather 80 percent of the vote.[43]

Similarly, Washington respected the strength and local credentials of Indonesian nationalism. In a cable to Secretary Marshall from Batavia, United States Consul General Charles Livengood underscored the "essential fallacy" of the Dutch view, their "consistent underestimation strength Republic [nationalist] support throughout Java, Madura, Sumatra and much of East Indonesia, and unshakeable determination to regard non-Republic Indonesia movements as something comparable. We stated frankly we believed Netherlands living in dream if believed elements constituting Republic would not completely dominate an independent Indonesia."[44]

Washington's reactions to these two powerful nationalist movements were markedly different, however. In the case of the Netherlands East Indies, the United States pushed unequivocally for independence under the aegis of the Hatta-Sukarno government. State Department documents convey the clarity of American thinking: The forces behind Hatta and Sukarno were fiercely anti-Communist, as had been demonstrated by the civil war around the Madiun incidents in the fall of 1948; but a prolonged confrontation with the Dutch would result in guerrilla warfare and would play into Communist hands. On the other hand, an independent Indonesia under Hatta and Sukarno would meet Washington's security concerns

while abolishing Dutch trade monopolies, and so would come
to rely on the United States commercially for its economic
development. Strong in these convictions, Washington warned
The Hague that should it press a military campaign against the
Republic, the United States might see fit to reduce its aid to the
Netherlands, to withdraw from the Good Offices Committee
mediating the dispute, to take the case against Holland before
the United Nations Security Council, even to recognize the
Republic and to enter into trade agreements with it.[45]

With respect to Indochina, however, the United States was
far less assertive, although Roosevelt had made it clear during
the war that he did not favor the return of France to this part of
Asia, and Truman refused French requests for American trans-
ports to convey troops to the area and arms to fight the insurgents in 1945.[46] The standard explanation for Washington's
policy was that it feared French refusal to go along with American security plans for Western Europe should the United States
press too hard: "Our aims in Europe require us to support a
friendly French government, and this has taken precedence
over Indochinese policy objectives," declared the State Department in September 1948.[47] But concern about the reaction of
The Hague had not deflected American pressures over Indonesia: Indeed Washington had actually hoped that as a result
of its efforts the Dutch government would fall, to be replaced
by one more amenable to reason.[48] Of course the fall of the
French government was a more risky affair: A more militant
Right or a more anti-American Left might pick up the pieces.
But the assertion that it was only European considerations that
shaped Washington's handling of France is not convincing.

More important than the difference between France and Holland in determining Washington's actions in Southeast Asia
after 1945 was the difference between Indonesian and Indochinese nationalism: The former was safely anti-Communist,
the latter most decidedly was not. In these circumstances,
Washington hesitated – hoping, as a government memorandum
put it, for "the establishment of a truly nationalist government
in Indochina which, by giving satisfaction to the aspirations of
the peoples of Indochina, will serve as a rallying point for the

nationalists and will weaken the Communist elements."[49] Would Paris permit the reunification of Vietnam, conferring upon its government the right to determine its internal and external affairs as it chose in full sovereignty? Because it was precisely on these points that the French proved reluctant (as were the Dutch in Indonesia), Washington could act only by backing Ho Chi Minh. This it refused to consider. Instead, hope was maintained that some solution along the lines of that found in Indonesia and the Philippines might be discovered: "truly" nationalist forces dedicated to checking the power of communism locally.

Here in microcosm was the crucial issue that American experience prior to World War II had done little to resolve. As it became apparent after 1945 that southern nationalism might find a variety of forms of expression and that the international role of the United States had altered markedly, the question naturally arose of on what basis these two changing historical forces could associate. On the one hand, the global character of the war and the ensuing retrenchment of America's Western European allies from the Near East to the Orient meant that for the first time United States interests were not regional but virtually worldwide in scope, and included the responsibility of protecting the international interests of its chief allies as well as its own. On the other hand, the character of southern nationalism was changing as well, partly as a result of internal developments, partly as a consequence of the global retraction of the principal prewar imperialist powers: It was growing more powerful and more militant. Were there variants of southern nationalism that could not be reconciled with American interests, but instead threatened to undermine them? And if such threats existed, how might they best be handled?

Rather than contemplating laying the foundations for a working relationship with indigenous Communist movements in the Far East and Latin America, where they showed themselves to be free of Moscow's control, the United States adopted a different tack: to try to split the Communists from the other nationalists, and to support the latter in their struggle with the former. Only in China, where the United States initially hoped to bring about a coalition government wherein Chiang Kai-shek would be dominant, did United States policy markedly differ. In pursuit of its strategy of separating Communists from other nationalists, Washington promised to give political satisfaction to the latter by sponsoring the membership of their country in the international community at the same time that it encouraged them in progressive reforms at home, reforms designed to curb the appeal of communism to the lower strata of society. Thus, the United States both gladly conferred independent status on the Philippines immediately after World War II and prompted that country to social and political reforms to counter the Hukbalahap Rebellion which began in 1946. Its ally in this process was Ramon Magsaysay, defense minister in 1949, and president in 1953, who responded to the intensification of the rebellion in 1950 with promises of progressive reforms in land tenure. Similarly, in Greece, the United States fully supported the military suppression of the Communist-led rebellion against the government established by Britain at the close of the war, but it pressured all the while for the formation of more socially progressive governments in Athens.[50] And in the case of China, there is an especially long and impressive record of American admonitions to Chiang Kai-shek to remake his government and to reform his country if he would save it from Mao Tse-tung Communists. As Truman wrote Chiang on August 10, 1946:

The hopes of the people of China are being thwarted by militarists and a small group of political reactionaries who are obstructing the advancement of the general good of the nation by failing to understand the liberal trend of the times. The people of the United States view with violent repugnance this state of affairs. It cannot be expected that American opinion will continue in its generous attitude toward your nation unless convincing proof is shortly forthcoming that genuine progress is being made toward a peaceful settlement of China's internal problems.[51]

In short, Washington would work to make southern governments internally progressive and internationally sovereign. In the process, it hoped that they would be able to resist becoming Communist. It should not be concluded from this that the United States was acting on the basis of some carefully calculated grand design. To the contrary, the policy flowed rather naturally from past American experience and the political shape of objective circumstances. If grand design there were, it would be better to see it on the part of the Communists, whose calculated Machiavellianism in this respect was a matter of public record and even pride (because it contrasted to the "hypocrisy" of the bourgeoisie and the imperialists). For it was the Communists who had deliberately formed the strategy of the united front in order to wage the "national-democratic revolution" against imperialism (in the case of China, for example), only to anticipate ending it and turning on their erstwhile allies once this first stage was successful.[52]

In Greece and the Philippines the American-backed efforts of nationalists opposed to the Communists were successful (although many of the conditions that prompted local insurgencies are still present today). But in China, the force of Communist nationalism could not be stopped by Chiang Kai-shek, and the United States was for the first time unable to control a regional situation through local allies. Washington's response to this development was crucial in the formulation of American policy toward the South over the next quarter century.

Throughout the war, as it was made especially clear at the Cairo Conference in December 1943, the United States showed that it hoped to see China emerge from the struggle under Chiang Kai-shek's leadership both internally united and regionally dominant. Neither Stalin nor Churchill took seriously Roosevelt's proposal that China be treated after the war as one of the Big Four (to be symbolized by its Security Council seat in the future United Nations), but both conceded that the Pacific and an independent China proper would be an American sphere of influence (loathe as the Americans were to think in such terms). Once again the general pattern of American policy was manifest: Chinese nationalism and American overseas interests could establish a working relationship.[53]

One obvious dilemma threatened this project, however. At any moment the latent civil war between the Communists and the Kuomintang might break out anew, raising the question of the degree and kind of support to offer Chiang in the face of the likelihood of Communist successes and the possibility of Soviet interference. The initial hope was therefore to prevent civil war. This might be accomplished on the one hand by encouraging the CCP and the KMT to enter into a coalition government under Chiang's authority (a plan advanced first by General Hurley, later by General Marshall), and on the other by shoring up the KMT militarily (as with the dispatch of 113,000 marines to China, the transport of Chiang's troops to North China, and General Order Number One instructing the Japanese to surrender only to the KMT command).

As Chiang's position worsened, Washington had to choose between one of three courses of action: intervening more actively on behalf of the KMT; continuing essentially the same policy of supporting the KMT materially and with advisers, but without the commitment of American soldiers, in the hope that some unforeseen development would occur; or substituting the Communists for the Nationalists in the American plan to have a united, regionally dominant China. Although the first option was supported by a number of men within the State Department and by certain prominent politicians and public leaders generally associated with the Republican party, the Truman administration never seriously considered such an undertaking. Under the terms of the Truman Doctrine and the Marshall Plan, the major American commitment was to Western Europe and the Mediterranean; no large-scale involvement on the Asian mainland was deemed feasible, although it was not until he had safely won the 1948 election that Truman was unequivocal in this regard.

At the same time, except among a small group of men that included John Paton Davies and John Carter Vincent, no one gave much consideration to a policy of working with Mao and a Communist regime in China. The commitment to Chiang was too strong, the potential liabilities of working with the Communists too large (at the polls at home as well as in foreign affairs) to warrant such a shift. American policy, therefore, was to temporize, pursuing a wait-and-see course that in due time turned out to have its own terrible difficulties.

Two questions concerning the Chinese Revolution appear to

have been uppermost in Washington's thinking: whether it genuinely expressed a deep-seated current in Chinese history, and to what extent it would identify itself with the Soviet Union in world politics. Despite his tendency on occasion to see the Chinese political scene as so chaotic as to be uncontrolled, Secretary Acheson left no doubts about the revolution's deep roots in his Letter of Transmittal of the China White Paper in the summer of 1949:

> The fact was that the decay which our observers had detected in Chungking early in the war had fatally sapped the powers of resistance of the Kuomintang. Its leaders had proved incapable of meeting the crisis confronting them, its troops had lost the will to fight, and the Government had lost popular support . . . The Nationalist armies did not have to be defeated; they disintegrated . . . The unfortunate but inescapable fact is that the ominous result of civil war in China was beyond the control of the government of the United States. Nothing that this country did or could have done within the reasonable limits of its capabilities could have changed that result; nothing that was left undone by this country has contributed to it. It was the product of internal Chinese forces which this country tried to influence but could not.[54]

By a single line of the letter, however, the secretary showed his mind on the other critical question – in what measure the new leaders of China would work with the Soviet Union: "The Communist leaders have foresworn their Chinese heritage and have publicly announced their subservience to a foreign power, Russia." Perhaps Acheson was forgetting the various efforts made during the war by the CCP to establish relations with Washington, but whatever the case it is certain that well before 1949 Mao had come to see the United States as his unremitting opponent. Thus when Acheson explained that the "active abuse" of this country by the CCP made it impossible to treat Mao like Washington had begun to treat Tito in 1948, and so to try to separate the Chinese and the Russians, he may have had in mind any of a number of statements by prominent Chinese Communist officials modeled on the bravura of Mao's August 1946 statement to Anna Louise Strong that "all reactionaries are paper tigers."[55] Or as Mao put it in June 1949:

> To sit on the fence is impossible. A third road does not exist . . . not only in China but also in the world, without exception, one either leans to the side

of imperialism or to the side of socialism. Neutrality is a camouflage and a third road does not exist.[56]

To be sure, the evidence now strongly suggests that until the summer of 1946 the CCP would have welcomed relations with Washington and that the United States actively resisted these initiatives.[57] But by 1948, American hostility had been repaid in kind, making an American démarche to establish contact with the Communists much more difficult, even if it had been Washington's conduct that was at the origin of the conflict.

Nonetheless, there is good reason to believe that by the end of 1949 thinking in Washington was finally coming around to the idea of working with a Communist China. In December, Mao traveled to Moscow to conclude a treaty with the Soviet Union, and as his stay extended until the following February, it became conceivable to assume that a number of serious differences divided the two parties. In an address before the National Press Club on January 12, 1950, Acheson claimed that the Soviets were trying to take over both Inner and Outer Mongolia, Manchuria, and Sinkiang; and he declared:

We must not undertake to deflect from the Russians to ourselves the righteous anger and the wrath and the hatred of the Chinese people which must develop. It would be folly to deflect it to ourselves. We must take the position we have always taken – that anyone who violates the integrity of China is the enemy of China and is acting contrary to our own interests. That, I suggest to you this afternoon, is the first and greatest rule in regard to the formulation of American policy toward Asia.[58]

In the same spirit, the secretary cabled to the American Embassy in Paris the following month: "In this oriental bazaar bargaining Kremlin is probably discovering Chi Delegation least submissive it has had to deal with in all its experience with 'peoples democracies.'"[59] Perhaps the Americans were finally coming to realize what the British had been saying all along: Chinese–Russian differences were substantial enough that concessions from the West might make the breach still more serious.[60] From this perspective, we can understand the great importance of the decision made by Truman late in 1949 to cut all aid to Chiang on Taiwan.[61] If his government were destroyed by the Communists, the American commitment would automatically end, opening the way for relations to be established between Peking and Washington. Of course, the China Lobby was already in action to prevent such developments and hard-liners within the administration had drafted by the spring of 1950 the important National Security Council Policy Paper Number 68 calling for a national crusade to scotch the Kremlin's "aggressive expansionist drive," which was bent on "world domination."[62] Yet clearly there were forces developing to counter these efforts, and it may plausibly be maintained that in the early months of 1950, the United States was moving into a position from which it could establish relations with the very Communists it had so long sought to avoid.

But in June, 1950, came the Korean War. It is idle to speculate on how history might have been different had the United States followed the sage counsel of Britain and recognized the People's Republic in 1949. What is certain is that the conflict made it virtually impossible to extend the containment of Russia into Asia through an understanding with Peking. Instead, in what was surely the most momentous turning point in world affairs in the quarter century following the outbreak of the Cold War, the containment of Russia came to mean the containment of China as well. The containment of China, in turn, seemed to dictate the suppression of communism in the South, particularly in Asia. Within short order, the Truman administration called for the rearmament of Germany and the increased integration of Western defense forces; concluded peace and security treaties with Japan; signed mutual defense pacts with the Philippines, Australia, and New Zealand (from these countries' viewpoint, to counter a potentially resurgent Japan); reversed its position on Taiwan, moving to defend the island; and sizably expanded the aid allotted France to prosecute the Indochina conflict. In the words of Robert W. Tucker, "The course of containment became the course of empire."[63]

American policy toward the South, 1951–1981

There is no need to document in any detail the course of American policy following Truman with respect to the South.

A number of able reviews in this regard exist, so that the emphasis here will be on the manner in which succeeding administrations tended, in their concern over communism, to grow suspicious of Third World nationalism in such a way that the earlier endorsement of political self-determination in these regions of the world became increasingly qualified. Nevertheless, one can exaggerate the change in American conduct: The memory of the wholesale intervention in Vietnam should not color our understanding of American policy elsewhere in the Third World. Indeed, an outstanding feature of American behavior prior to President Johnson's fateful decision to escalate the war in that unhappy Southeast Asian country was that the United States remained exceedingly reluctant to become involved in a situation on the periphery in which it could not work with viable local interests.

In the case of the Eisenhower administration, for example, the United States managed to avoid any disastrous encounters with southern nationalism not because of the president's narrow construction of the Communist threat, or from his reluctance to take counterrevolutionary measures – the interventions in Laos, Guatemala, Iran, and Lebanon attest to that – but primarily because of American reluctance to act when not invited by an important local party to the conflict. In Guatemala, it is true, the United States supported the CIA protégé Carlos Astillo Armas; although his very anonymity meant that he might have been disavowed in the case of failure. But in Iran, the United States cooperated closely with the Shah, just as in Lebanon its intervention was requested by President Camille Chamoun, and in Laos it worked in association with a prince of the royal family. Perhaps this helps to explain why Eisenhower escaped entrapment in more difficult situations: There was no one he could use directly to oppose Kassim in Iraq, Ho Chi Minh in Indochina, or Gamel Abdel Nasser in Egypt – so he kept his distance.

Certainly there is nowhere in Eisenhower's memoirs any trace of sympathy for the role of charismatic leaders in the Third World. He found Nasser, for example, "wholly arrogant," "volatile and unpredictable," and given to the "mock heroic."[64]

And Townsend Hoopes reports that the administration saw the first deliveries of Czech weapons to Egypt late in 1955, like the recognition of China the following year, as a signal that Nasser might be passing into the Communist orbit.[65] Furthermore, by his unilateral expropriation of the Suez Canal in 1956, it seemed Nasser not only meant to challenge the United States as a result of its cancellation of the Aswan Dam project but also to deliver a blow against the British effort to weaken the Arab League and contain Egypt. Yet, although the president admitted that "the use of force under *extreme* circumstances might become necessary," he warned Britain and France against military intervention in Egypt, and brusquely ordered their withdrawal when it occurred, initiating financial and petroleum blockades that added to their indignity. As Eisenhower explained it, none too convincingly, Nasser had shown that he could run the canal effectively with his own pilots, and that was the essential issue. Surely a much more important consideration was, as Eisenhower warned, that the United States should heed the danger of involving itself in the Middle East directly, of becoming "an occupying power in a seething Arab world."[66] As John Badeau, former ambassador to Egypt has pointed out, the most likely outcome of unseating Nasser would have been to drive Egyptian nationalism still further into the arms of Moscow.[67] Whatever his animosity toward Nasser, Eisenhower was able to distinguish the Soviet threat from that of Egypt and to appreciate the limits of his power that came from his lack of any allies who could be classified as Egyptian nationalists and who could be used against Nasser.

The latter consideration emerges as particularly important when the refusal to become involved against Egypt is compared with Eisenhower's reluctance to join the French in fighting the Viet Minh. In his memoirs Eisenhower reports he came very close to ordering direct military intervention there. But a serious obstacle was his expectation that the French would not end their ceaseless maneuvers to remain in Indochina and instead grant the area its independence. In line with traditional American policy, Eisenhower saw that French demands rendered impossible the creation of a significant non-Communist, nationalist group in Vietnam with which Washington could side. The president wrote that he was well aware of Ho's tremendous popularity in Vietnam, and that he therefore feared American involvement there would be extremely costly, leading to "a succession of Asian wars, the end result [being] to drain off our resources and to weaken our over-all defensive position."[68]

Yet although Eisenhower appears prudent to have avoided projecting the United States into situations where it did not have reasonably strong local allies to carry the burden of the effort, he did at the same time considerably expand the international network of American treaty obligations and so helped to set a trap that would spring on his successors. For it was the Southeast Asian Treaty Organization (SEATO), launched in 1954, that did so much to involve the United States in the affairs of South Vietnam; and it was Eisenhower's support for the Baghdad Pact in 1955, followed by his expulsion of France and Great Britain from their paramount positions in the Middle East after Suez in 1956 and the enunciation of the Eisenhower Doctrine relative to this area the following year, that brought this country into direct responsibility for events in the Middle East as well. Thereafter, save for Africa, the global structure of American political commitments – the international exercise of the Monroe Doctrine – was complete. Once this structure of obligations was in place, it seemed to take on a life of its own, dictating that a threat to any one of its constituent parts posed a threat to the whole. The United States had become an empire and was beginning to think more and more in imperial terms.

Ever since World War II, the United States had viewed developments abroad in a dual fashion: On the one hand, with a prudent appreciation of the power of local actors with whom America should work in order to realize its own interests locally; on the other hand, with a geopolitical sense that the resolution of local questions had a bearing on the global structure of American interests and obligations. As the network of United States obligations broadened after 1947, the seemingly compelling logic of the geopolitical vision grew with it, at times completely superseding any reading of the logic of local developments. The virtue of President Kennedy in this regard was that at least initially he saw how distinct these two domains of action might be. What comes as a surprise, therefore, is not that he handled problems that arose in Guinea, the Congo, Yemen, and British Guiana so skillfully, but that his record with respect to Vietnam and Cuba was so poor.[69] In each case, the flaw in his thinking was apparently the belief (despite American experience in China) that with relative ease he might use the traditional American association with foreign nationalism to counter Communist advances abroad. As he had put it in 1951, when he visited Vietnam:

In Indochina, we have allied ourselves to the desperate effort of a French regime to hang on to the remnants of empire. There is no broad general support of the native Vietnam government among the people of that area. To check the southern drive of Communism makes sense but not only through reliance on the force of arms. The task rather is to build strong native non-Communist sentiment within these areas and rely on that as a spearhead of defense rather than on the legions of General de Lattre. To do this apart from and in defiance of innately nationalistic aims spells foredoomed failure . . . Without the support of the native populations there is no hope of success in any of the countries of Southeast Asia.[70]

The same perspective informed his approach to Cuba. Incredible as it may appear, the principal reason the president failed to provide backup for the Bay of Pigs Invasion in April 1961 seems to be that he assumed there would be a mass uprising against Castro once the news was out that the "liberators" had arrived. Arthur Schlesinger indirectly quotes Kennedy as saying when it was evident the invasion had failed: "The test had always been whether the Cuban people would back a revolt against Castro. If they wouldn't, the United States could not by invasion impose a new regime on them."[71] Similarly, in the case of Vietnam, Kennedy trusted (as did many other Americans) in the person of Ngo Dinh Diem, the Catholic mandarin who had resisted attempts by both the Japanese and the Communists to include him in their governments for Vietnam, and who had spent time in a Maryknoll seminary in Maryland. "We saw a miracle take place," wrote Kennedy in 1960, speaking of Diem's emergence after the Geneva Agreements in 1954: "I should have had more faith in my own propositions about the potential power of free Asian nationalism."[72] But by early 1963, it was evident that Diem had not provided the leadership Kennedy had expected. Viet Cong successes in the countryside had begun to increase once again after a downturn in 1962. Far more ominously, however, Diem failed to project himself as the leader of the non-Communist nationalists, as the Buddhist demonstrations against his regime in the spring and summer of 1963 clearly indicated. In view of the failure of the non-Communist nationalists in Vietnam during 1963, it has been a matter of much debate whether Kennedy would have escalated the American involvement in the country as President Johnson was subsequently to do. On the one hand, Kennedy is reported to have said in the fall of 1963 that after the 1964 elections he would see to a withdrawal from Indochina, whatever the personal price he had to pay for the decision.[73] Such a course of action would have corresponded with a realistic assessment of the strength of non-Communist nationalism in the area and hence it would have been in line with many of the president's own prejudices as well as with that interpretation of the "lessons of China" that holds that communism in association with nationalism is an especially powerful opponent.

One important consideration suggests, on the other hand, that Kennedy might have been more reluctant to disengage, for his administration witnessed the implementation of a significant new approach to the question of how to act in regard to Third World nationalism. Since the late 1950s, serious concern had been raised about the methods by which "internal subversion" – the techniques of guerrilla warfare developed by Mao Tse-tung – was undermining the assumptions under which Washington had hitherto operated with respect to southern nationalism. It now began to appear that the United States needed to be prepared to intervene more directly in "limited wars" and to shore up through a variety of counterinsurgency tactics governments under siege from rebellions based on an organizational model exported from China.[74] In other words, it was no longer so clearly the case that non-Communist regimes in the Third World could be supported in power by traditional means. Theories of guerrilla warfare gave a new sense of urgency to the geopolitical view of the world.

Once he took office, therefore, President Kennedy gave substantial encouragement to counterinsurgency tactics, greatly increasing the budget for the "special forces" (of whom the best known were the Green Berets) and insisting that civilians in the Departments of State and Defense be aware of these new military doctrines.[75] As a result, despite his recognition that the non-Communist nationalists were in disarray in Saigon, the president might quite possibly have been convinced that his own, and the traditional, American practice of intervening abroad only where there was a viable nationalist force to be assisted was now outmoded; that Vietnam instead represented something of a testing ground for insurgency and counterinsurgency techniques and therefore should be viewed within a geopolitical understanding of American overseas obligations. As he put it in an address to Congress in May 1961:

The great battleground for the defense and expansion of freedom today is the whole southern half of the globe – Asia, Latin America, Africa and the Middle East – the lands of the rising peoples . . . And theirs is a revolution which we would support regardless of the Cold War . . . the adversaries of freedom did not create the revolution . . . but they are seeking to ride the crest of its wave, to capture it for themselves . . . the adversaries of freedom plan to consolidate their territory – to exploit, to control, and finally to destroy the hopes of the world's newest nations; and they have ambitions to do it before the end of the decade. It is a contest of will and purpose as well as force and violence – a battle for minds and souls as well as lives and territory. And in that contest we can not stand aside.[76]

Perhaps Kennedy would have managed an American withdrawal from Vietnam had he won the 1964 election. But with his reputation built on toughness toward communism and on his belief that nations, like individuals, realize the best in themselves by making heroic demands of their citizens; with his reliance on the methods of counterinsurgency; with the gradual escalation of the commitment there to nearly 17,000 men by late 1963; and with his perception of Vietnam as linked to the greater network of America's international obligations, there is no particular reason to be confident Kennedy would have withdrawn and permitted a Communist victory. One of the best indications of what he might have done comes from the thinking of the men surrounding him. Most of them later went on to be the chief advisers to President Johnson, and they were virtually unanimous in counseling him to escalate the war. There is a terrible irony in Kennedy's comment on the Eisenhower men who had carried him along with his predecessor's plan to invade Cuba in 1961: "My God, the bunch of advisers we inherited . . . Can you imagine being President and leaving behind someone like all those people there?"[77]

It was during the Johnson administration that the balance between seeing local events in the Far East and Latin America in their own terms and seeing them geopolitically – that is, in terms of their presumed impact on America's overall relations with the Communist world – finally gave way. The hitherto dominant pattern of American policy that sought to base relations in the South on the expectation of mutual interests to be served took a decidedly secondary place to the arguments for preemptive imperialism. To be sure, there was the familiar assertion on the part of the United States that it claimed no special privileges for itself in the South, only that it wanted to keep these areas free of Communist influence. Nor was there anything novel in putting the contests in Vietnam and the Dominican Republic within a geopolitical framework. What was different was the one-sidedness of the emphasis and the corresponding willingness of the United States for the first time to commit itself directly and massively (in the case of Vietnam) to an Asian government lacking credible domestic political support or even the apparent means of gaining it. But as Vice-President Johnson had put it in 1961:

The battle against Communism must be joined in Southeast Asia with strength and determination to achieve success there – or the United States, inevitably, must surrender the Pacific and take up our defenses on our own shores.

The basic decision in Southeast Asia is here. We must decide whether to help these countries to the best of our ability or throw in the towel and pull back our defenses to San Francisco. . . .More important, we would say to the world in this case that we don't live up to our treaties and don't stand by our friends.[78]

In an important sense, therefore, the Nixon Doctrine of 1970 was not so much a departure from standard American policy as a return to the dominant tradition: The doctrine insisted that the local political terrain must be reasonably receptive before the United States committed itself again. "Asia is for Asians," declared President Nixon on July 25, 1969, "and that is what we want, and that is the role we should play. We should assist, but we must not dictate . . . we must avoid the kind of policy that will make countries in Asia so dependent upon us that we are dragged into conflicts such as the one we have in Vietnam."[79] The essence of his doctrine was straightforward:

Its central thesis is that the United States will participate in the defense and development of allies and friends, but the Americans cannot – and will not – conceive *all* the plans, design *all* the programs, execute *all* the decisions and undertake *all* the defense of the free nations of the world.[80]

And at the same time that they recognized the dangers of being drawn into a conflict without reliable local allies, the president and Secretary of State Kissinger appeared to appreciate the risks of a certain form of geopolitical thinking as well: "We are not involved in the world because we have commitments; we have commitments because we are involved. Our interests must shape our commitments, rather than the other way around."[81]

Yet if he recognized potential problems in a geopolitical outlook, Secretary Kissinger meant to render it more useful than ever before to American leaders, to found a veritable "tradition" on its insights that he would leave as his legacy to his successors.[82] At the center of his calculations stood, of course, the Soviet Union. Through a process of détente, the secretary sought to recognize Soviet military parity with the United States by working to establish a relationship between the two countries based on recognition of the facts "that we have some parallel interests and that we are compelled to coexist. Détente encourages an environment in which competitors can regulate

and restrain their differences and ultimately move from competition to cooperation."[83] Moreover, Washington could encourage such a development through a mixture of "carrots,"
such as increased trade and arms-limitation agreements, and
"sticks," such as the potential of the new relationship with
China.

A major problem arose, however, over Soviet and American
relations in the Third World. For in practice the condominium
arrangement proposed by Kissinger turned out to mean that
Moscow should discipline its allies in Cuba, Vietnam, and
Syria, but that it was not to extend the range of its commitments any farther. Nor would the secretary allow local developments in the South to make their own contribution to Soviet
advances, as he demonstrated in 1973, when he collaborated
in the overthrow of the Allende regime because of what he
thought its existence would mean to other countries in Latin
America and to Communist movements in Western Europe,
and thus ultimately to the balance of power with the Soviet
Union. Or again, as Kissinger put it in 1976 in regard to his
proposal that the United States intervene more actively in Angola:

When one great power tips the balance of forces decisively in a local conflict
through its military intervention – and meets no resistance – an ominous
precedent is set, of grave consequence even if the intervention occurs in a
seemingly remote area. Such a precedent cannot be tolerated if a lasting
easing of tensions is to be achieved. And if the pattern is not broken now, we
will face harder choices and higher costs in the future . . . To claim that
Angola is not an important country, or that the United States had no important interests there, begs the principal question. If the United States is seen
to waver in the face of massive Soviet and Cuban intervention, what will be
the perception of leaders around the world as they make decisions concerning their future security? And what conclusions will an unopposed superpower draw when the next opportunity for intervention beckons?[84]

In short, something of an evolution had taken place in Kissinger's thinking between 1969 and 1976. Fearing that the United
States was retreating too far from its global responsibilities as
a consequence of the national trauma over Vietnam, he found
himself urging once again an insistence on geopolitical concerns in relative disregard of the character of the political ter-

rain into which the United States was to project its power and prestige.

In contrast, the Carter administration until the end of 1979 displayed a far more pronounced reluctance to view developments in the Third World in terms of Washington's relations with Moscow. Thus, the United States avoided a direct confrontation in Iran, where no Soviet presence was alleged; as well as in Nicaragua, despite the Castroite sympathies of the triumphant Sandinistas; and in Angola and the Horn of Africa, where the Soviet Union was playing a direct role in local conflicts. The predominant view in Washington, perhaps best expressed by United Nations Ambassador Andrew Young, was that intervention for the purpose of insisting on an American solution would in every case be self-defeating, arousing both local and regional opposition to the United States of a sort best calculated to work to Moscow's advantage. At the same time, President Carter rallied support for the ratification of the Panama Canal Treaty, which would cede the waterway back to Panama at the turn of the century; worked to secure a Middle East peace with due regard for the right of the Palestinians to a national home; and declared the United States to be in favor of majority rule in Zimbabwe. In short, Washington would work with the forces of southern nationalism in order to further its own interests of regional stability and access to economic resources in the Third World.

The fall of the Shah of Iran early in 1979, and the Soviet incursion into Afghanistan at the end of that year, raised serious questions as to the viability of the Carter policy, however. Although National Security Adviser Zbigniew Brzezinski spoke of associating the United States with an "Islamic Renaissance" to limit Soviet expansion, so sounding the traditional American theme of fending off the encroachment of rival great power spheres of influence by becoming friends with nationalist forces in threatened areas, such an orientation appeared increasingly untenable.[85] The taking of American hostages in Teheran in November 1979, followed by the outbreak of hostilities between Iraq and Iran the next year and the increase of international petroleum prices by 150 percent in the two-year period ending in December 1980, suggested that there were definite limits to the advantages Washington might gain if it assumed its basic interests were naturally compatible with those of southern nationalism. The challenge to America's international hegemony from the Soviet Union combined with the apparent instability of southern nationalism to augur another round of preemptive American imperialism with the coming of the Reagan presidency. Whereas it had taken some twenty years for the alleged "lessons of China" to be unlearned, the evident "lessons of Vietnam" were being rejected after scarcely five.

The pattern of American policy

Since the turn of the century, if not much earlier, the dominant pattern of American policy toward what may broadly be called the South has been Washington's preference to advance its interests through relations with sovereign governments there. Like the British before them, the Americans have favored a plural political world (a preference first forcefully indicated by the Monroe Doctrine), knit together economically by a nondiscriminatory, multilateral commercial system (best expressed by the Open Door Policy). The chief contradiction within this liberal tradition has been Washington's defense of private American property rights abroad even when this meant destabilizing governments there. In some circumstances, however, American willingness to work with southern governments has seemed meaningless when political instability has arisen in a region menaced by a rival great power and seen as important to American national security. Here the pattern has been for the United States to be preemptively imperialist, securing its interests by its direct intervention. Although these patterns have their separate identities, there have been occasions when the liberal mode of American policy has successfully established an American economic presence in the South that, in turn, has contributed to a subsequent political upheaval there and so encouraged preemptive American intervention. American policy toward Guatemala in 1954 or toward Nicaragua, El Salvador, and Guatemala after 1979 might be cited as cases in point. The same basic process may be said to have been at work in an analogous fashion during the period of British hegemony with respect to the Ottoman Empire, West Africa, and China. In every case, economic penetration contributes to local instability that then becomes a matter of concern in terms of great power rivalries.

So far as the dominant liberal pattern is concerned, the administration of Franklin Roosevelt made two significant innovations: After 1932, Washington championed international free trade against economic nationalism, and after 1939, it appeared to back democratic, national self-determination the world around and not only for Europeans. But these innovations of the Roosevelt years were not without their concessions to reality, nor were they startling new departures in terms of the political and economic world order this country had earlier promoted.

The dramatic shift that occurred in America's world role after 1945 reflected to some extent these changes in Washington's policies, but was even more a function of their global scope, the relative power at their disposal, objective world conditions, and the nature of the threat to the international order as the United States came to perceive it. Although the United States had been concerned since at least World War I with the global balance of power, it was not until World War II that it sought to make influencing the character of the international system the essential preoccupation of its foreign policy and so effectively to expand the scope of its actions. It was at this same moment that American power was unparalleled, standing supreme in the aftermath of the war. And it was shortly thereafter that Washington concluded that the chief obstacle it faced to the creation of the world order it desired after the chaos of war was the international spread of communism.

Hereafter, the United States was an imperial power in the sense that it became a country concerned to dominate the conduct of weaker peoples for the sake of certain domestic interests and in the name of an international order conforming to its design. Through its sponsorship of collective security in the United Nations, through agreements and organizations by which it sought to foster an open world economy, and through the range of bilateral and multilateral contacts it entered into, Washington was moving by 1945 through 1947 into a position from which it could control the essential framework of world affairs just as fully as London had for much of the nineteenth century. Not that every detail of this order was accounted for thereby; certainly there were always significant limits to what Washington could accomplish. Nor is there any reason to suggest that these developments reflected a detailed blueprint drawn up in Washington, because they were in large measure the product of outside circumstances, especially of the relative power of the United States internationally. There was nonetheless enough coherence and drive to American policy after 1945 (as well as before) to permit us to see distinct patterns in it.

Indeed, the relative power and the overall objectives of the United States were such after 1945 that the country would surely have functioned as an imperialist power had the Soviet Union never existed. Much as Britain alone had dominated world affairs in the years following 1815, so Washington possessed both the means and the will to impose certain practices upon the postwar world order. As the American hostility to British imperialism discussed previously suggests, this would have occurred whether or not the rival great powers were Communist, as whatever the case the United States opposed spheres of influence in world affairs. Thus, if the bluster of ambassador to China Patrick Hurley were not typical of all Americans, his opposition to European expansion certainly corresponded to a widespread sentiment in Washington. As he wrote to Truman in protest of what he believed were Lord Mountbatten's designs to assume control of Allied forces in China:

Should Lord Louis or any other British Admiral or General receive this appointment in preference to an American it would constitute an overwhelming victory for the hegemony of the imperialist nations and the principles of colonial imperialism in Asia. Such an appointment would also be a distinct setback for America and democracy in Asia ... The paramount political issue in Asia for many years has been the issue between democracy and imperialism. We supported Chinese democratic aspirations against the imperialism of Japan. The question is will we now permit British, French and Dutch imperialists to use the resources of the American democracy to reestablish imperialism in Asia. It is the old conflict between the aspirations of people to be free and the desire of predatory nations to rule . . . The appointment of Lord Louis or any other imperialist as Commander in China would constitute nullification of American principles and achievements in China.[86]

Under the guise of opposition to great power spheres of influence, the United States was licensing itself to make the world its sphere of influence. Antiimperialism was acquiring a decidedly imperialist tone of its own.

The Americans compounded the offensive force of this politically inspired antiimperialism by the effects of an innovation in United States foreign economic policy in favor of international free trade. Once again, the parallels with the British are obvious. The consequence of this shift in policy was that however friendly the United States remained to the political self-determination of peoples abroad, it proved much less warm to notions of economic nationalism. Indeed, as early as the Wilson administration, the idea was advanced that the political divisiveness latent in nationalism might be corrected through the interdependence fostered by an open world economy. But it remained for Secretary of State Cordell Hull to give concrete application to the concept after Franklin Roosevelt became president. His first success came quickly: At the Montevideo Conference in 1933, Hull persuaded the Latin American states to agree to a substantial liberalization of regional trade, which the secretary foresaw as the model for world trade thereafter. Because closed trading blocs seemed to be the basis of political rivalries at the time, the Americans were soon to contend that an open international economic system based on free trade would promote world peace. In their own way, the Americans were restating the arguments of British nineteenth-century free traders against mercantilism − except that now the irony was that the major country resisting such propositions was none other than Great Britain.[87]

It could therefore be anticipated that during World War II, the United States would use its substantial leverage to advance these goals. Whether rhetorically in the Atlantic Charter, or diplomatically in seeking concessions through Lend Lease, or institutionally in the organizations and procedures introduced at Bretton Woods, Washington sought to promote its plan for a liberal, multilateral economic order after the war.

So far as the Third World was concerned, these reforms occurred at a time when these countries were undergoing rapid economic and demographic changes that put enormous social pressures on political institutions usually ill suited by tradition or experience to deal with them. However different the various countries of the Third World may be, what makes them similar is the constant specter of civil or regional war (or both) that confronts them. In such potentially violatile circumstances, foreign economic actors may wield substantial influence: A loan withheld, an investment canceled, a trade channel abandoned can have significant repercussions for a weaker country either in terms of its regional competitors or with respect to the balance of forces among the social groups that determine its political stability. Similarly, the extension or expansion of trade, aid, and investment to these countries may be the source of significant influence on local affairs, consolidating the position of some groups or governments at the expense of their rivals. Given the general orientation of postwar American foreign economic policy and the relatively easy access business has to political decision making in this country, there is a built-in tendency to encourage Washington's intervention in this situation.[88] Nor has the United States been blind to the opportunities offered it thereby.

For example, in 1973 the United States held 25 percent of the votes (Europeans held another 36 percent) in the World Bank, the leading international institution lending to the South. Two historians of the bank leave no doubt but that the encouragement of domestic private and foreign investment in the South is one of the institution's major goals, and that "in the typical case . . . the Bank finds itself supporting certain elements in the government or in the community against others."[89] It is thus not surprising that several studies have found significant variations in the flow of publicly controlled American funds to the South depending on whether a particular regime has Washington's favor.[90] Just as the Marshall Plan proved so effective in Europe, so might economic leverage apply in the

Third World. In the words of a Rockefeller Foundation report drawn up by a group of prominent Americans: "Economics provides a channel of influence far deeper than it has been accorded in traditional diplomatic concepts . . . As an exporter of capital and technical skills, America has played an increasingly important role. It is important also to think of the power that is exerted by reciprocal or absorptive means. . . Too often the significance of this role has not been adequately appraised."[91] For instance, Washington's voting in the Inter-American Development Bank, where in 1974 it held 40.3 percent of the votes, is determined by the National Advisory Council on International Monetary and Financial Policies, whose membership includes the leading members of the Import-Export Bank, the Federal Reserve, and the secretaries of state, commerce, and the treasury.[92]

Notwithstanding American concern to foster an open international economic system after 1945 and the interest of many Third World regimes in gaining Washington's favor, what compelling evidence is there that this was the sole, or even leading, goal of United States policy, or that it was backed either by the basic needs of American industry and finance or by a clear and consistent political vision? Although Gabriel and Joyce Kolko are surely correct to insist that there was a virtual consensus that the South would be part of a new international economic order, it is much less obvious either that Washington had at its disposal a fully articulated program for what this meant, or that economic considerations of this sort were the first priority of American policy. "Essentially the United States' aim was to restructure the world so that American business could trade, operate and profit without restrictions everywhere," write the Kolkos: "On this there was absolute unanimity among the American leaders, and it was around this core that they elaborated their policies and programs."[93]

Consider, however, the case of China, on which the Kolkos base an important part of their argument. These authors apparently assume that because the Chinese Communists would not accept the tenets of the Open Door and free trade, they were unacceptable to Washington. But as they acknowledge, Chiang

Kai-shek was an economic nationalist, and in two works he published in 1943, *China's Destiny* and *China's Economic Theory*, he made it clear that he planned to reorient China's foreign economic relations more to the country's own advantage. A more important consideration, however, is that Chiang had relatively little to deliver to the United States economically. The Kolkos write that "no other area exceeded Manchuria in attractiveness for American economic expansion in the Far East," and that "perhaps more than any other region, the United States was interested in the future of Manchuria and economic access to it."[94] But this overlooks that first at Teheran, then later and more explicitly at Yalta, Roosevelt had conceded to the Soviets important rights in Manchuria irrespective of China's postwar regime. Nor is it so obvious that if economic interests were dictating policy the best political move was steadfast opposition to the Communists. When the British in 1949 pressed upon Washington the urgency of recognizing the new Chinese government, two reasons were uppermost in their thinking: A strong regime in Peking, regardless of its ideological temperament, could be counted on to quarrel with Moscow over Manchuria; and the safeguarding of Western *economic* interests called for a speedy accommodation with the new regime.[95] In short, it is difficult to perceive what clear economic interests the United States had in China other than the right to trade and invest there in a nondiscriminatory fashion (privileged access to Manchuria was not an issue), and whether such interest might not best have been advanced through cooperation with a strong Communist government, given the weakness of the KMT.

As the case of China suggests, although American projects for the place of the South in the international economy after the war were in line with the rest of thinking in Washington, there is no reason to conclude that such planning was rigid or that it was a matter of the highest priority. The most urgent tasks facing the United States concerned Western Europe – the emphasis of the international economic agencies and agreements supported by this country gave a back seat to the South. Trade and investment figures subsequently confirmed this orientation: Such exchanges between northern industrial states have grown at a relatively far greater pace than those between the North and the South. Indeed, the most frequent complaints today are that the South is being hurt by *neglect* and *exclusion* from the commercial networks established among the northern market states rather than by their wholehearted inclusion in a liberalized world economic order such as Hull had originally conceived.

Perhaps the most telling arguments against the contention that American policy toward the South was premised on economic considerations and that these were in turn important stakes to be pursued by Washington come from the economic evidence itself. Whether it is access to raw materials, or the search for profits and markets, it is difficult to establish a commanding need on the part of the American economy for guaranteed entry into the Third World. The chief exception to this generalization is the petroleum industry, where profit rates were tremendous and American control of the market reinforced Washington's political preeminence within the Atlantic Alliance. But even here, we are left with the problem of American support for Israel and the relative ease with which the Organization of Petroleum-Exporting Countries was formed. Mira Wilkins reports a telling statistic with respect to this question when she contrasts Britain's reliance on the international economic system before World War I with that of the United States today. By her calculation, the United States has the equivalent of approximately 7 to 8 percent of its gross national product invested abroad at present, whereas Great Britain was *annually* investing this amount abroad in the years before World War I – so that by 1914, that country had the equivalent of 150 percent of its gross national product in foreign investments. (A ratio of these holdings to Britian's domestic GNP is nearly twenty-five times greater than in the case of the United States, where, moreover, the South represent a minority and declining share of its stock.)[96]

Furthermore, an explanation for American policy toward the Third World that is based on economic motivations must account for Washington's decision to intervene in Vietnam, where commercial interests were simply nonexistent, as well as for its decision *not* to intervene where acts of economic nationalism potentially inimical to American interests, like those of the Organization of Petroleum Exporting Countries, were occurring. Stephen Krasner comments, for example, on the "relatively passive response" by the United States to economic nationalism after 1965. According to his figures, three American-owned raw materials firms were taken over in the South between 1951 and 1965, but thirty-four were taken during the following decade.[97] However skittish the United States was about economic nationalism on the part of its allies or clients in the years after 1945, it appears difficult to believe these considerations provide a full or satisfactory account for the pattern of American policy toward the Third World following the war.

What is most evidently lacking in such an approach is any recognition of the political repercussions that the contest with the Soviet Union had on American policy toward the South. Just as Britain turned a keener eye to southern affairs at the moment it was calculating shifts in the European power balance, so too Washington was examining the case of southern nationalism more intently as relations with Moscow deteriorated. Indeed it is possible that American imperialism based on economic grounds might have been much more pronounced than it was had political considerations not relegated economics to a zone of secondary importance. As it was, Washington clearly indicated that it could distinguish between the dangers of foreign economic nationalism and communism, and that its stronger opposition was to the latter.

For toward its northern allies as toward its southern clients, United States opposition to economic nationalism was moderated in light of political considerations having primarily to do with Washington's relations with Moscow. By 1947, the evident weakness of Britain gave pause to those insisting on the free convertibility of the pound, and with the intensification of the Cold War the United States actually found itself promoting the economic nationalism of its allies. Under the auspices of the Marshall Plan, the United States encouraged the kind of economic organization in Western Europe that ultimately led to the creation of the European Economic Community. With respect to the Japanese the Americans were equally lenient, permitting Tokyo in effect to bar foreign direct investment from Japan and to engage in a variety of import-restricting measures. In each instance, politics commanded economics, although the hope remained in Washington that in time a nondiscriminatory, multilateral economic community would create the basis of prosperity and cooperation in the postwar world. And despite these concessions to political concerns, America was in many ways successful in securing its goals.[98]

Because the United States' involvement with the South was less crucial than that with its allies in Europe or Japan, American flexibility with respect to Third World economic nationalism came later. But with Castro's success in Cuba, Washington began to reassess its economic ties with Latin America, and in 1961 it sponsored the Alliance for Progress. Whatever the ultimate failure of this plan, its support for Latin American economic nationalism (albeit with a place reserved for North American investments) was evident. The alliance aimed to diversify Latin American exports, encourage regional industrialization schemes, and foster the overall economic integration of the area as well.[99]

Although by virtue of both its foreign economic policy and its rival international position in respect to the Soviet Union, the United States was doubtlessly biased against the Socialist organization of southern societies – particularly when it involved the militant mobilization of workers and peasants either against established American property rights or under the banner of the slogans of the October Revolution – the decisive shift in American policy came with the Korean War. Had the war, which broke out in June 1950, not set China and the United States at odds for over two decades, Washington might conceivably have been able to reach an understanding with Peking in the early 1950s and thereafter to avoid identifying every association of communism and nationalism in the South with the global expansion of Soviet power. Once the opposite argument embodied in such positions as National Security Council Policy Paper Number 68 appeared vindicated by the conflict in Korea, however, America was on a self-aggravating course that led with a firm step to deeper involvement in Indochina as well as to a more rigid stance toward southern nationalism in general. Hereafter what Richard Barnet calls the "national security managers" were at work issuing their rationales for American counterinsurgency programs, and American public opinion was increasingly persuaded to turn out of office – as Daniel Ellsberg and Leslie Gelb have described – those officials who appeared to be "soft on communism."[100] Now instability at the global level intersected with regional conflicts in the South in such a fashion that each magnified the other's intensity. Global rivalries were projected into regional conflicts, while the latter in turn fed the former, in a vicious circle whose principal victims were the peasants of the Third World.

In the process, the United States became the bastion of international "counterrevolution." Like the word imperialism, the term counterrevolution has a host of pejorative connotations attached to it; many might prefer to do without it did it not indicate an outstanding feature of contemporary history: American support for groups and governments in the South working to repress the demands and the organization of the working class and poorest peasants in society rather than attempting to incorporate them into the institutions of government. From American policy toward China in the forties to that toward Chile in the seventies the pattern is virtually without exception. One might prefer to use some other term to label it, but that is of less concern than agreement on the persistence of the policy.

No doubt the United States became counterrevolutionary in part by virtue of its economic role in the South. Having set themselves up in partnership with one regime, American economic interests could easily come to feel a solidarity with the established order against those seeking basic social change, and would thereupon call to Washington for its support. Given the fragility of political institutions in these countries and the depth of social cleavages, the American presence would have been felt as imperialist had no Communist movement been in existence: American policy toward Mexico after 1917 is clear evidence on this score. By the 1940s, however, indigenous Communist movements were present in virtually all Third World countries, and the obvious question arose of whether they would make common cause with the Soviet Union. As we have seen, the decisive turn in Washington's policy came with the fate of its relations with China. Thenceforth, the tendency to think of communism as a geopolitical whole grew, much as the United States had earlier come to think of fascism. In a sense, then, Washington was doubly determined to be counter-revolutionary, as its political prejudices came to second its economic interests.

As Washington perceived the contest with the Soviet Union to include the internal political order of states as well as the nature of their external allegiances, its comparison with Anglo–German rivalry earlier in the century is less apt than that between revolutionary France and monarchical Europe. As Edmund Burke put it in his great diatribe against the Jacobin Republic, France was everywhere provoking "civil war":

It is a war between the partisans of the ancient civil, moral, and political order of Europe against a sect of fanatical and ambitious atheists . . . It is not France extending a foreign empire over other nations: it is a sect aiming at universal empire, and beginning with the conquest of France. The leaders of that sect secured *the centre of Europe*; and that secured, they knew that, whatever might be the event of battles and sieges, their cause was victorious. . . . the faction is not local or territorial. It is a general evil. Where it least appears in action, it is full of life. In its sleep it recruits its strength and prepares its exertion. Its spirit lies deep in the corruptions of our common nature. The social order which restrains it feeds it. It exists in every country in Europe and among all orders of men in every country, who look up to France as to a common head . . . everywhere else the faction is militant; in France it is triumphant.[101]

Substitute the Soviet Union for France (and the center of Eurasia for the center of Europe) and you find a statement that any of a series of American leaders might have delivered in the years after 1945. Moreover, in each case there was a decided class basis to the struggle: Just as Britain would struggle against the political liberalism of the rising middle class, so the United States was opposed to the socialism espoused by peasants and workers.

Even before Washington's failure to come to terms with communism in China in the late 1940s, the Truman administration had conveyed something of the same feeling about the postwar struggle that was beginning to grip the world. Thus, Truman gave aid to Greece and Turkey in 1947 not simply for the sake of these countries or to check a single instance of Soviet expansion but in terms of a more generalized threat and an American willingness to see the challenge in its just global proportions.

It is necessary only to glance at a map to realize that the survival and integrity of the Greek nation are of grave importance in a much wider situation. If Greece should fall under the control of an armed minority, the effect upon its neighbor, Turkey, would be immediate and serious. Confusion and disorder might well spread throughout the entire Middle East. Moreover, the disappearance of Greece as an independent state would have a profound effect upon those countries in Europe whose peoples are struggling against great difficulties to maintain their freedom.[102]

Although Truman consciously limited containment to the Soviet Union, his successors after the Korean War calculated more broadly. In April 1954, Eisenhower likened the French stand at Dien-Bien-Phu to Thermopylae, Bataan, and the Alamo, and wrote to Churchill that if "Indochina passes into the hands of the Communists the ultimate effect on your and our global strategic position with the consequent shift of power ratios throughout Asia and the Pacific could be disastrous.[103] Two years later, Senator John Kennedy echoed Eisenhower: "Vietnam represents the cornerstone of the Free World in Southeast Asia, the keystone to the arch, the finger in the dike. Burma, Thailand, India, Japan, the Philippines, obviously Laos and Cambodia are among those whose security would be threatened if the red tide of communism overflowed into Vietnam."[104] A similar form of thinking informed Kissinger's assessment of Allende in Chile:

In any circumstances, Allende's election was a challenge to our national interest. We did not find it easy to reconcile ourselves to a second Communist state in the Western hemisphere. We were persuaded that it would soon be inciting anti-American policies, attacking hemisphere solidarity, making common cause with Cuba, and sooner or later establishing close relations with the Soviet Union . . . It was his explicit program and long-standing goal to establish an irreversible dictatorship and a permanent challenge to our position in the Western Hemisphere . . . it was not absurd to take seriously the military implications of another Soviet ally in Latin America. Our concern with Allende was based on national security, not on economics. Nationalization of American-owned property was not the issue . . . He was not just nationalizing property; he avowed his dedication to totalitarian Marxism-Leninism. He was an admirer of the Cuban dictatorship and a resolute opponent of "American imperialism." His stated goal for over a decade before he became President had been to undermine our position in the entire Western Hemisphere by violence if necessary. Because it was a continental country, Chile's capacity for doing so was greater by far than Cuba's . . . Chile bordered Argentina, Peru, and Bolivia, all plagued by radical movements. Allende's success would have had implications also for the future of Communist parties in Western Europe, whose policies would inevitably undermine the Western Alliance whatever their fluctuating claims of respectability.[105]

The central problem for American policymakers after 1950 thus seemed to be to find allies among the southern elites who were able to contain and direct the changes taking place in these lands and who were at the same time likely to be dependable participants in a world order where a range of American security interests (including those of its allies in Western Europe and Japan) would be respected. There is no reason to doubt that Washington's initial hope was to be true to its progressive traditions and to sponsor elites in the South who were genuinely nationalistic and concerned to satisfy the demands of change – so long as they were anti-Communist. Although the United States continued to regret economic nationalism, this took a decided back seat to the issue of communism. The Marshall Plan might serve as a model: Sufficient funds and the correct economic environment would contribute substantially to the desired political outcome. On paper it sounded as though the same formula might work in the South: Change would be embraced, the poor fed, and local support for communism disappear.[106] But the obvious objection was that the social situation in southern countries was in no way analogous to that of Western Europe when Marshall Plan funds began to arrive, where modern forms of economic and political organization were already well rooted (and the challenge of domestic socialism dealt with long ago). Instead, the dilemma was that any broadly based, systemic change might be as likely to stimulate as to subvert the Communist presence. For in situations of rapid and unprecedented socioeconomic change such as most southern countries were experiencing, the task of strengthening political institutions and the risk of endangering them can turn on the marginally different outcomes of a series of delicate issues: the organization of the working class; the control of urbanization; the debate over recruitment and promotion within the military and the success of civilian control; the constitutional organization of government; the question of systems of land reform. That is, in certain phases of change, the road to reform and the road to revolution are one and the same.

The overriding question became, therefore, the degree of risk the United States was willing to run with respect to its nationalist allies in the South if support for reform courted revolution at the same time. In some places, the issue did not present itself too acutely. The problem, however, was that few countries could produce a man like Rómulo Betancourt, as Venezuela had, or a party like his Acción Democrática, a movement hostile to communism yet anticlerical, in favor of land reform and labor organizaton, and able to win elections.[107]

Where such movements were not in evidence (and this was typically the case), what policies should be pursued? It was President Kennedy who, by Arthur Schlesinger's report, uttered the reply in its classic form as he deliberated on alternative developments in the Dominican Republic after the assassination of Trujillo on May 30, 1961: "There are three possibilities in descending order of preference: a decent democratic regime, a continuation of the Trujillo regime or a Castro regime. We ought to aim at the first, but we really can't renounce the second until we are sure we can avoid the third."[108] Here was the spirit (not Kennedy's death) that doomed the Alliance for Progress: The fight against revolution would take precedence over the struggle for reform in those situations where the contradiction presented itself. The path to be followed in abandoning efforts at reform is clearly marked in Schlesinger's own thinking, although he always characterized himself as associated with the promise of the alliance and was one of its chief instigators. In the case of Cuba, for example, Schlesinger admitted that he could see some popular backing for Castro, but declared that he also grasped "the harsher truths and subtler corruptions." Accordingly, he worried about the "power and influence" of the United States as Castro came to be "the symbol not of social revolution but of Soviet penetration," which might "convert the Latin American social revolution into an attack on the United States itself."[109] One might well debate the logic of Schlesinger's fears, but a more crucial shortcoming is evident in his thinking: He is always confident that reform will inhibit rather than promote revolution. In this naiveté of the liberal mind lies a key to the toughness of American policy: It would support counterrevolution today, assuming that tomorrow's reform would undo the damage, all the while oblivious (unlike the radical or the conservative) to the role of reform in stimulating revolution. In short, liberalism had found a way to make its peace with counterrevolution.

A critical evaluation of the kind of thinking that saw in southern communism a threat with global ramifications for the United States must respect the limits within which such a perspective is both correct and natural. It is correct in the sense that this reasoning sees local developments as part of a larger historical movement and appreciates the cumulative significance of what on first inspection may seem to be chance or isolated occurrences. And it is natural that those charged by their position to think in global terms should adopt such a perspective: Their interests and their responsibilties permit no less. Certainly this was the lesson of World War II, when the United States had legitimately seen the growth of the Fascist threat in the Far East and Latin America as a political matter directly related to American security.[110]

World War II radically upset not only the international configuration of states, but in many instances the bases of domestic and regional stability as well. Alien to each other in their outlooks and practices, unaccustomed to their new roles as the internationally preeminent powers, the United States and the Soviet Union found themselves confronted by a rapid series of what might well be termed "wars of succession," into the midst of which they were projected both at the insistence of domestic interests and at the invitation of rival sides to the conflicts. To an extent any bipolar contest promotes imperialism against the weak, just as it encourages alliances with the relatively strong. How much more this is the case when the weak themselves in effect incite such intervention, either by their own internal collapse, as happened to the Ottoman Empire and to China prior to World War I, or by the outbreak of civil war, an event more familiar to our century.

Yet however natural and correct this 'perspective may be within certain bounds, it can overstep these limits and in the process both misinterpret reality and set self-defeating goals for national policy. The most significant blunder to beset this form of global reasoning is that it may fail to respect the weight of local circumstances and so extrapolate too quickly from events what it mistakenly assumes to be their wider meaning. Thus Dean Rusk, who as secretary of state under both Kennedy and Johnson repeatedly demonstrated his predilection for viewing history on the grand scale, is deservedly remembered for his 1951 comment (when he was assistant secretary of state for Far Eastern affairs) that "the Peiping Regime may be a co-lonial Russian government – a Slavic Manchukuo on a larger scale. It is not the government of China. It does not pass the first test. It is not Chinese." So to, Roger Hilsman, who under Kennedy was director of the Bureau of Intelligence and Re-search at the State Department and later assistant secretary of state for Far Eastern affiars, explicitly denied any *"pervasive national spirit as we know it"* in Vietnam, likened the Viet Cong to the Chicago Mafia in terms of its popular support, and pronounced General Giap with his "paid agents" to be an " 'ad-vance man' for Chinese Communist power."[111] Such citations could be multiplied many times over to the same end: Ameri-can leaders forced developments in the South into the terms of the rivalry with the Soviet Union in a way that made countries and peoples there little more than hollow pawns in the contest between the superpowers. The irony is that they were not alone in seeing events in this light. Lenin had spoken grandly of "world revolution"; Stalin had declared that "the road to victory of the revolution in the West lies through the revolutionary alliance with the liberation movement of the colonies and dependent countries against imperialism"; and then Chinese Vice-Premier Lin Piao had issued his famous likening of world revolution and the Chinese Revolution, describing North America and Western Europe as "'the cities of the world,'" and Asia, Africa, and Latin America as "'the rural areas of the world.'"[112] The fact that the Soviet and the Chinese could equal the Americans in their inflations of the global significance of local events did not necessarily bring such thinking any closer to reality.

This misperception contributed in turn to an aggressive and ultimately self-defeating policy. In the words of a Senate subcommittee report released in 1971:

With an eagerness and a "can-do" philosophy, the United States expanded its military presence abroad, to the point where it assumed, almost inadvertently and without notice, a role that has been described as policeman of the free world. As a result of these policies, by the mid-60's the United States was firmly committed to more than 43 nations by treaty and agreement and had some 375 major foreign military bases and 3000 minor military facilities all over the world, virtually surrounding the Soviet Union and Communist China in support of the policy of containment.[113]

By declaring that communism everywhere was in league with the Soviet Union, Washington tended to consolidate such alliances by forcing local movements to seek such support in order to counter America's foreordained hostility. It was a form of self-fulfilling prophecy wherein the United States assured the worst because it assumed the worst. Moreover, by viewing reality in this fashion, the United States lost the ability to discriminate among local communisms: Each of its varieties appeared linked to all the others; and every one of them, no matter how powerful it demonstrated itself to be locally, had to be resisted lest it lead to a crisis in confidence in the entire structure of containment that the United States had so painstakingly elaborated. "To understand Vietnam, it is necessary to understand that the issue is not Vietnam," wrote Senator Gale McGee in 1968 in a remark characteristic of this thinking.[114] Or as Senator Frank Church, chairman of the Senate Foreign Relations Committee put it in the fall of 1979 with respect to the several thousand Soviet troops in Cuba: "It's a test. The Russians deployed a combat brigade secretly in Cuba, attempted to conceal its presence, but they knew the brigade would be discovered by us. They're testing our resolve. We must decide where to draw the line against the deployment of Soviet combat troops. If not in Cuba, where would it be?"[115] Yet even if we accept the inevitability of some incompatability of interest between the United States and the Third World and acknowledge that on occasion Washington may have to defend its interests by force, this by no means constitutes a blanket endorsement of strong-arm American behavior in the South. It is difficult indeed to escape the conclusion that a combination of American ignorance and arrogance has contributed to the deaths of hundreds of thousands of Third World peasants and to the creation of military regimes in a series of countries there that otherwise might have been fortunate enough to avoid them.

It should be reiterated that within certain limits, globalist thinking that stresses the interrelated and cumulative nature of historical events must be respected. Isolationism before World War II has a host of lessons to teach in this respect. In recent years, however, we have been witness to a globalism run amok, wherein national security has been invoked to sanction brutal and needless interventions overseas. At the same time, however, this recognition should surely constitute no license to go to the other extreme – to believe that the United States should make no effort to anticipate or to influence the impact of events in accord with a general concept of its interests and responsibilities in the development of world order.[116] If the kind of globalism we have seen in past years shows serious shortcomings, neoisolationism provides no better answer to our dilemmas.

In sum, there is no mechanistic formula that can dictate what American policy toward the Third World should be. Liberals should be skeptical of the universal validity of their notions that southern nationalism can be counted on to work with American interests or that the exercise of force is always a self-defeating policy, just as conservatives should appreciate the danger that lies behind too ready a resort to arms or too quick a dismissal of the reality of Third World independence movements. Each group is quick to pick out the problems in perspective of its opponents, yet blind to its own dubious assumptions. If liberals are naive to believe that Soviet gains in the South will end only if America remains uninvolved, so conservatives are naive in the measure that they fail to see that the form of American political and economic involvement in the Third World breeds its own determined nationalist opposition there.

There is no need to conclude with the by-now standard complaint that the United States can act abroad only in terms of what Kissinger has called "our historical cycle of exuberant overextension and sulking isolationism."[117] Past experience is the catalog not only of serious mistakes but also of policies sensibly conceived and effectively executed. The principal legacy from the past is a liberal tradition of seeking to work with the force of southern nationalism in a way that advances United States interests. The chief limitation on this policy has come from the decision to defend private American property rights even when doing so threatened local political stability. Over the past two decades, however, such defense has appeared to be less and less important to Washington, so removing an important constraint on cooperation with Third World governments. One may nevertheless wonder whether the recurrent petroleum price hikes instituted by OPEC may not reverse this development and set Washington at loggerheads with Third World governments over economic issues once again.[118]

But there have been situations in which traditional policy simply has not been operative and something of a rival tradition has been born. In circumstances in which local instability in a region deemed of importance to the United States has raised the possibility of the expansion of another great power's sphere of influence, Washington has seen fit to intervene directly, to be a preemptive imperialist. Of course the center of the debate in the United States is over precisely how to define the degree of importance a region has to this country, and the likelihood that instability there will turn to the advantage of a rival great power. For all the "moralism" ascribed to American foreign policy deliberations, these eminently more realistic concerns have always been the heart of the matter. By this point, the United States has acquired enough experience from history to know that history provides no sure answer to the questions of the future. If, on balance, the dominant American tradition toward the South has been one of restraint, and the lessons those of the follies committed by intervention, it is by no means obvious that these conclusions constitute an iron-clad rule for either recommending or predicting policy in the years ahead. American experience can offer some general guidelines for the future, but tomorrow will have to be understood and acted upon in its own terms.

5

American imperialism in the early 1980s

The terrible quandary facing the United States with respect to its policy toward the Third World early in the 1980s is that neither of its two traditional patterns of conduct holds out clear hope for securing its interests. The success of the dominant liberal tradition in American policy, which expects a mutual accommodation of interests with southern governments, is most in doubt in the Middle East, by all odds the most important area of the Third World to this country. The fall of the Shah, the hostility of many Islamic nationalist movements to Washington, the unbridled rise in world petroleum prices engineered by the Organization of Petroleum Exporting Countries (OPEC), the instability of many governments in the region, and the expanding influence of the Soviet Union there are all testimony to the futility of the view that some kind of natural affinity will be found that serves the interests of the North and the South alike. But as America's resounding defeat in Vietnam demonstrated, the path of preemptive imperialism, whereby Washington imposes its will on southern countries by force, seems equally unpromising. This is all the more the case today, when the Soviet Union has reached military parity with the United States in conventional as well as nuclear terms. Thus liberals and conservatives ("doves" and "hawks") appear better able to point out the shortcomings in the line of action proposed by their opponents than to demonstrate convincingly the wisdom of their own proposals.

The first years of the 1970s were witness to two develop-

ments that strikingly underlined the growing power of southern actors in regional and international affairs and the relative
decline of United States imperialism: the American military
failure in Vietnam, as well as the unprecedented success of
Third World economic nationalism in the form of radical oil
and gas price hikes dictated by OPEC. The intersection of these
events with the dramatically expanded military power of the
Soviet Union and the sustained economic dynamism of the
European Community and Japan suggested the beginnings of a
new world order after 1975 wherein American power would
be far more constrained than had been the case since 1945.

Much more than the defeat of the Italians at Adua in 1896,
and more than the Japanese victory over Russia in 1904, the
ultimate triumph of nationalist communism in Vietnam appears to stand as a historical benchmark of the first order in the
process of halting European-North American overseas expansion (unless the Soviets provide the relay). Direct leverage over
the political and bureaucratic institutions in the South may
have ended with colonialism, but the North could retain the
belief that were a southern state to fail to respect basic northern
interests, defined not only economically and strategically but
in some cases ideologically (or symbolically) as well, it ran the
risk of military intervention. So it had been in Asia, for example, at least since the time of the Opium War (1839–42) – a
conflict of which the United States approved, as Commodore
Perry remarked to the Japanese when he arrived there in 1854.
(At the same time he pointedly provided them with magazines
illustrating the American occupation of Mexico City under
Winfield Scott in 1847.) Washington failed to continue this
tradition. As George Liska expressed it in a widely read book
that appeared in 1967:

The Vietnamese War . . . may well come to rank on a par with the two world
wars as a conflict that marked an epoch in America's progress toward definition of her role as a world power . . . This role implies the necessity to
define – by force if necessary – the terms on which regional balances of power
are evolved and American access to individual regions is secured . . . Had it
been less dramatized, the Vietnamese War would have been an ideal ground
for evolving, training, and breaking in . . . a combined political-military es-

tablishment as well as for educating the American people to changing facts of life. It may still prove retrospectively to have been such.[1]

Nor has the United States been easily able to promote local military forces acting as American proxies in the provision of domestic or regional security. For what the turmoil of the Iranian Revolution has demonstrated above all else in this respect is the failure of any such policy in situations where the government lacks organized domestic support. Once again, the character of southern nationalism and political organization had not been sufficiently appreciated.[2] In short, just as Vietnam put into doubt the effectiveness of massive commitments of men to struggles in the Third World, so the experience of Iran questioned the wisdom that held that northern interests might well be served by building up client militaries within these regions.

Yet these apparent "lessons" are not without their ambiguities. For if the experience of Vietnam does counsel against large-scale, long-term involvement in struggles to "win the hearts and minds" of a foreign people for a particular regime, it would not appear to rule out smaller-scale interventions designed to achieve more limited goals. Soviet-Cuban initiatives in Angola and the Horn of Africa as well as French moves in Zaire and the Central African Republic (Empire) offer examples of successful action undertaken in this respect. Nor has the Vietnam experience shown the inutility of conventional aims of warfare – to physically punish an enemy, or the enemy of an important ally or client. In the single month of October 1979, for example, the American government announced military assistance to Thailand against Vietnam, the Caribbean states against Cuba, South Korea against the North, and Morocco in its efforts to secure part of the former Spanish Sahara against Algerian wishes. Moreover, in all these cases, including Morocco, there was the implied understanding that the United States would be willing to intervene more directly and forcibly should its client be directly threatened.[3] America (as well as other industrial countries) thus retains the ability to use military sanctions in the appropriate setting, and it would be unrealistic to suppose that this kind of strength is not a substantial power resource in a host of respects in North–South relations.[4] Indeed, it may be that the Soviet occupation of Afghanistan prefigures a new scramble of military action in the South reminiscent of the scrambles of the late nineteenth century. The obvious area of concern is the Middle East, from Libya to the Persian Gulf.

Nor does the Iranian experience unambiguously refute the argument that a foreign military might be a source of support for American interests in certain circumstances. When a military has the general support of what might broadly be called the middle class, as is the case in some Latin American countries, its role may be both more secure and more predictable. This was clearly the understanding, for example, behind the United States' effort between 1950 and 1969, to train over 50,000 Latin American officers not only on how to handle American weapons but also on how to combat local Communist organizations.[5] And in its own terms, the gambit succeeded: Brazil in 1964 and Chile in 1973 are its testament. Furthermore, in arms shipments alone, the United States transferred some $30 billion worth of equipment directly to the Third World between 1967 and 1976.[6] Although a great deal of this failed to achieve its purpose (nearly a quarter went to Vietnam, and over a tenth to Iran), in other instances the support was successful for its own ends – keeping in power, or promoting to office, regimes that otherwise might have been unable to counter domestic or regional opponents. For their part, the Soviet have similarly worked to gain regional influence by supporting with military aid Third World regimes they favor. If Egypt proved a major disappointment, Soviet military aid in Africa (especially to Libya, Angola, and Ethiopia), South Asia (India), and the Middle East (Iraq, Syria, and South Yemen) has tended on balance to expand Moscow's voice in the South.[7]

It was under the shadow of America's military reversal in Vietnam (although clearly for other reasons as well) that the spectacular rise in petroleum prices occurred. In 1972, OPEC members received $29.2 billion for their exports, which constituted 7 percent of world exports by value; but by 1979, with a current value of $207 billion, this trade constituted some 14 percent of world commerce (after exceeding 16 percent in

1974). A new round of price rises in 1979 and 1980 raised oil costs some 150 percent, amounting to a tax of about 2 percent on the GNP of the OECD countries.[8] Other figures suggest the unprecedented magnitude of the transfer of wealth to those countries. In 1973, the twenty-four members of the Organization for Economic Cooperation and Development (OECD) showed a current account surplus of $2.8 billion. But from 1974 through 1977, they registered a combined deficit of $95.6 billion. OPEC's current account balance indicates part of the cause: From a $9 billion surplus in 1973, OPEC's claims in the next four years grew by another $172 billion in a display of southern economic power quite without precedent.[9]

The manner by which OPEC scored such a success may not be duplicated by other southern countries; there is good reason to believe that few other commodities can be subjected to cartel control in the way of petroleum.[10] Nevertheless, a strong case can be made that for some years most of the developing world has demonstrated a vigorous economic life. Of course not all societies in Asia, Africa, and Latin America have participated equally in growth – most indexes prepared by international agencies are careful to discriminate the very poorest areas from middle- and higher-income southern lands. And it is also true that not all groups within the various countries have benefited equally from the growth that has occurred. Nonetheless, development has been wide and sustained enough to throw serious doubt on the belief that southern countries are forever destined to be the "hewers of wood and drawers of water" (as the favored cliché has it) of the international economic order. Compared with the earlier diffusion of know-how at the time of the so-called agrarian revolution (after 8,000 B.C.), the spread of the technics of the industrial revolution which began a scant 200 years ago in the British Isles has been extremely rapid.[11] As we saw in Chapter 2, there are those for whom all the problems of underdevelopment today are to be laid at the doorstep of capitalist imperialism, which has moreover compounded its enormities by maintaining these weaker lands in a position of self-perpetuating subordination to the rhythms of the world economic system. But the empirical evidence raises strong

Table 3. *Industrial output as a percentage of 1970 production*

Area	Year	Heavy industry	Light industry	Total
Developed Market				
Countries	1960	53	65	57
	1974	124	115	121
	1975	111	113	111
	1976	122	118	121
	1978	134	126	132
Developing Market				
Countries	1960	45	64	56
	1974	151	127	138
	1975	151	133	142
	1976	166	140	152
	1978	192	154	172

questions about such a perspective except in its most qualified form.

Given the available figures, probably the best way to measure the economic strength of the Third World is to look at industrial output, particularly the place of heavy industry, and to compare this with developments in the North, especially at a time of international economic downturn, when we might expect to see a reversal in the developed world translate into problems for the South. In all these respects, United Nations statistics (which are subject to a margin of error) offer striking evidence of southern economic growth. Thus, even during the recession of 1974, the so-called middle-income countries – those with a per capita income of $200–$700 a year – managed to expand their manufacturing output by 8 percent, whereas OECD countries registered a zero growth rate in this domain. The comparative index numbers of industrial production over nearly two decades, presented in Table 3,[12] are especially revealing. Certainly, when the small base from which these advances are made and the rapid growth of population in the developing world are factored into these figures, their significance diminishes. But it is difficult to avoid the conclusion, these reservations notwithstanding, that the technics of the industrial revolution have taken root in many parts of the Third World and are drawing more and more strength from local circumstances. Of course, serious obstacles remain, except that they are not the product of northern actions. Thus, OPEC price hikes in 1973–4 and in 1979–80 resulted each time in a transfer of some 2.5 percent of the GNP of the non-oil-producing Third World into the coffers of OPEC, according to figures published by the OECD in *Economic Outlook* (no. 27, July 1980).

This point is important because there is some truth to the charge that the earlier impact of the industrial core countries on the rest of the world either deliberately or unwittingly worked to inhibit their industrialization. Albert Hirschman cites the case of Nazi policy toward Southeastern Europe, where Germany paid artificially high prices for raw materials in order to keep these markets open for German manufacturers:

To maintain this position [of dominance] it was one of the great principles of German foreign economic policy to prevent the industrialization of her agricultural trading partners. Particular insistence on this point has been noted in all the commercial negotiations of Germany with her Southeastern neighbors and even, to some degree and with some success, with Italy.[13]

In the case of the impact of imperialism on the preindustrial economies of the last century, the design may not have been so premeditated, but the result was in some instances analogous. Thus Richard Graham reports the problems Brazil encountered late in the nineteenth century after its initial success in developing an important export sector:

When the economy began to pulse with its own life and some energies began to turn to industrialization, they found the forces that had given birth to growth now seeking to smother it . . . The grip which the British held upon the railroad, the exporting firm, the import business, the shipping company, the insurance agency, the financial bank and even the government treasury now tended to choke off any efforts to reduce the reliance on British exports.[14]

In their undertaking, the British discovered they could count on the local export forces created by their presence: "Coffee interests were usually against tariffs, government loans to industries, crop diversification, land reform and education." As

Chapter 2 recounted, British policy in India and Egypt at the turn of the century similarly tended to stifle what might otherwise have been a more vigorous industrial development.

But is this the consequence, premeditated or not, of multinational investment today in the Third World? Surely it is not the deliberate ambition of the states that are home to these corporations. Where is the evidence that the countries of the Organization for Economic Cooperation and Development, acting in unison, or Washington, working alone, have either the cunning or the organizational ability to draw up such a scheme? If it did exist, where is the wholehearted effort to prevent southern industrializatin, monopolize their raw materials, break up their domestically integrated markets, oppose their regional integration programs, or develop a degree of international specialization so as to heighten their reliance on northern goods and markets? Neither the OECD nor the United States would get high marks for sound imperialist maneuvering were these the criteria to be used. To the contrary, unlike the conduct of Britain in Egypt or India in the late nineteenth century (and one should not overstate its impact) and unlike German policy toward its southeastern neighbors in the twentieth, the impact of the North today would seem quite clearly to accelerate rather than to retard southern industrialization.

Certainly Lenin (and after him Stalin, and later still Brezhnev) did not doubt that such foreign investments could improve Soviet economic performance. As E. H. Carr describes the 1920 decree on concessions:

The decree noted that the rate of recovery of the Russian economy could be "increased many times over" by bringing in foreign firms or institutions "for the exploitation and development of the natural riches of Russia," . . . Concession of sufficient duration would be granted to ensure an adequate return with a guarantee against nationalization or confiscation. Soviet workers could be employed under the conditions prescribed in the Soviet labor code.[15]

In the last few years, China too has been actively soliciting foreign investments. In a similar vein, Algeria had entered into a $13.8 billion debt by the end of 1977 (roughly $1,000 per inhabitant of the country), with the United States as its chief trading partner and creditor.[16] Yet one would mistake this involvement with the outside world if one saw it as anything other than an Algerian effort to practice that skill of the martial arts whereby the strength of the opponent is used against him. Indeed, the gains to the Third World from the loans and investments made by the North are so substantial that the labor movement in the United States has begun seriously to question whether home investment and industries are not suffering as a consequence. According to a study made at the Brookings Institution, there may be substantial merit to at least some of these charges.[17] Much as industry in the northern part of the United States moved to the "Sun Belt" in order to take advantage of cheaper labor and energy as well as more lenient public policies such as those in regard to taxation, so American industry is threatening to move abroad in response to a variety of incentives that may well not be in the national interest. It is legitimate to speculate whether the United States is hereby repeating the British experience of the turn of the century, when apparent success in foreign commercial operations helped to mask problems in that country's domestic system. This matter aside, the multinational corporations emerge as the primary vehicle for the international dessemination of the know-how of the industrial revolution.

It may be objected that however impressive these developments at first appear, they are nevertheless deceptive, and that "market" economy developing countries suffer from problems their "Socialist" brethren can avoid. Thus it is often alleged that by the vehicle of multinational investment, southern industry is being "decapitalized" and "denationalized." The favored way to document the alleged decapitalization is to present figures of capital inflow and outflow over time showing that foreign investment is taking more out of the Third World than it is bringing in. In the case of Latin America, for instance, Dale Johnson repeats the standard charge: "Between 1950 and 1961, 2,962 million dollars of U.S. private capital flowed into the seven principal countries of Latin America, while the return flow was 6,875 million dollars."[18] Although it is evident that such capital flows do not help southern balance of pay-

ments, it is glaringly obvious that these figures, cited by themselves, cannot establish the case for the exploitation or retar-
dation of southern industrial development as the term
"decapitalization" implies. For unless we know what this surplus in favor of the United States (amounting to $4 billion
during the period) means either in relation to American investment already in Latin America or to the output of American firms there, the sum says virtually nothing. And in these
respects, the available statistics indicate that the charge is a
mythical one, at least in the terms it is usually advanced. For
example, in 1975, Latin America received $178 million from
the United States to be invested in private manufacturing
there. At the same time, American corporations remitted from
this sector to the United States $359 million in profits and $211
million in fees and royalties. (In other years the return was
much lower or even negative.) Apparently, in 1975, United
States private investments "decapitalized" Latin America of
$392 million in terms of manufacturing alone. Yet if we com-
pare this amount to United States total manufacturing investment in Latin America, $8.6 billion, the sum repatriated to the
North amounted to a mere 4.6 percent, hardly an extortionist
outflow. The sum of $392 million is all the more insignificant
when we compare it to the total sales of United States manufacturing affiliates in Latin America in 1974 (figures are available for only the preceding year at present): $20.9 billion (less
than 2 percent). In short, if we consider the $392 million as
return either on investment or on volume of business generated, it can scarcely be maintained that Latin America is being
"decapitalized." (And should the suggestion come from these
theorists, who seem never to consult statistical tables closely,
that the business generated serves the international economic
system and not the local economy, the figures again offer an
impressive refutation: Of the $20.9 billion in manufacturing
sales generated in 1974 by American corporations in Latin
America, $19.4 billion were local.)[19]

"Denationalization" – a term that refers to the tendency of
northerners to buy out successful local businesses in the South
and to control local capital through encouraging its minority

participation in northern ventures there – is a bit more difficult to refute unambiguously because less information is available. For example, the Department of Commerce provides figures showing that from 1968 to 1972, Latin Americans provided from 33 to 54 percent of the capital called for by United States companies in the region.[20] Should this be interpreted as southerners financing the takeover of their own countries? Similarly, Richard Barnet and Ronald Müller cite a Harvard Business School study for the years 1958–67 to underscore the familiar allegation of the *dependencistas* that Americans are buying up able southern firms and so stifling southern entrepreneurs: "About 46 per cent of all manufacturing operations established in the period were takeovers of existing domestic industry."[21] Nevertheless, a closer inspection of the evidence suggests that once again the dependency school is selectively presenting its statistics. For if we look through the material the Harvard Business School assembled, it appears that through liquidations or expropriations or sales of an entire affiliate or a substantial part thereof, American interests had divested themselves of nearly as many manufacturing concerns as they had acquired: 332 lost as compared with 337 gained.[22] Nor are sheer numbers the most interesting statistics; it is the value of affiliates bought or sold that may be more important. And insofar as 1975 and 1976 are concerned, official statistics show that United States firms sold off about as much in value of their manufacturing affiliates in the South as they acquired through takeovers.[23] The emerging pattern of relations between the multinationals and southern governments would seem to indicate a growing tendency for the state to restrict foreign investment to those areas of the economy where local abilities cannot yet provide the necessary kind of capital or skills – and to push these foreigners out once conditions warrant it. To be sure, in many instances foreigners continue to operate behind the scenes: The *prestanombres*, or "borrowed names," arrangements whereby locals act as figurehead directors and owners of establishments actually controlled from abroad are by no means restricted to Latin America, as the Spanish word might suggest. However, as state and domestic interests gain in strength, there is little reason to think the letter of the law will not be increasingly applied.[24] And in this process of "nationalization," might not the investors with minority holdings documented in the Commerce Department survey be likely to become the next majority owners? "Denationalization" would seem to be a charge as difficult to substantiate as "decapitalization."

As was the case with military questions, there should be no illusion that trends suggesting an increasingly autonomous Third World are unambiguous. Trade patterns suggest that the South is far more dependent on the North for markets and commercial credits than is the North on the South.[25] Moreover, foreign-owned multinational corporations control the "commanding heights" of many of the leading sectors of these southern economies, and in most cases it is difficult to believe that rapid industrial development could continue in their absence.[26] On occasion, this foreign economic power has shown itself to be fungible with local political leverage. "Make the economy scream," Richard Helms is reported to have noted after a September 1970 meeting with President Nixon.[27] And if the Senate staff report detailing how American pressure was brought to bear in Chile is accurate, United States power in this stuation was considerable: It subsidized strikes against the regime; encouraged the military to intervene in part with commercial credits; supported American corporate action to resist expropriation; and denied Chile credit on the international financial market. Partly as a consequence, imports had to be curtailed by some 58 percent in nonagricultural consumer goods, creating a real impact on a nation of only 10 million people, all highly dependent on the international system.[28] Certainly this is not to suppose that the United States single-handedly overthrew Allende. Local forces clearly possessed a strength and determination all their own. Indeed, Allende would probably have fallen – although perhaps not until the next election – had the United States conducted business as usual with Chile. But Washington did have the ability to aggravate – or to quiet, if it had so chosen – the conflict there and so to shift the delicate balance.

The advantage of using economic linkages as the basis for international political order is that, properly organized, they provide benefits for all, and hence a stake in a stable world for Third World governments. At the same time, control over the avenues of trade and investment is an aspect of power, and with the important exception of petroleum products a clear advantage lies with the North. Just as domestic economic actors with goods to trade or capital to invest or to loan may have local political power, so may an international actor or group. In situations of incipient civil or regional conflict, typical of much of the Third World, the power to trade (or not), to extend loans (or not), to invest (or not) represents a mode of conduct fungible on occasion with respect to the social tranquillity or political stability of foreign lands.[29] This is all the more the case given the relative inability of the Soviet Union and its allies to compete with the members of the OECD. To be sure, there are Soviet speeches aplenty affirming that country's coming expansion in the international economy, and articles appear in the Western press that seem to give them substance.[30] But the available evidence casts doubt on the validity of such contentions. For if Soviet and Eastern European trade with the developing world has substantially increased in absolute terms in recent years, it amounted to only some 3.2 percent of the exports and 5.3 percent of the imports of the Third World in 1979. By contrast, developed market economies took 71.6 percent of the exports and provided 65.2 percent of the imports of the Third World in 1979.[31] Nor do Soviet bloc loan, aid, or credit arrangements compensate for the relative weakness of trade ties. The amount of aid is small – for example, in 1978, the Soviet Union is estimated to have disbursed some $300 million to Third World countries (not including Vietnam), whereas the United States disbursed $5.7 billion – and the terms of this aid are less favorable than those provided by the members of the OECD.[32] As a consequence, whatever the long-standing talk about a "world socialist system" complete with an "international socialist diversion of labor" to be found in Soviet sources (with no sense of the irony with which this reproduces, even to its flaws, capitalist arguments for comparative advantage, it might be added), steps toward creating any such thing outside the Soviet bloc remain quite modest.[33]

Nevertheless, the utility of economic advantage for the purpose of political leverage should not be overstated. In the capitalist world, where the power of the state over the corporations is limited, and where both are split along national lines, such force is difficult to organize. The wielders of power work indirectly and at a distance, with a mode of influence that is blunt, not delicate, and that has a tendency to fracture. Thus, if economic coercion played a part in toppling Allende, it was less potent against Castro, Idi Amin, and Ian Smith; if economic assistance has proved critical in keeping Mobutu afloat and preventing chaos in Turkey, it was useless with respect to forestalling the falls of the Shah and Somoza. If in certain circumstances economic resources provide some political leverage, this in itself is seldom decisive and sometimes impotent.

The experience of the 1970s indicates a marked decline in the instruments of American power with respect to the Third World. Vietnam and Iran showed the weakness of certain American military doctrines, and the actions of OPEC signaled the strength of southern economic nationalism. If United States influence with respect to the South remains substantial in each of these two respects, the constraints on this power and the need to find new avenues by which to exercise it are nonetheless apparent. Such a conclusion is all the more evident when we consider that the erosion of American power is due not only to the growing relative military and economic capacities of the South, but also – indeed, perhaps primarily – to the growing constraints the Soviet Union puts on the United States militarily, and to the dynamism the European Community and Japan have demonstrated economically. In short, Washington's ability to define unilaterally the basic rules of international order has declined not only as a consequence of new-found strength on the part of the weak, but as a function of changes among the powerful themselves as well.

"Look what has happened since 1975, in the space of little more than four years," declared former Secretary of State Henry Kissinger to *The Economist* on February 3, 1979: "We have had Cuban troops in Africa, Cuban troops in Ethiopia, two invasions of Zaire, a Communist coup in South Yemen, and the occupation of Cambodia by Vietnam, all achieved by Soviet

arms, with Soviet encouragement, and in several cases protected by the Soviet veto in the United Nations." His message
was clear. The quick collapse of the American position in
South Vietnam in the spring of 1975 was followed by an
equally dramatic erosion of the American presence world-
wide. Indeed, in the time since Kissinger made his pronounce-
ment, the relative position of the Soviet Union with respect to
the Third World would appear to have improved still more.
The fall of Somoza in Nicaragua to the Sandinistas, a group
with undisguised sympathies for Cuba, has occurred in what
is historically America's most inviolable sphere of influence.
At the same time, the fall of the Shah has destroyed the principal pillar of support for a regional order favorable to the
United States in the Middle East, and the Soviet takeover of
Afghanistan and the outbreak of hostilities between Iraq and
Iran point up Moscow's strategic superiority in military terms
in the area of the Third World that is today most important to
Washington and its allies in the Organization for Economic
Cooperation and Development. In short, events of the past five
years (building, of course, on earlier developments) have
shown the limits of American power and caused a reduction in
its world role, whereas by contrast, the Soviet Union has enjoyed an unprecedented surge of activity and success in regions where hitherto its interests have been minimal, or where,
as in the days of Khrushchev, the overall correlation of forces
(to use the Soviet phrase) did not favor pursuits such as Moscow is now engaged in.

Soviet interest in the Third World is nothing new, of course.
Ever since the founding of the Third International in 1919,
Moscow has maintained that its own fortunes were linked to
the struggle against "imperialism" in Asia and Africa.[34] In this
regard, Lenin's Imperialism: The Highest Stage of Capitalism
(1917) remains a central canon in Soviet theoretical thinking.
It has a double message: that imperialist squabbles can be
counted upon to divide the capitalist states from one another;
and that because imperialism has artificially prolonged the life
of capitalism, its retreat will hasten the day of its internal collapse.[35] To be sure, Communist reverses in China after 1926,

the doctrine of "socialism in one country," the vicissitudes of the struggle against fascism, and the need for internal regeneration after 1945 spelled a long period of quiet in Soviet conduct toward Africa, Asia, and Latin America. But shortly after Stalin's death, his successors began to move away from his "two-camp" view of international affairs and to look for ways to harness the strength of anticolonial nationalism in the Third World to serve Moscow's interests. Two obstacles nonetheless stood in the Soviet path: One was the inherent instability of politics in the Third World, so that early friends of Moscow such as Nkrumah, Ben Bella, Keita, and Sukarno fell from power in short order; the other was the overall correlation of forces that favored Washington and so put distinct limits on the aid the Soviet Union could offer its clients, such as those in Cuba or Vietnam. Today, if the first of these handicaps remains commonplace enough, the second – the inferiority of Soviet power relative to that of the United States – is no longer apparent.

Despite the relative weakness of Soviet trade and aid with the Third World, the leading item in Soviet exports to these regions is the clue to the success of Soviet expansion there: military hardware. (For example, there are estimates that in 1977, the Soviet Union extended $21 million in economic aid to sub-Saharan Africa, but $600 million in military aid.) United States sources calculate that from 1973 through 1977, the Soviet Union exported approximately $16.5 billion worth of armaments to the Third World. Although some important recipients of these arms, such as Egypt and China, subsequently turned against Moscow, the profile of those who received such aid (presented in Table 4)[36] is a good indication of Soviet clients in the Third World, and a map as well of the areas of Soviet influence in these regions.

As the Soviets plainly perceive, however, military aid alone is not enough to guarantee either Soviet interests in these countries or the strength of client regimes there. Third World governments are notoriously unstable, unable as they so frequently are to develop the political and bureaucratic infrastructure necessary to organize their people in order

Table 4. *Soviet military aid to the Third World, 1973–7 (principal recipients in terms of degree of Soviet aid relative to other countries)*

	Military aid extended (in millions of dollars)	Total military aid received from all sources
Africa		
Angola	340	640 (with 260 from "other," presumably largely from Cuba)
Benin	10	20
Congo	30	40
Equatorial Guinea	5	5
Ethiopia	340	537
Guinea	40	45
Guinea-Bissau	10	10
Mali	50	50
Mozambique	40	60
Uganda	80	95
South Asia		
Afghanistan	310	325
Bangladesh	60	106
India	1100	1292
Southeast Asia		
Vietnam	560	700
Middle East		
Algeria	470	710
Egypt	1200	1748
Iraq	2600	3748
Libya	1800	2694
South Yemen	160	170
Syria	3001	3006
Latin America		
Cuba	480	480
Peru	550	898

either to contain the social conflicts bred by economic change or to defend their regional interests against hostile neighboring states. Just as the Soviets impressed upon Sun Yat-sen in 1921 the importance of a strong party and a solid military base on

Table 5. *Distribution of Soviet, Eastern European, and Cuban military and technical personnel in the Third World in 1977*

	Soviet/Eastern European military	Cuban military	Soviet/Eastern European technicians	Cuban technicians
Algeria	1615	15	6200	15
Libya	600	15	15000	0
Angola	500	19,000	10	4,000
Ethiopia	500	100	250	400
Iraq	1150	150	6100	0
Syria	2175	0	4900	0
South Yemen	350	350	950	0
Mozambique	200	50	500	400

which to unify China, so today Moscow clearly understands that it must translate its military aid into an effective local political force if its influence is to be expanded. American sources calculate that in 1977, Third World countries hosted some 10,250 military and 58,755 technical personnel from the Soviet Union and Eastern Europe, as well as some 21,850 soldiers and 6,575 technicians from Cuba.[37] These figures, which are estimates, are presented in Table 5. Moreover, a Central Intelligence Agency review published by the *New York Times* on December 15, 1980, reported that in 1979, Soviet and Eastern European technicians in the Third World numbered 81,000, while military personnel totaled some 15,875. At the same time, the number of Cuban technicians grew to some 13,000, while its military personnel totaled 34,315. An already substantial foreign presence was being significantly increased.

In at least three distinct ways the presence of these advisers serves to strengthen their host regimes. First, in countries where the government is weak relative to the domestic forces to be controlled, foreign advisers may serve in effect as palace guards, loyal in their commitment and strong in the power they can bring to bear in isolated instances. (In this respect, the French have shown the way in Africa.) Second, in lands where regional animosities run high, a Soviet or Cuban military presence serves as a token of commitment to a specific regime, a warning to others that more force will be brought to bear in the event of an unacceptable challenge to the client regime. And finally, through its advisers, the Soviet Union may be able to provide instruction in authoritarian organization useful for political "development" or "modernization". Both Mustafa Kemal in Turkey and Sun Yat-sen in China turned to Moscow after World War I not only for both material and ideological aid against imperialist encroachments, but also – indeed especially – for insights and guidance as to how they might organize their countries politically in order to secure the kind of independence that the Soviet Union had achieved.[38]

What, then, does the Soviet Union hope to obtain from these relationships? The economic advantages to be gained have been fairly limited to date. A trade surplus with the Third World provides Moscow with currency to help finance its debt with the West, and certain resources difficult to procure domestically may be found there. (The largest project at present is the $2 billion, thirty-year Meskala phosphate mining enterprise undertaken in Morocco.) But unless the Soviet Union reaches a ceiling in domestic petroleum production later in this decade, it is difficult to believe that any crucial economic interests are involved in the developing world. A second limited interest pursued by the Soviet Union in the South may be regional hegemony of a kind that would enhance Soviet military security. Increased influence with Turkey or in South Asia might, for example, improve Soviet access to the Mediterranean or the Indian Ocean.

Rather than thinking of the expansion of Soviet influence in the South as in the service of any specific, limited goal, however, it would be better to place it within the context of Soviet power in the global sense. That is, in the shifting balance of power between the Soviet Union and its adversaries led by Washington, Moscow's connections to the Third World might add strength to its overall geopolitical position. On the one hand, this might occur directly, as regimes explicitly aligned with Moscow come to power in the South. So the Afghan leader Babrak Karmal has asserted his country's part "in our day, in this epoch of transition from capitalism to socialism on a world scale," and Nicaraguan leader Alvaro Ramírez has declared: "The overthrow of the Somoza dictatorship must be seen not merely as a local event due to a concurrence of circumstances and isolated from world developments. What made it possible was the new world balance in favor of the revolutionary process."[39] On the other hand, Soviet gains might be the product of less direct or premeditated events, as isolated acts, perhaps undertaken for essentially defensive reasons, come to have a cumulative significance for the organization of world power. Were the Soviet Union to become hegemonic in such a crucial region of the South as the Persian Gulf, for example, this might well serve as a wedge to fragment the alliance centered around the United States. The relatively low-risk opportunities provided by penetration in the Third World complement the potential long-term, cumulative benefits of such a policy.

Certain situations appear inherently to favor the expansion of Soviet influence in the Third World. One of these is where domestic class or ethnic conflict is so severe that revolution is in the offing. Particularly when the United States has allied itself with a corrupt and repressive regime that a commanding majority of the population despises, circumstances may be ripe for Moscow to gain a local following behind the banner of national liberation. Nevertheless, there are problems with such efforts, chief of which are the difficulties of penetrating a territory controlled by another state and the resentment of other governments over what they will see as subversion directed from abroad. Considerations such as these have restrained Soviet moves in Latin America, for example, even where ready "fraternal" parties exist. A second opportunity for the expansion of Soviet influence comes when other states seek to imitate the Soviet form of political organization. Although imitation may be the highest form of flattery, this has not necessarily meant that such regimes intend to stay in step with Moscow. If Havana indicated some such commitment with its plans for internal reorganization based on the Soviet model beginning around 1970, neither Peking nor Belgrade lets such matters stand in the way of marking its distance from the Soviet Union, and there is little reason to doubt that most countries in Eastern Europe would do the same if they did not fear Soviet military reprisals. By contrast with these circumstances, an even more promising environment for Soviet gains exists when regional conflicts open the way for great power involvement on the side of rival states. Here the Soviets choose to back a strong party with a good case: Vietnam in Southeast Asia, India in South Asia, the "progressive" Arabs in the Middle East, and different movements and states in Black Africa opposed to white minority rule. Where the problem seems intractable and the Western position the weakest, there the strongest push may be expected: against Israel in the Middle East, against South Africa below the Sahara. Moreover, as the Soviet involvement grows it may gain in strength. For client regimes may come to find themselves increasingly reliant on the strength of their foreign patron, either because local contests mount in intensity or because the penetration of state services by foreign agents makes these outsiders increasingly active power brokers in domestic affairs. The Soviet experience in Egypt nevertheless indicates that this approach is by no means assured of success. Indeed, these very factors may ultimately conspire against the growth of Soviet influence. As other imperialists have found before them, the Soviets may discover that their presence serves as a focal point for the unification of nationalist resentment against them. This may be all the more the case in situations where regional conflicts are quieted, either through the successful negotiation of differences or by the victory of one party to the dispute.

The main element of power the Soviet Union can bring to bear in these contexts that serve Soviet interests is its military strength. Alongside this power, Moscow's other sources of leverage in the South – economic, ideological, and cultural – are only frail reeds. No later than 1971, the Soviet Union was able to match the United States in overall nuclear capability, and by 1975–6, as it demonstrated in Angola and later in Ethiopia, the Soviet Union had acquired the ability to project conventional forces beyond the Eurasian land mass and so became a truly global superpower. Even if American forces remain on balance superior to those Moscow could marshal in most regions of the Third World, the change of roles (perhaps best illustrated by the expansion of the Soviet fleet) is nonetheless of great significance.[40]

Whether the projection of Soviet military power in the South will translate into Soviet international rank depends on at least two issues that Moscow may be able to influence, but not to control. As we saw earlier, one of these lies in the development of political relations in the Third World considered both domestically and regionally. If regimes develop greater domestic governing capacities in these areas, and if serious regional conflicts can be limited by an awareness on the part of neighboring states that their differences invite the interference of powerful outsiders – interference that may escalate dangerously the level of hostilities – Soviet influence may be restrained. There is, however, little likelihood of either of these developments occurring in the foreseeable future, even if there are hopeful developments (such as the new government of Zimbabwe) that can be cited. The other major question concerns the future of the Western alliance centered on the United States, as to an important extent the Soviet advance reflects the decline of America. The victory of the Viet Cong, the rise of the Organization of Petroleum Exporting Countries, the political legacy of Watergate, the rigidity of the commitment to Israel, and the mix of serious, long-term economic difficulties that set in during the early 1970s – all these combine to limit Washington's ability to act in the global manner to which it had grown accustomed in the quarter century following World War II. How the United States will adjust to these domestic and international constraints in the coming years will obviously have its impact on the course of Soviet policy as well.

As was mentioned above, a key issue with respect to the growth of Soviet influence in the Third World has to do with how this development impinges on the character of Soviet relations with Western Europe, Japan, and the United States. The era of Western colonialism is barely two decades behind us, and the dependence of a resource-poor Western Europe and

Japan on trade and investment with Africa, Asia, and Latin America is difficult to dispute, even if it is frequently overlooked how self-reliant this alliance might be were the need to arise, exception made for the crucial case of petroleum. Thus, despite the Soviet contention that it seeks to play no more of a role in these regions than befits its superpower rank, the status quo will be decidedly different if Moscow achieves its purpose and becomes a power broker in every significant issue relating the South to the members of the OECD. Great powers have always sparred with each other in weaker areas, where local instability in effect invites outside participation yet where the dangers of escalation appear limited. The Third World appears to be no different, except that it is the home of economic resources increasingly vital for the livelihood of the northern industrial countries. In this respect, the reiterated Soviet pledge to help spread "wars of national liberation" in the South might be considered to be not only a traditional great power stance with respect to rival spheres of influence made all the more sincere by Moscow's Marxist-Leninist commitments, but also a genuine claim to a stake of substance in determining the global balance of power.[41]

Although it is fortuitous that the rise of Soviet military power should accompany the development of a multitude of economic problems in the United States, such a coincidence sets the stage for potentially volatile changes in the international order. By virtually every measure, Washington's management of global economic relations began to falter noticeably in the summer of 1971, when the crisis of the dollar finally broke. Several indexes reflect the underlying problems. Thus, for some time the European Economic Community has been the world's preeminent international trading body. In 1978, for example, the Community exported $222 billion worth of goods (excluding intra-Community trade) – whereas the United States exported only $144 billion, taking a second place to the Community in every part of the world except the Western Hemisphere, Japan, and Australia.[42] Such a figure might be no cause for concern were it not accompanied by statistics showing the sluggish growth of the American economy. So, from

1965 through 1976, the United States ran behind every major country in the OECD in terms of rise in gross national product, exception made for Great Britain (average OECD growth rate was 4.1 percent, with the United States trailing at 2.7 percent).[43] Or again, in terms of labor productivity, the United States has registered an even more disappointing showing relative to its allies, falling very far behind Japan, and comparing unfavorably as well with Germany, France, and Italy.[44] Another salient failing has appeared in the area of energy. Despite some limited progress in conservation and the development of alternative sources of energy, Washington has seemed unable, even if willing, to check private interests that successfully opposed comprehensive planning to deal with this urgent problem. Washington has seemed obliged to leave in relative neglect sources of energy that might either conflict with or be outside the domain of control of certain large corporations. That the economic health of the country was still best measured in 1980 by the health of the automobile industry is surely the best single example of the illness from which the country seemed unable to rouse itself. This weakness and lack of internal discipline understandably alarmed America's closest allies. The distance these capitals now considered putting between themselves and Washington could only compound the obstacles to using the international economic system for political ends. Weakness was breeding weakness in a manner no optimistic talk about the virtues of a decentralized world order could serve to disguise.

In short, whether we consider United States relations with the Third World, the Soviet Union, or its partners in the OECD in 1980, we see a reduction in the means at Washington's disposal to influence, if not to control, the conduct of southern states. The greater internal industrial strength of the Third World intersected with certain centrifugal forces within the OECD to spell a decline in America's ability either to assure global economic management or to use its economic resources as a means of political power. At the same time, the evident potential militancy of southern nationalism as witnessed in Vietnam intersected with the expanded military power of the

Soviet Union to make Washington's decision to use either conventional or nuclear threats far more costly. Of course, neither in economic nor in military terms was the United States any less than a great power; and its preeminence in each of these power hierarchies made it still the single most important actor in world politics. But in contrast with the quarter century after World War II, the United States operated in an international environment that presented far more obstacles to its unfettered will.

Models of domestic revolutions typically take into account three primary variables: the cohesion of the ruling group, the organizational capacity of the ruled to act, and the menace of foreign powers by war. Although the field of international relations prides itself on the uniqueness of its categories of analysis, much the same distinctions might be made in studying the current transformations of world politics. For the postwar world order largely established by the efforts of the United States is faced by a series of overlapping, if somewhat independent, challenges: by divisions in the North on economic, and to a lesser extent military, matters; by unrest in the South, which is better than ever able to direct itself politically; and by the new military parity of the Soviet Union. Could some combination of these forces bring about a "revolution" in the shape of the international system? What would be required here would probably be no less than some measure of Soviet conventional military superiority tied into a split in the Western alliance, and the association of key Third World states (such as the Arab members of OPEC) within a Soviet security system. Or if not revolution, then what of some mode of reform or restoration of the international order?

Let us then speculate, in concluding, on how the current decline of Western imperialism and the rise of that which is Soviet may affect the global organization of power in the next generation. Three alternate scenarios, or models of future developments, might be proposed, taking into account different potential patterns of change among the chief actors in questions – even if history never falls into such neat, ideal frameworks as those to be suggested here.

The first model of future developments proposes that the Soviet Union will go from success to success, each step forward preparing the ground for the next. According to this scenario, as the degree of Soviet power available for projection into the Third World comes to be appreciated, more and more states will gradually accommodate to a Soviet interpretation of an acceptable world order. Thus, faced with the unchallenged Soviet success in Afghanistan and the evidence of a stunning Soviet rescue of an Ethiopian regime in bad repair, other Middle Eastern countries (particularly if pressured by Libya, Algeria, Syria, South Yemen, and perhaps Iraq) might well be tempted to settle their differences with Moscow, or even to see their security linked to a greater regional assertion of Soviet power, and this despite their possible fear (or perhaps because of it) they might be the next to experience the fate of Afghanistan. Such a development might in turn encourage a loosening of the Atlantic Alliance as Western Europe and Japan, already chafing at American leadership for a variety of reasons (particularly, with respect to the Middle East, over Washington's connection to Israel), came to see their access to Middle East petroleum mediated by a Soviet presence.[45] Such events might at the same time chasten the Chinese, turning them from their growing involvement with the United States toward a role of limited regional preeminence with deference to Moscow. According to this perspective, there is no particular reason to think such developmnts would be forestalled by aggressive American actions. Rather the reverse might be true, as America's allies, reacting against a belligerence in Washington which seemed to them uncalled for and from which they thought they had only to lose, sought to separate their destinies from that of the United States.

Nor is there any reason to believe that such an eventuality goes unthought of in Moscow, where messianic talk of a "world socialist system" has replaced Lenin's talk of "world revolution," where a Soviet bureaucracy lacking deep-seated legitimacy seeks an ideological base with which to justify itself (and where international "détente" may be construed in the same terms as domestic "united front" – that is, as a prelude to Communist success), and where a rising military bureaucracy cloaks its will to power behind fine theoretical pronouncements on the future course of world history. Thus, alongside the statements in the Soviet press concerning that country's restraint and essentially defensive reactions to world events, one finds as well the note sounded that "capitalism in its historical competition with socialism is surrendering one position after another."[46] One need not give credence to such statements, of course, but it is worth considering how widely spread the notion is among Soviet opinion and decision makers that the decline of Western imperialism is synonymous with the decline of the West *tout court*, and therefore anticipates the coming age of "proletarian internationalism" centered, we must presume, around a beneficent Moscow. Indeed, even if this is not Moscow's premeditated intention it may nonetheless be the eventual consequence of its actions. For even if the Soviet Union is acting today for what it sees as basically defensive reasons and in full realization of its inability to gain military superiority over the United States, the growing Soviet role in the Third World might nonetheless profoundly influence the structure of international power in a decidedly favorable way from the point of view of the Kremlin.

A second scenario, quite different from the first although as hypothetically plausible, suggests that Soviet expansion will breed a broad series of countermeasures on the part of its rivals, which in turn will seriously endanger world peace. In other words, the movement toward "revolution" in world affairs might be met by a still more powerful drive for "restoration." Already the aggressive Soviet moves into Africa and Afghanistan have begun to mobilize parts of the American establishment that wish to counter them, groups that not long before confidently sought to decouple "North–South" affairs from "East–West" affairs. Similarly, the election of Ronald Reagan expressed the sentiments of a vocal and powerful segment of American society that would substantially accelerate a military response to Soviet gains. Nor has Europe been found wanting, ready to retreat into a self-imposed "Finlandization." Rather, France has announced new defensive nuclear plans, and the West Germans have served notice that they may consider a serious buildup of conventional forces. So too, China gives every indication that Soviet advances will only confirm its opposition to Moscow's "hegemonism"; and one can only wonder whether Japan might ultimately follow suit. The remilitarization of Japan and Western Europe is all the more probable given the domestic and regional instability rampant in the Third World, especially where conflicts such as that between Iran and Iraq might call for outside intervention irrespective of Soviet intentions. To these dangers another must be added: the danger that the Soviet Union may overextend itself abroad by entering into unrealistic commitments that it cannot hope to maintain but that it fears to abandon. The result could be that Moscow would lash out in a defensive fury, provoking the very catastrophe it may genuinely be seeking to prevent. For in situations where patron–client and alliance politics become rigid, local matters that might otherwise be trivial, or weaker actors that might otherwise be ignored, come to provoke chain reactions, escalating matters that under different circumstances might be handled more moderately into issues of global importance. The lessons of World War I are clear on this account.[47]

To be sure, there is no reason to believe that this eventuality, any more than the one described earlier, has not been considered in Moscow. The Soviet Union has traditionally been reluctant to become involved in entanglements abroad that might ultimately jeopardize the existence of the Communist state itself. Lenin talked much of "world revolution," but even more thoroughly he taught a prudent, strategic pragmatism in word and action which the terrible sufferings of the Soviet people in two world wars have amply served to confirm. Fear of "adventurism" is deeply implanted in Soviet political culture. And the Soviets are doubtlessly well aware that despite their striking military gains in relative terms over the past decade, there is no reason to think that such force will alone provide a way out of their growing "encirclement," as they by no means yet possess the capability to go on the offensive whatever "windows of advantage" may be attributed to them by foreign observers.[48]

We should speculate as well on a third, more moderate model for the future, which might be called "reform." Perhaps by its assertive actions in the Third World, Moscow may come to find itself treated more seriously than has hitherto been the case by its major rival, the United States. For although the Carter administration acted with restraint toward the Third World (in Central America with respect to Nicaragua and the canal, in Africa toward Angola and the Horn, and in relation to Iran), its policy toward the Soviet Union was far less careful. Whether by its initial position on arms agreements with Moscow, by its human rights campaign, by its outcry over Soviet troops in Cuba, or by its tilt toward China, the Carter administration failed to exhibit the kind of behavior that might have encouraged the Soviet Union to be more confident about détente.[49] By demonstrating its strength alongside its restraint (as with respect to China's attack on Vietnam), the Soviet Union may encourage a seriousness in Washington that soft words could not elicit, a seriousness that would show the magnitude of the stakes involved in failing to have a clear and long-term policy with respect to superior relations. Were such an understanding to be accompanied by a revitalization of ties among the members of the Atlantic Alliance (including Japan) and innovation with respect to relations with the Third World, a new, substantially stronger international order might emerge from the effort to confront the present dilemmas.

The problem with optimism in regard to such proposals is that in the early 1970s some such developments appeared to be in the offing, but they never materialized. With the slogans of "détente" with the Soviet Union and "devolution" with regard to the leading members of the OECD, Washington demonstrated that it possessed at least the idea of international reform. Détente was to signify the regularization of Soviet–American competition and the search for accommodation on interests of mutual concern, with the frank recognition of Soviet superpower status. Although the reform of relations among members of the Western coalition was never so high a priority among policy makers as were relations with Moscow, there was a conviction shared by many that should the United States oversee a devolution of its power in favor of pluralism the alliance might grow in strength. As Stanley Hoffmann expressed the notion:

The goal would be, not to reproduce the conditions of domestic integration at a higher level, but to translate these conditions: no central power, but effective international institutions; no social or political consensus on a broad range of values, but a dense web of ties signifying the prevalence of mixed interests over adversary relationships and a code of behavior corresponding to a minimum of common values . . . We would be relieved from playing Atlas, and others would be rescued from the frustrations, humiliations, narrowing of vision, self-doubts, or petulance that dependence breeds. We would become, in effect, a more responsible player by being less intoxicated by world responsibility, and others would become more responsible by having to deal with world (and not just parochial) issues. Above all, the perils of a centralized system in which every local crisis involves the great powers and feeds their contest would be reduced.[50]

At the same time, the members of the OECD might further institutionalize their relations with the Third World. In this sense, the call in the mid-1970s for a "new international economic order" corresponded to northern as well as southern interests. For as debt financing, market access programs, and buffer stocks and earning stabilization schemes become more highly institutionalized, what initially appeared to be concessions to the Third World might ultimately become limited forms of leverage over it. At one and the same time, northern interests might establish more harmony of understanding among themselves while forging new links with the South. There is no reason to exaggerate the amount of power that would accrue to the members of the OECD as a result: Interests would not be highly enough synchronized on most matters to make this a potent form of influence except on rare occasions. A model for such a relationship might be found in the Lomé Conventions, which link the European Community with some fifty less developed states in Africa, the Caribbean, and the Pacific. With agreements on trade cooperation (including a price stabilization scheme for commodities exported by the developing countries), with financial and technological transfer agreements, with an understanding on investment rights, and with an institutional mechanism designed to oversee the working of the accords, Lomé stands as an example of what can be accomplished in terms of integrating the policies of northern states with each other and with those of the South.[51]

Whether the international order will see "revolution," "restoration," "reform," or some mix of changes other than those sketched above, the outcome obviously depends on far more than the conduct of the United States alone. The American defeat in Vietnam, the rise of OPEC, the Sino–American rapprochement, the new Soviet military capability in conventional as well as in nuclear terms, the recurrent problems plaguing the Western economies, and the serious domestic and regional political divisions bedeviling the Third World – the issues are too numerous, too complex, too weighty, and by now too long-standing for us to see the history of the last decade as any more than a time of transition between a period of unquestioned American hegemony and the future. As the decade of the 1980s opens, it is difficult to conceive of how we may emerge safely from the present dangers. In terms of the concerns of this book, the key question is whether America can, or will, protect its interests in the Third World by working with strong nationalist movements in these areas, as has been its historical preference. The rise of Soviet military power, the continued instability of many parts of the South at a time of unprecedented importance of secure access to energy resources there, and the domestic appeal within the United States to act forcefully in these circumstances indicate a more interventionist policy on the part of Washington.[52] Whether this can succeed is a matter of foremost concern. The room for debate will be wide and its outcome important. There is nothing foreordained either in the domestic structure of the United States or in the international configuration that will determine how American policy should be conducted. If the South has secured a notable degree of economic and political independence in the period since 1945, there is no guarantee that these gains will be consolidated, and some reason to believe that they may well be reversed in the years to come.

APPENDIX

A note concerning moral issues and American imperialism

Like all questions involving unequal parties in a political relationship, moral issues are a fundamental part of contemporary North–South affairs, and today they present themselves with unprecedented vigor. In the past, the powerful assumed the mandate of civilization, whereas the weak were left to manage as best they could (which in cultural as well as political terms usually meant not very well at all). In the nineteenth century, conservatives in Europe generally had the most sympathy with the plight of the preindustrial areas, for their form of thought encouraged respect for the social integrity of foreign peoples, however much their ways might differ from those of Europeans. Liberals, to the contrary, gravely took up the burden of empire in such a fashion that even outspoken critics of colonial rule such as J. A. Hobson thought more of reforming than of ending Europe's overseas presence. Marx and Engels, for their part, could relegate the question of morality in international affairs, like that in domestic politics, to the period after the revolution. As Engels remarked of the French victory over Abd el-Kader in Algeria:

> Though the manner in which brutal soldiers, like Bugeaud, have carried on the war is highly blamable, the conquest of Algeria is an important and fortunate fact for the progress of civilization ... All these nations of free barbarians look very proud, noble and glorious at a distance, but only come near them and you will find that they, as well as the more civilized nations, are ruled by the lust of gain, and only employ ruder and more cruel means ... the modern bourgeois, with civilization, industry, order, and at least rela-

tive enlightenment following him, is preferable to the feudal lord or to the marauding robber, with the barbarian state of society to which they belong.[1]

Today, as southern nationalism expresses itself more forcefully in world affairs, Third World leaders are denouncing the usurpations of the past and linking their current problems with this inheritance. The result is a tone of moral imperative in their deliberations with the North that has by now far overstepped the bounds of manifestos issued by intellectuals and has become common rhetoric at public forums. Although the roots of this movement go as far back as the Bandung Conference of 1955, its current form depends more on the strength of the Group of 77 (whose name reflects the number of Third World states that joined together at Algiers in 1967). Thereafter the ranks of the Group of 77 grew in number and the movement found its opinions most widely expressed at the periodic meetings of the United Nations Conference on Trade and Development (UNCTAD), which had been inaugurated under the chairmanship of Rául Prebisch in 1964.

However much the Group of 77 may be concerned with the variety of technical questions concerning the international economic order – including debt relief, commodity pricing schemes, aid packages, tariff agreements, and investment expropriation rights – a tone of moral indignation at the operations of the international system dominated by the North is seldom lacking. As the opening sentence of the Charter of Algiers, the founding document of the Group of 77, declares: "The lot of more than a billion people of the developing world continues to deteriorate as a result of the trends in international economic relations."[2] Similarly, in his address to UNCTAD-III when it met in Santiago in 1972, Salvador Allende offered the delegates an example of investment exploitation. In 1931, he declared, copper companies invested some $30 million in Chile. No fresh capital followed, but over the ensuing decades at least $4 billion (American billion) in profits were repatriated to the United States. And this in a country of 10 million, where perhaps half a million children in 1972 were mentally stunted from malnutrition. According to Allende, this process came about when an unscrupulous local elite, eager to fill its own pockets but unmindful of the national interest, created a large external public debt in order to encourage foreign investment. Thus, in 1971, nearly one-third of the total export earnings of Chile went to service a debt that was "largely contracted in order to offset the damage done by an unfair trade system, to defray the costs of the establishment of foreign enterprise on our territory, [and] to cope with the speculative exploitation of our resources . . . "[3] The pervasiveness of this sentiment explains the general support given by these countries to the OPEC price hike in 1973, even when many Third World states found their problems exacerbated by the financial distress caused by the hike. They could take heart from the words of Algerian President Houari Boumedienne, who addressed the Sixth Special Session of the United Nations General Assembly in April 1974:

> The OPEC action is really the first illustration, at the same time the most concrete and most spectacular illustration, of the importance of raw material prices for our countries, the vital need for the producing countries to operate the levers of price control, and lastly, the great possibilities of a union of raw material producing countries . . . This action should be viewed by the developing countries . . . as an example and a source of hope.[4]

Boumedienne's initiative led to the adoption of what was called the "Programme of Action on the Establishment of a New International Economic Order" by the UN, which in January 1975 endorsed a companion declaration sponsored by Mexican President Luis Echeverría, "The Charter of Economic Rights and Duties of States." As it turned out, the "rights" were those of the South, whereas the "duties" pertained to the North's obligation to respect these rights. Article 2 stated:

> Every State has and shall freely exercise full permanent sovereignty, including possession, use and disposal, over all its wealth, natural resources and economic activities.[5]

This right was to include the competence to "nationalize, expropriate or transfer ownership of foreign property" with the "question of compensation . . . settled under the domestic law of the nationalizing State." Furthermore, by the terms of Article 5:

All States have the right to associate in organizations of primary commodity producers in order to develop their national economies . . . all States have the duty to respect that right by refraining from applying economic and political measures that would limit it.

The Group of 77 reasserted the moral basis for these demands in 1976 in their Manila Declaration, in which they "affirm their conviction that it is necessary and urgent to bring about radical changes in economic relations in order to establish new relations based on justice and equity which will eliminate the inequitable economic structures imposed on developing countries, principally through the exploitation and marketing of their natural resources and wealth."[6] There was, then, something of a background to Fidel Castro's declaration before the United Nations in October 1979 that "we were forced into underdevelopment by colonization, imperialism and neocolonialism"; and hence that there is a "moral obligation" to rectify this state of affairs on the part of those "who benefited from the plunder of our wealth and the exploitation of men and women for decades and for centuries." In addition to calling for the cancellation of the external public debt of the poorest countries, Castro demanded the North distribute $300 billion (American billion) over the next decade, claiming that otherwise "the future will be apocalyptic."[7]

In the United States, the response to the current demands by the South for a more just and equitable international order has been, predictably, varied. Whereas to the Left such claims seem eminently justified, to some men of the Right, such as Daniel Patrick Moynihan or Irving Kristol, these demands carry no moral weight whatsoever. Or rather, as Kristol put it in his much-cited *Wall Street Journal* article of July 17, 1975, the moral imperative is to resist such demands:

When the poor start "mau-mauing" their actual or potential benefactors, when they begin vilifying them, insulting them, demanding as of right what is not their right to demand – then one's sense of self-respect may take precedence over one's self-imposed humanitarian obligations.

What I shall call the liberal position, despite the wide range of opinions within it, is quite different. It assumes that the power of the South is real (even if not equivalent to the

North's), and that as some, although certainly not all, of the demands for a new international economic order are not inimical to northern interests (and others may be turned to advantage), they should be satisfied. It is from this general perspective that the World Bank, the Trilateral Commission, groups at Brookings, and the Overseas Development Council – whatever their differences – have pressed for accommodation.

But liberals are particularly likely to defend their policies in moral terms as well: Because the reforms aim to increase the economic productivity of the developing world, it can be claimed that they are instrumental in easing the strains of world poverty. The famines in the Sahel and in Bangladesh are only the most dramatic forms of the malnutrition that afflicts from 700 million to over 1 billion persons in the South.[8] A constituency of conscience is growing in the North – people who are somewhat embarrassed at their affluence alongside such desperate poverty, and aware that the Care packages and Food For Peace are only stopgap measures when more enduring reforms are necessary. The focus is on food for the world's hungry. The moral imperative behind reform is therefore that of the Good Samaritan: When it is in your power to do good for another who needs it at no serious risk to yourself, your duty is to do so.[9]

But as we have seen, it is decidedly not the morality of the Good Samaritan that so many in the Third World, especially radical governments and intellectuals, expect from the North. For them, it is not simply that poverty exists alongside affluence, but that the one is *structurally* a function of the other. In the words of Frantz Fanon, one of the first to articulate fully this "structuralist" position:

The mass of the people struggle against the same poverty . . . their shrunken bellies outline what has been called the geography of hunger . . . Confronting this world, the European nations sprawl, ostentatiously opulent. This European opulence is literally scandalous, for it has been founded on slavery, it has been nourished from the blood of slaves, and it comes directly from the soil and from the subsoil of that underdeveloped world. The well-being and progress of Europe have been built up with the sweat and the dead bodies of Negroes, Arabs, Indians and the yellow races. We have decided not to overlook this any longer.[10]

From this perspective, it is intolerable that the rich nations should strike the pose of the Good Samaritan, that they should affect historical innocence (in the manner of Albert Camus, who, like Fanon, was primarily interested in Algeria) and even pretend that their wealth should be the salvation of this misery which in fact it created and continues to perpetuate. If there be a moral imperative behind international reform, it is the recognition of historical responsibility and of the justice of reparations.[11]

~ In a formal sense, this is a serious moral argument. It maintains that an established procedure of only apparently neutral rules and regulations has demonstrably resulted in the self-perpetuating misery of a part of humanity even as it has served the interests of another group. Power created this structure of domination and only power preserves it. Its victims have the "right" to change the system, and those profiting from it, would they act justly, have the "duty" to do so. Similar arguments have served to legitimize reformist as well as revolutionary action around the globe in this century. They are essentially the justification, for example, behind "affirmative action" and other claims for "reparations" by disadvantaged groups in the United States today. Thus Charles Beitz has extended John Rawl's theory of justice from domestic to international application, maintaining that global interdependence and cooperation is great enough today to justify raising questions of distributive justice in a broader context.[12]

To be morally persuasive, however, this argument must be empirically valid as well as formally sound. The issue therefore has its scientific, as well as normative, dimension. Note that the principal charge against the North is not fundamentally concerned with what might be simply called crimes against humanity, such as the plunder of Bengal, forced labor in the Congo and in the mines of Peru and Mexico, African slavery, or the dispossession of the Irish peasantry. Nor does the principal charge deal with the damage wrought by imperialist political acts, such as the overthrow of Colonel Arabi in Egypt by the British in 1882, or American conduct in Vietnam from 1965. Reprehensible as these deeds were, they are secondary to the contention that imperalism set in place an international division of labor whose consequence in normal operation has been to delay and distort the economic development of the South, thus breeding the manifold human miseries we see today in underdevelopment, including the prevalence of authoritarian-military governments in these regions.

The evidence reviewed in Chapter 2, in Chapter 4 (section entitled "The pattern of American policy"), and in Chapter 5 does not substantiate such a severe indictment against imperialism on these grounds. Although the course of development in Africa, Asia, and Latin America depended mightily in all its dimensions on the expansion of Western Europe, this should serve as no license to ride roughshod over the force of local circumstances in determining the character of change in these regions. For there have been substantial differences in the way various areas have reacted to their exposure to modern economic forces, and an understanding of how the general features of the international economic system – capital, technology, markets – came to be integrated into local social and political structures must recognize the relative autonomy of life on the periphery and its leading role in determining what to make locally of these influences coming from abroad. Imperialism played its part in these developments without any doubt, but never was it able to make the world over in its image, as is so frequently alleged by southern nationalists and Marxists, whose interests are served by promoting such a picture. (It is ironic indeed that leaders and governments in the South that systematically repress the demands of their citizenry – whether in favor of a national bourgeoisie or a national Communist party – should adopt a tone of self-righteous indignation to protest infringements on "justice" and "equity" by the North when it would seem that their own conduct would be as well addressed.) Admittedly, the link between American business and local elites made the former a part of the power structure on the periphery, and so tended to make subsequent efforts to displace the established governments there anti-American. And it is a matter of public record that even before the Mexican Revolution of 1910, long before communism was a concept of any relevance to the South, Washington would protect these economic interests so long as it did not jeopardize geopolitical concerns in the process. What the indictment against the strength of international capitalism nonetheless omits are recognition of the stimulus these economic forces have given to the growth and modernization of southern economies and appreciation of the politically based balance of power considerations that have led Washington to intervene in the South in a counterrevolutionary fashion. Why else did the United States intervene in Vietnam where economic interests were simply not at stake, or fail to act decisively against startling acts of economic nationalism such as those engineered by Colonel Qaddafi in Libya? One need not deny the importance of the business community in Washington in order to maintain that this alone cannot provide the primary, much less the sole, explanation for the pattern of American policy toward the South since 1945.

Although we may dispute the blanket charge that imperialism is responsible for all the woes afflicting the South, we should not rally to the other extreme and suppose that imperialism has done no harm, or indeed that it has been an unmitigated boon to mankind. Especially in regard to the years since 1945, when the United States has viewed with special interest the internal organization of southern lands, it is impossible to overlook the role American imperialism has played in lending support to repressive governments and forms of economic development in the South. At one time, analysts in Washington may have believed that economic growth was a good in itself, that what was good for some was good for all (in the sense of that questionable process known as the "trickle down"). But in due course, reports revealed that the form economic development was taking in many parts of the South was actually adding to the privations of certain groups.[13] In the case of agricultural programs, for example, irrigation efforts, credits for seed or fertilizer, or access to markets frequently ended up benefiting the rich and middle-income farmers while the poor were squeezed all the more.[14] Or again, agribusiness may move into an area and begin producing crops or livestock for export while destroying the bases of traditional cultivation, the mainstay of the peasantry. If jobs were provided for the displaced in the industrial sector, or if the profits reaped from these new enterprises were redistributed to the population at large, such developments would be positive for all concerned. But as it often is, certain class and ethnic groups profit not only relative to others, but to their absolute disadvantage. It was said that "sheep ate men" during the enclosure movement in England, when serfs were turned off the land to make way for sheep, the basis for the wool trade so crucial to the later industrial revolution. Such scenes are repeating themselves in our day *with the active support of investment and trading interests in the North.*[15]

Moreover, as we saw in Chapter 4, because of its fear of communism the United States has actively intervened to oppose efforts by peasants and workers to redress such circumstances. Although the United States may favor reform over reaction in the South, it will back reaction over revolution wherever this is the only alternative presenting itself. Consider as a test case the Alliance for Progress, initiated by the Kennedy administration in 1961 to bring economic development and political stability to Latin America. Even a radical like James Petras concedes that the alliance's inspiration was valid: It looked to remedy the continent's problems by remaking a part of its socioeconomic structure.[16] As the program was first laid out, it encouraged regional industrialization schemes, export diversification, land reform to end "unjust structures" of ownership, special attention to the needs of weaker countries in the hemisphere, and health, housing, and employment projects "to meet the most pressing social needs and benefit directly the greatest number of people." Twenty billion dollars were pledged over a ten-year period.[17]

In short order the alliance proved to be a failure. It lacked the sustained support of any established organizations in the United States and was opposed by vested interests in Latin America who found ways to turn local programs to their own advantage.[18] Its chief shortcoming might have been predicted. By mounting the alliance as an antidote to Castroism in the Americas, Washington made its projects hostage to anticommunism in the region. Because bids at genuine reform risk sponsoring revolution (for they involve the creation of new power structures and the dismantling of the old), the alliance soon degenerated into a counterrevolutionary ploy. As the chairman of the House Committee on Foreign Affairs put it in 1965 with respect to the American role in the overthrow of constitutional government in Brazil:

Every critic of foreign aid is confronted with the fact that the Armed Forces of Brazil threw out the Goulart government and the U.S. military aid was a major factor in giving these forces an indoctrination in the principles of democracy and a pro-U.S. orientation. Many of these officers were trained in the United States under the AID program. They knew that democracy was better than communism.[19]

Or as then Secretary of Defense Robert McNamara presented the issue just two years later:

Social tensions, unequal distribution of land and wealth, unstable economies, and the lack of broadly based political structures create a prospect of continuing instability in many parts of Latin America. The answer to these and other associated problems, if one is to be found, lies in the Alliance for Progress, to which we and our Latin American friends are devoting large resources. But the goals of the Alliance can be achieved only within a framework of law and order. Our military assistance programs for Latin America thus continue to be directed to the support of internal security and civic action measures.[20]

In this final sentence the familiar American pattern of thinking reemerges: Reform is to be preferred to reaction unless it leads to revolution – in which case it will be abandoned. Although the United States had deliberately and publicly committed itself to influencing the course of development in the South, its record to date with respect to improving the quality of life there is far from brilliant.

In modified form, therefore, it would appear that the "structuralist" as opposed to the "Good Samaritan" argument for American responsibility for suffering in part of the Third World may be maintained. Nevertheless, the qualifications on this argument are substantial. First, American (as well as European and Japanese) responsibility would not appear to be engaged in a structuralist sense in the misery in most of Africa or in South Asia (India, Pakistan, and Bangladesh). Here resides the great majority of the world's poorest and most desperate people – some 76 percent.[21] And here the morality of the Good Samaritan would seem to be appropriate, as neither the international economic system nor the political conduct of the United States or its allies would seem to play any part in the worsening situation there. To be sure, the introduction of modern medicine in these regions has played an important role in the creation of a dilemma typified by a situation in which, in the words of Carlo Cipolla, an agrarian birthrate exists alongside an industrial death rate.[22] But this structural link is not to be associated with patterns of profit or domination so much as with earlier expressions of Good Samaritan concern.

The structuralist argument must be qualified in the second place by the suspicion that there can very likely be no such thing as "just" and "equal" development under the conditions of change that a society experiences as it moves from an agrarian to an industrial structure. The political infrastructure that alone could make such a transition is either lacking or finds itself obliged to act in an authoritarian manner against the inevitable obstacles to a social reorganization so profound and so rapid. Except that a country culturally inherits the complement of skills and organizations that makes the process a natural one (as in the case of Australia), justice and equality can in all probability be only long-term goals that a state sets for itself. Certainly the experience of Western Europe, the Soviet Union, and Japan gives little reason to think things can work out differently (although in saying this we should not discourage the effort). Therefore, to blame imperialism for what appears to be a well-nigh inevitable state of affairs is to look for scapegoats; a wiser route would be to confront honestly the difficult and painful choices that all but the most fortunate will be obliged to deliberate.

This second qualification suggests a third: that in most development processes the primary responsibilities lie with the southern states and not with Washington or the capitals allied to it. Multinational corporations have proved their ability to operate in virtually any political climate – bringing technology to totalitarian Russia as well as to democratizing Spain and authoritarian Brazil. How their presence will affect a host country thus has far more to do with how the country is organized than with any power the multinationals have to control affairs in their interest. This is not to deny that multinationals exercise a definite influence in the distribution of power locally, and that therefore their presence has a moral dimension; but it is to affirm that they can scarcely be held solely responsible for morally indefensible developments in the South.

There is a final qualification to the structuralist argument as well: Washington is limited in its ability to promote justice in the South by virtue of its finite stock of power and its pursuit of other interests in these regions that it may have good grounds to deem more important. President Carter's human rights campaign is a perfect case in point. Initially the Carter administration apparently assumed that there would be no significant trade-offs between active support for human rights abroad and effective understandings with foreign governments on other matters of importance to Washington. Apart from the irony of a nation that had only recently extricated itself from the tragic war in Vietnam lecturing others as if it were a paragon of virtue, a number of other difficulties cropped up. More powerful nations such as the Soviet Union were incensed that the United States would intervene in their internal affairs and threatened to prove uncooperative on the resolution of other issues of concern to America.[23] Weaker regimes such as those in Korea and Iran, on which the United States depended as key parts of its global security network, began to give evidence that these campaigns were weakening them further.[24] And the campaign prompted countries like Argentina, which was considering its own nuclear development and expanded grain trade with the Soviet Union, to go their own way. Ultimately the United States came to look something of the hypocrite, pushing its values where the cost of doing so was low, but abstaining from criticism where the price in terms of other interests seemed high. Arthur Schlesinger put the case for many when he questioned the good sense (and hence basic morality) of such an itinerant morality, and suggested that the United States would be better occupied attending to its own problems than conducting abolitionist crusades abroad.[25]

Of course, not everyone shares this view. For example, Gunnar Myrdal again and again has insisted on a morally proper exercise of power by the members of the OECD in their relations with the Third World. Thus he writes that "aid policies cannot be morally neutral," and he approvingly cites a 1962 statement by the Swedish government on foreign assistance:

> We can reasonably try so to direct our assistance programs that they do, to the best of our judgment, tend to promote political democracy and social equality. It is not consistent with the motives or aims of Swedish assistance that it should help preserve anti-progressive social structures.[26]

Yet if Sweden may allocate all its aid to Latin America to Castro's Cuba or Allende's Chile (as it did prior to 1973), Stockholm's range of goals is not so broad or so complex as Washington's, and the Swedes can therefore live a moral life less at conflict with itself. Franklin Roosevelt summed up the American dilemma years ago, by contrast, when he declared that Rafael Trujillo was "an s.o.b. but our s.o.b." And so we have what is so often a dialogue of the deaf, in which the "realists" defend themselves from accusations of "cynicism" by insisting that no great power can be innocent, that there can be no end to trafficking with the Devil, while the "liberals" refuse to be called "sentimentalists" for their contention that those who would use cruel means must clearly justify their decisions in terms of the ends supposedly served thereby. The debate surrounding Kissinger's actions with respect to Bangladesh, Cambodia, and Chile might serve as an example.

The foregoing qualifications to the structuralist argument for American responsibility for the suffering of the world's poor do not constitute by any means a rejection of the thesis. American power may be far more limited than this perspective usually concedes, and there may be room aplenty for the ethic of the Good Samaritan to be applied, but these provisos do not constitute ground enough to dismiss the structuralist charge. The truth at the core of this position is that wealth and power are often defended in bad faith – rationalizations and justifications for their existence and conduct are presented that are transparently self-serving – and that a close accounting of the behavior of the powerful in terms of the ends they have sought with the means at their disposal often shows their reasoning to be intellectually shallow and morally indefensible. American political and economic actors have deliberately made themselves part of the domestic power structures in the South, particularly in Latin America and the Far East, and so are bound up with the question of justice in the form of the social organization that has been created in these regions. In such circumstances, it obscures the issue of structural responsibility to assert that, because the behavior of our authoritarian "friends" is no worse than that of our totalitarian opponents, the former should not be the object of our special concern. Even should we accept that, for example, dissidents in the Soviet Union suffer more than blacks in South Africa, the latter might legitimately be more a matter of our moral concern owing to the strength that the South African government draws for its apartheid policies from its membership in a Washington-dominated international order. We are, therefore, structurally implicated in the affairs of South Africa in a way we are not in the Soviet Union. The companion argument – but for Third World dictators these lands would become Communist – ignores the fact that the fortunes of communism frequently rise precisely because of the character of these "friendly" governments. Indeed, the moral shortcomings of many of these regimes are basic aspects of their institutional weakness. The dictates of simple morality (e.g., "the land to those who till it") would thus appear to coincide with the national interest (e.g., inhibiting Soviet expansion) far more often than many "realists" with their proclivity for strong-arm behavior ever concede.

Such a conclusion is all the more compelling in the measure that this book takes issue both with those neo-Leninists who maintain that American economic organization permits no less than a counterrevolutionary posture on Washington's part, and with those geopoliticians who hold that radical governments almost anywhere in the South have the potential to shift the balance of world power in favor of the Soviet Union. Were either of these "iron laws of necessity" so demanding, the possibility of political choice would in effect be canceled and the issue of moral responsibility (except perhaps to overthrow the economic system or to remake the world order) would be irrelevant. But as Chapter 4 argued, neither the neo-Leninist nor the geopolitical contention is warranted – except in a modified sense (in the case of Leninism), or in special instances (with respect to geopolitical concerns). As a whole range of activities from trade and investment with Communist countries to accommodation with OPEC demonstrates, there is a great deal of flexibility in the way the United States operates in the world economy. The Leninist explanation casts American behavior into a far more rigid mold than the historical record allows. Short of some extreme measure such as a prolonged OPEC embargo, there is little reason to believe that economic nationalism in the South of a sort designed to answer the needs of its poorest peoples would unduly trouble the economies of the OECD, or even a significant part of the multinational actors engaged in the Third World. (And in the case of an OPEC embargo the reaction of alarm would be the same if all the members of the OECD were Socialist: Leninism scores no points here.) The burden of the argument, then, is on those who assert that the established patterns of trade and investment are so crucial to the North that such changes would have a significantly unsettling economic effect there. Similar reservations apply to the calculations of geopoliticians such as Henry Kissinger. When a country gains a revolutionary regime, even with Moscow's support, it is not invariably a test of American "credibility" and "resolve" or a sign of a global shift in favor of the Soviet Union. Indeed, Washington has weakened itself and thus made serious errors of precisely a geopolitical sort by following exactly such assumptions. Of course there may be instances when gains would accrue to Moscow that Washington might well have reason to oppose, just as there are acts of southern economic nationalism America might find intolerable. But to admit such constraints on American policy is not tantamount to subscribing to a version of history run either by economic or geopolitical laws of motion.

We have seen that there are two very different ways of approaching the question of America's moral responsibility for the suffering of the world's poor. Those who might be called the liberal moralists generally adopt a utilitarian approach labeled Good Samaritanism and call for remedies such as donating a certain percentage of northern GNP to the needy of the South under conditions that will improve their well-being. Those who might be called the radical moralists generally see a structural relationship between America's international economic and political conduct and the plight of the world's poor. Although these two camps seldom enter into dialogue with each another, there is no inherent reason that their views are mutually exclusive, except that the liberals believe they can work within the system whereas the radicals more often despair of trying. Nevertheless, if the liberals can be convinced that much more than charity is called for would they aid the poor, and if the radicals might be persuaded that the room for maneuver is not so tight as they believe, Americans might succeed in addressing these moral issues more realistically and hence more usefully.

Yet even were the United States to become more critical of the trade and investment arrangements it is sponsoring in the South that work to the detriment of the poor, even were it to become more open to working with revolutionary regimes dedicated to improving the lives of the hundreds of millions suffering there from malnutrition, it should be understood that there are no panaceas. There are many indications from the examples offered by China, and especially by the Soviet Union, that the price of correcting the abuses of the old order may itself be a high one. And as much as the Cuban Revolution offers an example of economic justice in a Latin America singularly without it elsewhere, Cuba's record on political freedom after more than two decades is distinctly more somber. The belief that the diminution of American imperialism will herald a bright new day for mankind is an illusion to be subscribed to by those whose notion of the origin of social suffering and injustice is equally simplistic. Is it any more than realistic to suspect that in the future the term imperialism will be useful to describe the practices of some of the former victims and most outspoken critics of the Anglo-American variety?

Notes

Preface

1 Tony Smith, ed., *The End of the European Empire: Decolonization after World War II* (Heath, 1975); and Smith, *The French Stake in Algeria, 1945–1962* (Cornell University Press, 1978).

Introduction

1 United Nations, *Yearbook of National Account Statistics*, 1977, vol. 2, table 1A; United Nations, *World Statistics in Brief* (1978).
2 United Nations, *Demographic Yearbook*, 1977, p. 137. It is difficult to locate figures on southern industrial output as a percent of the world total. However, in 1973, the United Nations Industrial Development Organization (UNIDO) estimated that, by 1970, the less developed countries were producing 11.4 percent of the world's light manufactured goods, and 4.5 percent of its heavy manufactures. See UNIDO, *Industrial Development Survey*, 5 (1973), table 1.
3 On the domestic forces behind imperialist expansion, the "classic" texts include: for economic interests, J. A. Hobson, *Imperialism: A Study* (1902); for military machines, Joseph Schumpeter, *The Sociology of Imperialism* (1919); for deep-seated psychological reasons, William Langer, "A Critique of Imperialism," *Foreign Affairs*, October 1935. On the ability of the international system, by its distribution of power, to incite imperialism against the weak (just as it encourages alliances among the strong) see Hans J. Morgenthau, *Politics Among Nations: The Struggle for Power and Peace*; Raymond Aron, *Peace and War: A Theory of International Relations* (Doubleday, 1967); Robert W. Tucker, *Nation or Empire? The Debate over Ameri-*

can *Foreign Policy* (Johns Hopkins University Press, 1969). On the role of southern countries themselves in these matters, see John Gallagher and Ronald Robinson, "The Partition of Africa," in *The New Cambridge Modern History*, vol. 2 (Cambridge University Press, 1962); and D. K. Fieldhouse, *Economics and Empire, 1830–1914* (Cornell University Press, 1973). For a parallel, if very different, attempt to understand the identity of weaker peoples in terms of their own resources and their influence on the overall structure of the society in which they lived, see the outstanding work by Eugene D. Genovese, *Roll Jordan Roll: The World the Slaves Made* (Pantheon Books, 1972).

4 For a more extended discussion, see Theda Skocpol and Margaret Somers, "The Uses of Comparative History in Macrosocial Inquiry," *Comparative Studies in Society and History*, 22, 2, April 1980. See also Skocpol, *States and Social Revolutions: A Comparative Analysis of France, Russia, and China* (Cambridge University Press, 1979), pp. 33ff.

5 R. R. Palmer and Joel Colton, *A History of the Modern World* (Knopf, 1971), p. 673.

Chapter 1. The dynamics of imperialism: the perspective of a century, 1815–1914

1 C. J. Bartlett, *Great Britain and Sea Power, 1815–1853* (Oxford University Press, 1963); Gerald S. Graham, *Tides of Empire: Discussions on the Expansion of Britain Overseas* (McGill-Queen's University Press, 1972).

2 For trade figures, see E. J. Hobsbawm, *Industry and Empire* (Pelican, 1969), p. 139; and J. Forbes Munro, *Africa and the International Economy, 1800–1960* (Rowman and Littlefield, Totowa, N.J., 1976), p. 40; for investment figures, see Michael Barratt-Brown, *After Imperialism* (Humanities Press, 1970), p. 93, and William Woodruff, *Impact of Western Man: A Study of Europe's Role in the World Economy, 1750–1960* (St. Martin's Press, 1967), p. 150.

3 John Gallagher and Ronald Robinson, "The Imperialism of Free Trade," *Economic History Review*, second series, 6, 1, 1953.

4 Lenin, *Imperialism, the Highest State of Capitalism* (1917).

5 D. C. M. Platt, *Finance, Trade, and Politics in British Foreign Policy, 1815–1914* (Oxford University Press, 1968), p. 361.

6 D. C. M. Platt, "Further Objections to an 'Imperialism of Free

Trade,' 1830–60," *Economic History Review*, second series, 26, 1, February 1973.

7 Rhodes Murphey, *The Treaty Ports and China's Modernization: What Went Wrong? Michigan Papers in Chinese Studies*, 7, 1970, reprinted in Mark Elvin and G. William Skinner, eds., *The Chinese City between Two Worlds* (Stanford University Press, 1971); and Murphey, *The Outsiders: The Western Experience in India and China* (University of Michigan Press, 1977).

8 H. S. Ferns, *Britain and Argentina in the Nineteenth Century* (Oxford University Press, 1960), pp. 487–8.

9 Ibid., p. 489.

10 Ibid., pp. 296–7.

11 Ibid., p. 290; p. 314–15.

12 Platt, *Finance, Trade and Politics* (n. 5), p. 360.

13 Woodruff, *Impact* (n. 2), p. 313.

14 Ibid., pp. 314–17 (table 7/14) (Note obvious error in Woodruff's text p. 316 concerning exports for Asia; it is corrected here to 17 percent.).

15 Ibid., p. 150. Important questions have been raised about the size of these figures (although not about the relative weights of the countries involved) by D. C. M. Platt, "British Portfolio Investment Overseas before 1870: Some Doubts," *Economic History Review*, second series, 33, 1, February 1980.

16 Herbert Feis, *Europe, the World's Banker, 1870–1914: An Account of European Foreign Investment and the Connection of World Finance with Diplomacy before the War* (Yale University Press, 1930), p. 23.

17 Murphey, *The Treaty Ports* (n. 7), pp. 34–5.

18 Charles Issawi, ed., *The Economic History of the Middle East, 1800–1914* (University of Chicago Press, 1966), p. 9.

19 Feis, *Europe* (n. 16), p. 463.

20 Cited in Bartlett, *Great Britain* (n. 1), p. 68.

21 See, for example, the case of Argentina, discussed in Ferns, *Britain and Argentina* (n. 8), chapter 4.

22 In the case of the Ottoman Empire, see, for example, Issawi's introduction in, *The Economic History of the Middle East* (n. 18); for China, see John King Fairbank, *The United States and China* (Viking Press, 1958, 2nd ed.), pp. 122–3, 147, 167. Also, J. C. Hurewitz, *Diplomacy in the Near and Middle East: A Documentary Record: 1535–1914* (Van Nostrand, 1956).

23 Cited in Ronald Robinson and John Gallagher with Alice Denny,

Africa and the Victorians: The Climax of Imperialism (Doubleday, 1968), p. 2.

24 Eugene Staley, *War and the Private Investor: A Study in the Relations of International Politics and International Private Investment* (Howard Fertig, N.Y., 1935; reprinted 1967), pp. 398–9.

25 David S. Landes, *Bankers and Pashas: International Finance and Economic Imperialism in Egypt* (Harvard University Press, 1958), p. 96.

26 For Turkey, see Feis, *Europe* (n. 16), chapter 14; on Egypt, ibid., pp. 128, 329; on the occupation of Egypt, Robinson and Gallagher, *Africa and the Victorians* (n. 23), chapter 4.

27 Cited in Lloyd C. Gardner, *Wilson and Revolutions: 1913–1921* (Lippincott, 1976), pp. 64–5.

28 Cited in Bartlett, *Great Britain and Sea Power* (n. 1), pp. 261–2.

29 Ibid., pp. 262–7.

30 Landes, *Bankers and Pashas*, (n. 25), pp. 91–2.

31 Cited by Richard Graham, "Robinson and Gallagher in Latin America: The Meaning of Informal Imperialism," in William Roger Louis, ed., *Imperialism: The Robinson and Gallagher Controversy* (Franklin Watts, N.Y., 1976), p. 220.

32 On this issue, I believe D. C. M. Platt has offered conclusive evidence. In addition to *Finance, Trade, and Politics* (n. 5), see *Latin America and British Trade, 1806–1914* (Harper & Row, 1973), and his edited volume *Business Imperialism, 1840–1930: An Inquiry Based on British Experience in Latin America* (Oxford University Press, 1977).

33 Benjamin J. Cohen, *The Question of Imperialism: The Political Economy of Dominance and Dependence* (Basic Books, 1973), chapters 2 and 4; and D. K. Fieldhouse, " 'Imperialism': An Historiographical Revision," *The Economic History Review*, second series, 14, 2, 1961.

34 Michael Barratt-Brown, *After Imperialism* (Heinemann, 1963), pp. 81–2; Fritz Fischer, *Germany's Aims in the First World War* (Norton, 1967), p. 12; Charles P. Kindleberger, *Economic Growth in France and Britain, 1851–1950* (Harvard University Press, 1964), pp. 271–2.

35 Hans-Ulrich Wheler, "Bismarck's Imperialism, 1862–1890," *Past and Present*, 48, August 1970; Henry Ashby Turner, Jr., "Bismarck's Imperialist Venture: Anti-British in Origin?" in Prosser Gifford and William Roger Louis, eds., *Britain and Germany in Africa* (Yale University Press, 1967).

36 Platt, *Finance, Trade and Politics* (n. 5), p. 153.

37 Ibid., pp. xvi–xvii.

38 J. A. Hobson, *Imperialism: A Study* (University of Michigan Press, 1965; first published in 1902), pp. 81, 89, 93.

39 A. K. Cairncross, *Home and Foreign Investment, 1870–1913* (Cambridge University Press, 1953), p. 225.

40 Platt, *Finance, Trade and Politics* (n. 5), part 1 especially. Moreover, although Feis (n. 16) documents that bankers seldom loaned except to allies of their home nation, the City of London loaned to Russia even during the Crimean War: Albert H. Imlah, *Economic Elements in the Pax Britannica* (Harvard University Press, 1958), p. 10.

41 David S. Landes, *The Unbound Prometheus: Technological Change and Industrial Development in Western Europe from 1750 to the Present* (Cambridge University Press, 1969), pp. 329–31.

42 Hobsbawm, *Industry and Empire* (n. 2), pp. 151, 192.

43 W. Arthur Lewis, *Growth and Fluctuations, 1870–1913* (Allen & Unwin, 1978), p. 133.

44 Issues of *Foreign Trade* published by the Ministry of Foreign Trade, Moscow, are replete with such observations. For their theoretical defense by Soviet writers, see, for example, O. V. Kuusinen et al., *Fundamentals of Marxism-Leninism* (Foreign Language Publishing House, Moscow, 1963, 2nd rev. ed.), chapter 25; and Shalva Sanakoyev, *The World Socialist System: Main Problems, Stages of Development* (Progress Publishers, Moscow, 1972).

45 For an elaboration on this point, see Otto Hintze, "Economics and Politics in the Age of Modern Capitalism," in Felix Gilbert, ed., *The Historical Essays of Otto Hintze* (Oxford University Press, 1975).

46 Peter Temin, "The Relative Decline of the British Steel Industry, 1880–1913," in H. Rosovsky, ed., *Industrialization in Two Systems: Essays in Honor of Alexander Gerschenkron* (Wiley, 1966), p. 143.

47 For a discussion see Landes, *Unbound Prometheus* (n. 41), chapter 5.

48 J. S. Hoffman, *Great Britain and the German Trade Rivalry* (Russell and Russell, N.Y., 1964; first published 1933), pp. 115, 129, 158, 295.

49 David Gillard, *The Struggle for Asia, 1828–1914: A Study in British and Russian Imperialism* (Holmes and Meier, 1977).

50 George Monger, *The End of Isolation: British Foreign Policy, 1900–1907* (Thomas Nelson, N.Y., 1963), chapters 1 and 2. For some interesting speculation on what such a rapprochement might have entailed, see George Liska, *Quest for Equilibrium: America and the*

Balance of Power on Land and Sea (Johns Hopkins University Press, 1977), chapters 3, 4, 5.

51 Winston S. Churchill, *The World Crisis, 1911–1914* (Scribner, 1924), chapter 1. See also the discussion in Cohen, *Question of Imperialism* (n. 33), chapter 7.

52 An early and especially powerful essay on this subject is Eckart Kehr, "Anglophobia and Weltpolitik," in Kehr, *Economic Interest, Militarism and Foreign Policy: Essays on German History*, edited by Gordon Craig (University of California Press, 1977; orig. pub. 1920s). See also Thorstein Veblen, *Imperial Germany and the Industrial Revolution* (Macmillan, 1915), chapters 3 and 7; Joseph Schumpeter, *The Sociology of Imperialism* (1919); Fischer, *Germany's Aims* (n. 34), chapters 1 and 2, and Fischer, *World Power or Decline: The Controversy over Germany's Aims in the First World War* (Norton, 1974), thesis 1. For additional arguments tending to sustain this position, see Wolfgang J. Mommsen, "Domestic Factors in German Foreign Policy before 1914," and Hans Rosenberg, "Political and Social Consequences of the Great Depression of 1873–1896 in Central Europe," reprinted in James J. Sheehan, ed., *Imperial Germany* (Franklin Watts, N.Y., 1976); see also Gordon A. Craig, *Germany, 1886–1945* (Oxford University Press, 1978), pp. 98f. and chapter 9.

53 Kenneth Bourne, *The Foreign Policy of Victorian England, 1830–1902* (Oxford University Press, 1970).

54 Although the emphasis in this chapter has fallen on the domestic economic and international political factors in European rivalries, the independence of political from economic considerations allows us to consider matters of psychological makeup and their influence on historical developments. Three categories of psychological analysis seem appropriate in this respect: (1) what might be called the psychology of mass movements, which stresses general ideological factors and their popular acceptance for no particularly better reason than that mankind must live by myths – in very different veins, see Hannah Arendt, *The Origins of Totalitarianism* (Harcourt Brace Jovanovich, 1951), part 2, and Martin Green, *Dreams of Adventure, Deeds of Empire* (Basic Books, 1979); (2) what might be called the psychology of interest articulation as expressed, for example, in Bernard Semmel, *Imperialism and Social Reform: English Social-Imperial Thought, 1895–1914* (Harvard University Press, 1960), and *The Rise of Free Trade Imperialism: Classical Political Economy and the Empire of Free Trade and Imperialism, 1750–1850* (Cambridge University Press, 1970); and (3) what might be called the psychology of decision making as discussed, for example, in Robert Jervis, *Perception and Misperception in International Politics* (Princeton University Press, 1976). All three of these approaches shed important light on European imperialism and the movement to World War I.

55 Cited in Richard W. Sterling, *Macropolitics: International Relations in a Global Society* (Knopf, 1974), p. 56.

56 See, for example, the account given by A. J. H. Latham, *Old Calabar, 1600–1891: The Impact of the International Economy upon a Traditional Society* (Oxford University Press, 1973).

57 A. G. Hopkins, *An Economic History of West Africa* (Longman, 1973), p. 145.

58 John Gallagher and Ronald Robinson, "The Partition of Africa," in *The New Cambridge Modern History*, vol. 2, 1962, reprinted in Louis, *Imperialism* (n. 31); D. K. Fieldhouse, *Economics and Empire, 1830–1914* (Cornell University Press, 1973).

Chapter 2. The impact of imperialism: the perspective of a century, 1815–1914

1 Kwame Nkrumah, *Neo-Colonialism: The Last Stage of Imperialism* (International Publishers, N.Y., 1966), p. ix.

2 William Woodruff, *Impact of Western Man: A Study of Europe's Role in the World Economy, 1760–1960* (St. Martin's Press, 1967), pp. 313–17, 150; W. Arthur Lewis, *Growth and Fluctuations, 1870–1913* (Allen & Unwin, 1978), pp. 169, 177; Simon Kuznets, *Modern Economic Growth: Rate, Structure and Spread* (Yale University Press, 1966), p. 322.

3 Ronald Robinson, and John Gallagher with Alice Denny, *Africa and the Victorians: The Climax of Imperialism* (Doubleday, 1968), pp. 3–4.

4 Lewis, *Growth and Fluctuations* (n. 2), p. 202. See also chapters 7 and 8.

5 Ibid., p. 205, 220.

6 D. C. M. Platt, "Dependency in Nineteenth Century Latin America," *Latin American Research Review*, 15, 1, 1980.

7 In some cases, the argument against the Europeans is obviously overwhelming, such as with respect to African slavery, mining in Mexico and Peru, the plunder of Bengal, or the treatment of the Irish peasantry. Two other charges are far more problematic, however. One is that local artisans were destroyed by cheap European products. The other is that local development was either delayed or distorted by incorporation into the international economic system. In the case of China, for example, see Robert F. Dernberger, "The Role of the Foreigner in China's Economic Development, 1840–1949," in Dwight H. Perkins, ed. *China's Modern Economy in Historical Perspective* (Stanford University Press, 1975); Kang Chao, *The Development of Cotton Textile Production in China* (Harvard University Press, 1977); and Alexander Eckstein et al., "The Economic Development of Manchuria: The Rise of a Frontier Economy," *The Journal of Economic History*, 34, 1, March 1974. For a general discussion of the economic dynamism of the periphery (except Latin America), see A. J. H. Latham, *The International Economy and the Underdeveloped World, 1865–1914* (Rowman and Littlefield, Totowa, N.J., 1978). For a polemical but not unjustified treatment of the subject, see P. T. Bauer, "The Economics of Resentment: Economics and Underdevelopment," *Journal of Contemporary History*, 4, 1, January 1969.

8 Claudio Véliz, *The Centralist Tradition of Latin America* (Princeton University Press, 1980). See also Howard J. Wiarda, "Toward a Framework for the Study of Political Change in the Iberic-Latin Tradition: The Corporative Model," *World Politics*, 25, 2, January 1973.

9 Lewis, *Growth and Fluctuations* (n. 2), pp. 163, 196.

10 E. A. Boehm, *Twentieth Century Economic Development in Australia* (Longman, 1971), pp. 32–3 and chapter 6. Also N. G. Butlin, "Some Perspectives on Australian Economic Development, 1890–1965," in Colin Foster, ed., *Australian Economic Development in the Twentieth Century* (Praeger, 1971).

11 Lewis, *Growth and Fluctuations* (n. 2), p. 196; Robinson and Gallagher, *Africa and the Victorians* (n. 3), p. 6; H. S. Ferns, *Britain and Argentina in the Nineteenth Century* (Oxford University Press, 1960), pp. 492–3; A. G. Ford, "British Investment and Argentine Economic Development, 1880–1914," in David Rock, ed., *Argentina in the Twentieth Century* (University of Pittsburgh Press, 1975).

12 D. C. M. Platt, *Latin America and British Trade, 1806–1914* (Harper & Row, 1973).

13 Richard Graham, *Britain and the Onset of Modernization in Brazil, 1850–1914* (Cambridge University Press, 1968), pp. 27–8.

14 Platt, "Dependency" (n. 6).

15 Carlos F. Díaz Alejandro, *Essays on the Economic History of the Argentine Republic* (Yale University Press, 1970), pp. 2, 11.

16 Carlos Manuel Pelaez, "The Theory and Reality of Imperialism in the Coffee Economy of Nineteenth-Century Brazil," *Economy History Review*, second series, 29, 2, May 1976.

17 Platt, *Latin America* (n. 12), pp. 78, 84.

18 Díaz, *Essays* (n. 15), p. 138.

19 Calculated from Woodruff, *Impact of Western Man* (n. 2), p. 253.

20 Frederic Wakeman, Jr., "High Ch'ing: 1638–1839," in James B. Crowley, ed., *Modern East Asia: Essays in Interpretation* (Harcourt Brace Jovanovich, 1970).

21 Mary Clabaugh Wright, *The Last Stand of Chinese Conservatism: The T'ung-Chih Restoration, 1862–1874* (Stanford University Press, 1962), pp. 9–10. On British support for the Restoration, see chapter 3. See also Paul A. Cohen, "Ch'ing China: Confrontation with the West, 1850–1900," in Crowley, *Modern East Asia* (n. 20).

22 Frank Edgar Bailey, *British Policy and the Turkish Reform Movement: A Study in Anglo-Turkish Relations, 1826–1853* (Howard Fertig, N.Y., 1970); Z. Y. Hershlag, *Introduction to the Modern Economic History of the Middle East* (E. J. Brill, Long Island City, N.Y., 1964); Charles Issawi, ed., *The Economic History of the Middle East, 1800–1914* (University of Chicago Press, 1966); Stanford J. Shaw, "The Nineteenth-Century Ottoman Tax Reforms and Revenue System," *International Journal of Middle East Studies*, VI, October 1975; Edward C. Clark, "The Ottoman Industrial Revolution," *International Journal of Middle East Studies*, V, January 1974; Z. Y. Hershlag, *Turkey: The Challenge of Growth* (E. J. Brill, Long Island City, N.Y., 1968); and Ellen Kay Trimberger, *Revolution from Above: Military Bureaucrats and Developments in Japan, Turkey, Egypt and Peru* (Transaction Books, New Brunswick, N.J., 1977).

23 Charles Issawi, *Egypt in Revolution: An Economic Analysis* (Oxford University Press, 1963), chapters 1 and 2; A. E. Crouchley, *The Economic Development of Modern Egypt* (McKay, 1938), chapter 2; *The Encyclopedia Britannica*, "Mehemet Ali," 11th ed., vol. 18. The figures for industrial workers may be found by comparing Hershlag, *Introduction* (n. 22), p. 86 with Issawi, *Egypt in Revolution*, p. 43. For an interesting study of the intellectual thought in this period, see Peter Evans, *Islamic Roots of Capitalism: Egypt, 1760–1840* (University of Texas Press, 1979).

24 E. R. J. Owen, "Lord Cromer and the Development of Egyptian Industry, 1883–1907," *Middle Eastern Studies*, II, 4, July 1966; and "The Attitudes of British Officials to the Development of Egypt's Economy, 1882–1922," in M. A. Cook, ed., *Studies in the Economic History of the Middle East* (Oxford University Press, 1970).

25 Robert L. Tignor, "Bank Misr and Foreign Capitalism," *International Journal of Middle East Studies*, 8, 2, April 1977; and Charles

Issawi, "Shifts in Economic Power," in Issawi, *The Economic History of the Middle East* (n. 22).

26 See the discussion of the rise of British consular power in the area in K. Onwuka Dike, *Trade and Politics in the Niger Delta, 1830–1885: An Introduction to the Economic and Political History of Nigeria* (Oxford University Press, 1956), chapter 7.

27 On slave revolts see ibid., chapter 8. For a case discussion of other problems, see A. J. H. Latham, *Old Calabar, 1600–1891: The Impact of the International Economy upon a Traditional Society* (Oxford University Press, 1973).

28 Barrington Moore, Jr., *Social Origins of Dictatorship and Democracy: Lord and Peasant in the Making of the Modern World* (Beacon Press, 1966), chapter 5; Trimberger, *Revolution from Above* (n. 22); Angus Maddison, *Economic Growth in Japan and the USSR* (Allen & Unwin, 1969); G. C. Allen, *A Short Economic History of Modern Japan: 1867–1937* (Praeger, 1962); Henry Rosovsky, "Japan's Transition to Modern Economic Growth, 1868–1885," in Rosovsky, ed., *Industrialization in Two Systems: Essays in Honor of Alexander Gerschenkron* (Wiley, 1966).

29 S. N. Eisenstadt, "Post-Traditional Societies and the Continuity and Reconstruction of Tradition," *Daedalus*, 102, Winter 1973.

30 Theda Skocpol, "France, Russia, China: A Structural Theory of Social Revolution," *Comparative Studies in Society and History*, 18, 2, 1976, p. 185; Skocpol, *States and Social Revolutions: A Comparative Analysis of France, Russia and China* (Cambridge University Press, 1979), pp. 24ff. See also Trimberger, *Revolution From Above* (n. 22).

31 Alexander Gerschenkron, *Europe in the Russian Mirror: Four Lectures in Economic History* (Cambridge University Press, 1970), pp. 99, 102–3. See also Rondo Cameron, ed., *Banking and Economic Development: Some Lessons of History* (Oxford University Press, 1972).

32 Moore, *Social Origins of Dictatorship and Democracy*. (n. 28).

33 See Robert R. Kaufman et al., "A Preliminary Test of the Theory of Dependency," *Comparative Politics*, VII, 3, April 1975; David Ray, "The Dependency Model and Latin America: Three Basic Fallacies," *The Journal of Interamerican Affairs and World Studies*, XV, 1, February 1973; Patrick J. McGowan, "Economic Dependency and Economic Performance in Black Africa," *The Journal of Modern African Studies*, XIV, 1, 1976; and Elliot J. Berg, "Structural Transformation versus Gradualism: Recent Economic Development in Ghana and the

Ivory Coast," in Philip Foster and Aristide R. Zolberg, eds., *Ghana and the Ivory Coast: Perspectives on Modernization* (University of California Press, 1971).

34 Fernando Henrique Cardoso, "Associated-Dependent Development: Theoretical and Practical Implications," in Alfred Stepan, ed., *Authoritarian Brazil: Origins, Policies, and Future* (Yale University Press, 1973), and Cardoso, "Dependent Capitalist Development in Latin America," *The New Left Review*, 74, July-August 1972. In the jargon used by proponents of this approach, such countries become part of the "semi-periphery." Although the term is Immanuel Wallerstein's, the earliest use of the concept of which I am aware occurs in the idea of "go-between" countries as expressed in Johan Galtung, "A Structural Theory of Imperialism," *Journal of Peace Research*, 8, 2, 1971. Note how countries obtain their comparative labels by virtue of international, not domestic, characteristics.

35 Although the local economies as well as the international system are seen to change over time, the dominant partner and therefore the shaper of the overall movement is always the world economy in these analyses. See, among others, Susanne Bodenheimer, "Dependency and Imperialism: The Roots of Latin American Underdevelopment," in K. T. Fann and Donald C. Hodges, eds., *Readings in U.S. Imperialism* (Porter Sargent, Boston, 1971); and Stanley J. Stein and Barbara H. Stein, *The Colonial Heritage of Latin America: Essays on Economic Dependency in Perspective* (Oxford University Press, 1970).

36 Immanuel Wallerstein does not forsee the end of the system for another century or two. See "Dependence in an Interdependent World: The Limited Possibilities of Transformation within the Capitalist World Order," *African Studies Review*, XVII, 1, April 1974, p. 2.

37 Samir Amin, *Accumulation on a World Scale: A Critique of the Theory of Underdevelopment* (Monthly Review Press, 1974), vol. 1, p. 3.

38 André Gunder Frank, "The Development of Underdevelopment," in James D. Cockcroft et al., *Dependence and Underdevelopment: Latin America's Political Economy* (Doubleday, 1972), p. 9.

39 Walter Rodney, *How Europe Underdeveloped Africa* (Bogle-l'Ouverture, London, 1973), pp. 21–2.

40 Frances V. Moulder, *Japan, China, and the Modern World-Economy: Toward a Reinterpretation of East Asian Development* (Cambridge University Press, 1977), pp. vii–viii.

41   Stein, *The Colonial Heritage*, p. viii (n. 35).

42   Kurt Grunwald and Joachim O. Ronall, *Industrialization in the Middle East* (Council for Middle Eastern Affairs Press, 1960), p. 331.

43   Immanuel Wallerstein, *The Modern World-System: Capitalist Agriculture and the Origins of the European World-Economy in the Sixteenth Century* (Academic Press, 1974).

44   Georg Lukács, "Rosa Luxembourg, Marxiste," in *Histoire et conscience de classe* (Editions de Minuit, Paris, 1960), pp. 47–8.

45   Immanuel Wallerstein, "The Rise and Future Demise of the World Capitalist System," *Comparative Studies in Society and History*, XVI, 4, September 1974, p. 390. In the fall of 1977, Wallerstein launched the journal *Review* to encourage the dissemination of these ideas.

46   Paul Baran, *The Political Economy of Growth* (Monthly Review Press, 2nd ed., 1962), p. 149.

47   Ibid., p. 150.

48   Morris D. Morris, "Towards a Reinterpretation of Nineteenth-Century Indian Economic History," *The Indian Economic and Social History Review*, V, March 1968, pp. 6–7.

49   See Moore, *Social Origins of Dictatorship and Democracy* (n. 28), chapter 6; Angus Maddison, *Class Structure and Economic Growth: India and Pakistan since the Moghuls* (Allen & Unwin, 1971); and M. D. Morris, "Trends and Tendencies in Indian Economic History," *The Indian Economic and Social History Review*, V, 4, December 1968, and Morris, "Towards a Reinterpretation" (n. 48).

50   Romesh Dutt, *The Economic History of India: In the Victorian Age, 1837–1900* (Ministry of Information and Broadcasting, Government of India, 2nd ed., 1970), book 2, chapter 12; book 3, chapter 9; Daniel Houston Buchanan, *The Development of Capitalistic Enterprise in India* (Macmillan, 1934), pp. 465–7. Radhe Shyam Rungta, *The Rise of Business Corporations in India, 1851–1900* (Cambridge University Press, 1970); B. R. Tomlinson, *The Political Economy of the Raj, 1914–1917: The Economics of Decolonization in India* (Macmillan, 1979), chapter 1; and Clive Dewey, "The End of the Imperialism of Free Trade: The Eclipse of the Lancashire Lobby and the Concession of Fiscal Autonomy to India," in Dewey and A. G. Hopkins, eds., *The Imperial Impact: Studies in the Economic History of Africa and India* (Athlone Press, 1978).

51   Moore, *Social Origins of Dictatorship and Democracy* (n. 28), pp. 354–5.

52   Baran, *The Political Economy of Growth* (n. 46), p. 158.

53 André Gunder Frank, "Sociology of Underdevelopment and Underdevelopment of Sociology," in Cockcroft, *Dependence and Underdevelopment* (n. 38); and Susanne J. Bodenheimer, *The Ideology of Developmentalism: The American-Paradigm-Surrogate for Latin American Studies* (Sage Professional Papers in Comparative Politics, 1971).

54 André Gunder Frank, "The Development of Underdevelopment," and "Economic Dependence, Class Structure, and Underdevelopment Policy," in Cockcroft, *Dependence and Underdevelopment* (n. 38); Wallerstein, "The Rise and Future Demise" (n. 45).

55 Colin Leys, *Underdevelopment in Kenya: The Political Economy of Neo-Colonialism, 1964–1971* (University of California Press, 1974), pp. 198–9.

56 Jean-Paul Sartre, *Critique de la raison dialectique* (Gallimard, 1960), p. 44. For a criticism of Sartre on precisely the grounds that he also occasionally rides roughshod over the individual case, see Tony Smith, "Idealism and People's War: Sartre on Algeria," *Political Theory*, I, 4, November 1973.

57 Immanuel Wallerstein, *The Modern World-System* (n. 43), p. 355.

58 Immanuel Wallerstein, "Class Formation in the Capitalist World-Economy," *Politics and Society*, 5, 3, 1975, p. 375.

59 Theda Skocpol, "Wallerstein's World Capitalist System: A Theoretical and Historical Critique," *American Journal of Sociology*, 82, 5, March 1977.

60 Alexander Gerschenkron, "Economic Backwardness in Historical Perspective," in his *Economic Backwardness in Historical Perspective* (Harvard University Press, 1973).

61 Peter C. W. Gutkind and Immanuel Wallerstein, eds., *The Political Economy of Contemporary Africa* (Sage, 1976), pp. 11, 14.

62 Ibid., pp. 12, 27.

63 See, for example, James A. Caporaso, "Dependency Theory: Continuities and Discontinuities in Development Studies," *International Organization*, 34, 4, Autumn 1980.

64 Guillermo A. O'Donnell, *Modernization and Bureaucratic-Authoritarianism: Studies in South American Politics* (Institute of International Studies, Berkeley, 1973).

65 Guillermo A. O'Donnell, "Corporatism and the Question of the State," in James M. Malloy, ed., *Authoritarianism and Corporatism in Latin America* (University of Pittsburgh Press, 1977), p. 54; and see O'Donnell, "Reflections on the Patterns of Change in the Bureaucratic-Authoritarian State," *Latin American Research Review*, 13, 1, 1978, pp. 29–30.

66 Albert O. Hirschman, "The Turn to Authoritarianism in Latin America and the Search for its Economic Determinants," in David Collier, ed., *The New Authoritarianism in Latin America* (Princeton University Press, 1980), p. 68.

67 José Serra, "Three Mistaken Theses Regarding the Connection between Industrialization and Authoritarian Regimes," and Robert R. Kaufman, "Industrial Change and Authoritarian Rule in Latin America: A Concrete Review of the Bureaucratic-Authoritarian Model," in Collier, *The New Authoritarianism* (n. 66).

68 For a rebuttal of attempts to refute such criticisms, see Tony Smith, "The Logic of Dependency Theory Revisited," *International Organization* (in press).

Chapter 3. Decolonization

1 For a discussion of the conference, see D. Bruce Marshall, *The French Colonial Myth and Constitution-Making in the Fourth Republic* (Yale University Press, 1973), pp. 102–15.

2 *Brazzaville: 30 janvier–8 fevrier 1944* (Ministère des Colonies, 1944), p. 32.

3 Tony Smith, "The French Colonial Consensus and People's War, 1945–1958," *The Journal of Contemporary History*, 9, 4, October 1974.

4 See Hubert Deschamps, "French Colonial Policy in Tropical Africa between the Two World Wars," William Cohen, "The French Colonial Service in West Africa," and Leonard Thompson, "France and Britain in Africa: A Perspective," in Prosser Gifford and William Roger Louis, eds., *France and Britain in Africa: Imperial Rivalry and Colonial Rule* (Yale University Press, 1971).

5 Cited in Gabriel Kolko, *The Politics of War: The World and United States Foreign Policy, 1943–1945* (Random House, 1968), p. 83. See Robert Dallek, *Franklin D. Roosevelt and American Foreign Policy, 1932–1945* (Oxford University Press, 1979), pp. 459ff.

6 A. W. DePorte, *DeGaulle's Foreign Policy, 1944–1946* (Harvard University Press, 1968), chapters 2 and 3. See also Kolko, *The Politics of War* (n. 5), chapter 4.

7 Charles de Gaulle, *The Complete War Memoirs of Charles de Gaulle* (Simon & Schuster, 1967), p. 574.

8 Anti-Americanism flared in France each time the dependent role became evident: over the Marshall Plan, the EDC, the "nuclear shield," and American funds for the Indochinese War. See, among others, Georgette Elgey, La République des illusions (Fayard, Paris, 1965), pp. 101, 133, 139–41, 248; and Alfred Grosser, La Politique extérieure de la Ve République (Seuil, Paris, 1965), pp. 17, 47ff.

9 Max Beloff, "The Special Relationship: An Anglo-American Myth," in Martin Gilbert, ed., A Century of Conflict, 1850–1950: Essays for A. J. P. Taylor (Hamish Hamilton, London, 1966), p. 156. Beloff also insists on British realism as early as the 1890s: "It would need a profound belief in providence to make one refrain from wondering why a group of foggy islands off Europe's north-western shores, populated beyond the means of subsistence that the islands could provide, endowed with no great natural assets outside the coalfields, should have become the center of a world empire" (p. 5).

10 Kolko, The Politics of War (n. 5), pp. 71–84; Anthony Eden, Full Circle (Houghton Mifflin, 1960), chapter 9.

11 Leon D. Epstein, British Politics in the Suez Crisis (University of Illinois Press, 1964).

12 David Goldsworthy, Colonial Issues in British Politics, 1945–1961 (Oxford University Press, 1971).

13 On party politics during decolonization, see especially Miles Edwin Kahler, External Sources of Domestic Politics: Decolonization in Britain and France (Ph.D. diss., Harvard University, 1977).

14 Goldsworthy, Colonial Issues (n. 12), pp. 166ff.

15 Patrick Keatley, The Politics of Partnership (Penguin Books, 1963), pp. 393ff.

16 Ibid., part 5; Goldsworthy, Colonial Issues (n. 12), chapter 8 and pp. 352ff.; Rudolph von Albertini, Decolonization (Doubleday, 1971), pp. 245–7.

17 Charles de Gaulle, La France sera la France (F. Bouchy et Fils, Paris, 1951), p. 193.

18 The following comments are drawn from Smith, "French Colonial Consensus" (n. 3).

19 Philip Williams, Crisis and Compromise: Politics in the Fourth Republic (Doubleday, Anchor Books, 1966); Stanley Hoffmann, ed., In Search of France (Harper & Row, 1965); Raymond Aron, Immuable et changeante: De la IVe à la Ve République (Calmann-Lévy, Paris, 1959); Michel Crozier, The Bureaucratic Phenomenon (University of Chicago Press, 1964); D. MacRae, Parliament, Parties and Society in France, 1946–1958 (St. Martin's Press, 1967); Jean Barale, La Constitution de la IVe République à l'épreuve de la guerre (Librairie

Générale de Droit et de Jurisprudence, 1963); Nicholas Wahl, "The French Political System," in Samuel Beer and Adam Ulam, eds., *Patterns of Government* (Random House, 1962); Nathan Leites, *On the Game of Politics in France* (Stanford University Press, 1959).

20 Hugh Dalton, *High Tide and After: Memoirs 1945–1960* (Frederick Muller, London, 1962), p. 211.

21 For the very different attitudes of Prime Ministers Attlee and Ramadier, see the excerpts of parliamentary debates of 1946–7 reprinted in Tony Smith, *The End of European Empire: Decolonization after World War II* (Heath, 1975).

22 For a fuller discussion of Communist policy, see Tony Smith, *The French Stake in Algeria, 1945–1962* (Cornell University Press, 1978); and Irwin M. Wall, "The French Communists and the Algerian War," *The Journal of Contemporary History*, 12, 3, July 1977.

23 Kahler, *External Sources* (n. 13), chapter 6. For supporting evidence in the case of India, see B. R. Tomlinson, *The Political Economy of the Raj, 1914–1947: The Economics of Decolonization in India* (Macmillan, 1979).

24 Ruth S. Morgenthau, *Political Parties in French-Speaking West Africa* (Oxford University Press, 1964), p. 181.

25 Aristide Zolberg, *One Party Rule in the Ivory Coast* (Princeton University Press, 1969), p. 163.

26 Marshall, *The French Colonial Myth* (n. 1), chapters 5, 7, 8; Morgenthau, *Political Parties* (n. 24), chapters 2 and 3.

27 Zolberg, *One Party Rule* (n. 25), pp. 131ff.; Morgenthau, *Political Parties* (n. 24), pp. 188ff.

28 Zolberg, *One Party Rule* (n. 25), pp. 143, 237; Morgenthau, *Political Parties* (n. 24), pp. 207ff.

29 Cited in Zolberg, *One Party Rule* (n. 25), p. 151. Tribal cultivators are, of course, very different from peasants, so that for reasons of social structure they may be more difficult to mobilize in revolution.

30 Elliot J. Berg, "The Economic Basis of Political Choice in French West Africa," *American Political Science Review*, LIV (1960), p. 290; Zolberg, *One Party Rule* (n. 25), p. 165.

31 In 1944, there were 40,000 of these farms. By 1956, there were 120,000, while the population total was under 3 million: Zolberg, *One Party Rule* (n. 25), p. 27.

32 On taxes and migrant labor, see Zolberg, *One Party Rule* (n. 25), pp. 159ff., 41; and for more recent figures on migrant labor, see U.S. Department of State, *Handbook for the Ivory Coast*, 1973, p. xvii.

33 This judgment is shared by Morgenthau, Zolberg, Michael Crowder, and Pierre Gonidec, among others.

34 Colin Leys argues that the British effectively created such an elite in Kenya in the few years before their departure. See his *Underdevelopment in Kenya: The Political Economy of Neo-Colonialism, 1964–1971* (University of California Press, 1974).

35 Berg, "The Economic Basis," (n. 30). A. G. Hopkins suggests a more complicated and long-term relationship between economic changes and the process of colonization and decolonization when he maintains that different stages in the development of the economies of West Africa can be tied to specific political developments. See *An Economic History of West Africa* (Longman, 1973), especially pp. 168ff. For an extension of this analysis to India, although with less political detail, see Tomlinson, *The Political Economy of the Raj* (n. 23).

36 Smith, *The French Stake* (n. 22), chapters 4–6.

37 George M. Kahin and John W. Lewis, *The United States in Vietnam* (Dial Press, 1967), pp. 14–15.

38 John T. McAlister, Jr., *Viet Nam: The Origins of Revolution* (Knopf, 1969), chapter 6; and Joseph Buttinger, *Vietnam: A Political History* (Praeger, 1968), chapter 9.

39 George Kahin estimates that by 1925 perhaps half the families on Java and Madura (together accounting for two-thirds of the country's population) were landless, and that this percentage increased during the 1930s. Françoise Cayrac-Blanchard puts the proportion of landless there at 60 percent of the population in the early 1970s. Apparently a combination of communal mutual aid, strong patron–client relations, and the existence of two opposed tendencies of Islam discouraged class conflict at the village level. See Kahin, *Nationalism and Revolution in Indonesia* (Cornell University Press, 1952), pp. 17ff.; Cayrac-Blanchard, *Le Parti communiste indonesien* (Armand Colin, Paris, 1973), pp. 33–4; Clifford Geertz, *The Religion of Java* (University of Chicago Press, 1960), pp. 127ff.; Ruth McVey, "The Social Roots of Indonesian Communism" (speech published by the Centre d'Etude du Sud-Est Asiatique et de l'Extrême-Orient, l'Université Libre de Bruxelles); and Rex Mortimer, "Class, Social Cleavage, and Indonesian Communism," *Indonesia* (Cornell University Press), no. 8. October 1969.

40 I have been unable to find a comparative study of Communist organization in Indonesian and Vietnamese villages.

41 Barrington Moore, Jr., gives central importance to this alliance for the political development of India. See his *Social Origins of Dic-*

tatorship and Democracy: Lord and Peasant in the Making of the Modern World (Beacon Press, 1966), pp. 370ff.

42 Angus Maddison, *Class Structure and Economic Growth: India and Pakistan since the Moghuls* (Allen & Unwin, 1971), chapter 3.

43 Moore, *Social Origins* (n. 41), pp. 373ff.

44 See, among others, Francis Hutchins, *India's Revolution: Gandhi and the Quit India Movement* (Harvard University Press, 1973).

45 Maddison, *Class Structure* (n. 42), p. 106; Moore, *Social Origins* (n. 41), pp. 368ff.

46 Maddison, *Class Structure* (n. 42), p. 89; Moore, *Social Origins* (n. 41), pp. 385ff.

47 Leys, *Underdevelopment in Kenya* (n. 34).

48 Eden, *Full Circle* (n. 10), p. 230.

49 Ibid., pp. 474, 481.

50 Elizabeth Monroe, *Britain's Moment in the Middle East, 1914–1956* (Johns Hopkins University Press, 1963), chapter 4; Harold Macmillan, *Riding the Storm: 1956–1959* (Macmillan, 1971), chapter 16.

Chapter 4. "The American Century"

1 In the following pages some ambiguity is inevitable concerning the terms "sovereign national governments" and "national self-government." These terms should not be understood to imply either that these states are democratically constituted (as in "self-determination") or that they necessarily govern a homogeneous "national" community, but simply that these regimes are locally constituted and from the standpoint of international law may be considered sovereign.

2 Mary Clabaugh Wright, *The Last Stand of Chinese Conservatism: The T'ung-Chih Restoration, 1862–1874* (Stanford University Press, 2nd ed., 1962), chapter 3; Dorothy Borg, *American Policy and the Chinese Revolution, 1925–1928* (Macmillan, 1947), and Borg, *The United States and the Far Eastern Crisis of 1933–1938* (Harvard University Press, 1964); Tang Tsou, *America's Failure in China* (University of Chicago Press, 1963), chapter 1; Akira Iriye, *The Cold War in Asia: A Historical Introduction* (Prentice-Hall, 1974), chapter 2; Paul W. Schroeder, *The Axis Alliance and Japanese-American Relations, 1941* (Cornell University Press, 1958), pp. 200ff.; and the collection of documents usefully assembled in Paul Hibbert Clyde, *United*

*States Policy Toward China: Diplomatic and Public Documents,
1839–1939* (Russell and Russell, N.Y., 1964).

3 *Treaties and Conventions Concluded between the United States
of America and Other Powers since July 4, 1776* (Government Printing Office, 1889), p. 907.

4 Although this has been documented by a number of "revisionist"
historians (such as Walter LaFeber, *The New Empire: An Interpretation of American Expansion, 1860–1895* [Cornell University Press,
1963], and Charles S. Campbell, *The Transformation of American
Foreign Relations, 1865–1900* [Harper & Row, 1976]), it is often overlooked to what extent the more "mainstream" historians recognized
these developments. See, for example, Samuel Flagg Bemis, *The
Latin American Policy of the United States: An Historical Interpretation* (Harcourt Brace Jovanovich, 1943), p. 123: "It was widely believed [in the 1890s] that the home market for manufactured goods
was saturated, that in the future the United States must compete for
world markets with the great industrial nations, the world powers,
and that to sustain this competition it must be prepared to have a
navy and naval bases more than enough to protect the continental
United States." See, too, J. Fred Rippy, *British Investments in Latin
America, 1822–1949: A Case Study in the Operations of Private Enterprise in Retarded Regions* (University of Minnesota Press, 1959),
pp. 197–8.

5 Department of State, *Foreign Relations of the United States* (hereinafter referred to as *FRUS*), 1903, pp. 91ff. (article 7 on mining); and
1914, p. 134.

6 David A. Wilson, "Principles and Profits: Standard Oil Responses
to Chinese Nationalism, 1925–1927," *Pacific Historical Review*,
XLVI, 4, 1977.

7 Other instances may be found discussed in Eugene Staley, *War
and the Private Investor: A Study in the Relations of International
Politics and International Private Investment* (University of Chicago
Press, 1935; reprinted by Howard Fertig, N.Y., 1967), pp. 398ff.; and,
for the period after World War I, see William Roger Louis, *British
Strategy in the Far East, 1919–1939* (Oxford University Press, 1978),
pp. 120, 126ff.

8 Mira Wilkins, *The Emergence of Multinational Enterprise:
American Business Abroad from the Colonial Era to 1914* (Harvard
University Press, 1970), pp. 120–1.

9 Charles C. Cumberland, *Mexico, The Struggle for Modernity* (Oxford University Press, 1968), chapter 8.

10   Staley, *War and the Private Investor* (n. 7), p. 396.

11   Cole Blasier, *The Hovering Giant: U.S. Responses to Revolutionary Change in Latin America* (University of Pittsburgh Press, 1976), chapter 5; Karl M. Schmitt, *Mexico and the United States, 1821–1973* (Wiley, 1974), chapter 6.

12   William Appleman Williams and the group of historians that acknowledges his influence generally advance this interpretation. See his *The Tragedy of American Diplomacy* (Dell, 1962).

13   Rupert Emerson, *From Empire to Nation: The Rise to Self-Assertion of Asian and African Peoples* (Beacon Press, 1964).

14   Ernest R. May, *American Imperialism: A Speculative Essay* (Atheneum, 1968).

15   Joseph Stalin, *Foundations of Leninism* (Moscow, 1924), part 6.

16   Paul A. Varg, "The Economic Side of the Good Neighbor Policy: The Reciprocal Trade Program and South America," *Pacific Historical Review*, 95, 1976, pp. 56–61.

17   Cited in Theodore Friend, *Between Two Empires: The Ordeal of the Philippines, 1921–1946* (Yale University Press, 1965), p. 105. For the debate over independence, see Part 3 of Friend's book. On Philippine immigration and the problems it created in the United States, see Robert A. Divine, *American Immigration Policy, 1924–1952* (Yale University Press, 1957), pp. 68–76.

18   An excellent discussion of Wilson's economic policies remains William Diamond's *The Economic Thought of Woodrow Wilson* (Johns Hopkins University Press, 1943).

19   In the case of the Far East, Williams's *The Tragedy* (n. 12) makes a biazarre case for the central importance of the Open Door Policy in American thinking despite the fact that force was not used to protect it. For a contrary, and more credible, reading, see Paul A. Varg, *The Making of a Myth: The United States and China, 1897–1912* (Michigan State University Press, 1978), and Christopher Thorne, *Allies of a Kind: The United States, Britain and the War Against Japan, 1941–1945* (Oxford University Press, 1978), pp. 22ff.

20   Bryce Wood, *The Making of the Good Neighbor Policy* (Columbia University Press, 1961), p. 5; Alexander DeConde, *A History of American Foreign Policy* (Scribner, 1971), p. 536.

21   Benjamin H. Williams, *Economic Foreign Policy of the United States* (Howard Fertig, N.Y., 1967; first printed in 1929), chapter 3 and passim.

22   Bemis, *Latin American Policy* (n. 4), pp. 108ff.

23 Holger H. Herwig, *Politics of Frustration: The United States in German Naval Planning, 1889–1901* (Little, Brown, 1976), p. 68.

24 Bemis, *Latin American Policy* (n. 4), chapter 9; Dana G. Munro, *Intervention and Dollar Diplomacy in the Caribbean, 1900–1921* (Princeton University Press, 1964), chapter 12 and passim.

25 Article 27 is reprinted as an appendix in Robert Freeman Smith, *The United States and Revolutionary Nationalism in Mexico, 1916–1932* (University of Chicago Press, 1972).

26 See ibid. and the sources cited in note 11. For later instances of North American tenaciousness on these issues see, for example, the letters and memoranda of Cordell Hull reprinted in *FRUS*, 1938, "Mexico."

27 Cited in Arthur S. Link, *Wilson: The New Freedom* (Princeton University Press, 1956), p. 379.

28 Stephen D. Krasner, *Defending the National Interest: Raw Materials Investments and U.S. Foreign Policy* (Princeton University Press, 1978), pp. 156–78.

29 Blasier, *The Hovering Giant* (n. 11), chapter 7; and Krasner, *Defending the National Interest* (n. 28), pp. 178–88.

30 Robert Dallek, *Franklin D. Roosevelt and American Foreign Policy, 1932–1945* (Oxford University Press, 1979), pp. 175ff. Dulles is cited in Christopher Mitchell, "Dominance and Fragmentation in U.S. Latin American Policy," in Julio Cotler and Richard R. Fagen, eds., *Latin America and the United States: The Changing Political Realities* (Stanford University Press, 1974), p. 183.

31 Jane Degras, ed., *The Communist International: Volume I, 1919–1923* (Oxford University Press, 1956), p. 43.

32 Jane Degras, ed., *The Communist International: Volume II, 1923–1928* (Oxford University Press, 1960), pp. 25–6.

33 For Anglo-American relations, see the two comprehensive studies: William Roger Louis, *Imperialism at Bay: The United States and the Decolonization of the British Empire, 1941–1945* (Oxford University Press, 1978); and Thorne, *Allies of a Kind* (n. 19).

34 John Lewis Gaddis, *The United States and the Origins of the Cold War, 1941–1947* (Columbia University Press, 1972), pp. 17, 173. See, too, Daniel Yergin, *Shattered Peace: The Origins of the Cold War and the National Security State* (Houghton Mifflin, 1977), chapter 2; Diane Shaver Clemens, *Yalta* (Oxford University Press, 1970), chapter 8; Dallek, *Franklin D. Roosevelt* (n. 30), pp. 436ff., 524–5, and passim. For a review of rival interpretations of the period in American policy that is an interesting argument in its own right, see Geri

Lundestad, *The American Non-Policy Towards Eastern Europe, 1943–7* (Humanities Press, 1975).

35 *FRUS*, 1944, V, pp. 119–20 for Department of State; p. 121 for FDR. The general theme is reiterated on pp. 113–31.

36 Cordell Hull, *The Memoirs of Cordell Hull*, vol. 2 (Macmillan, 1948), p. 1599.

37 On India, *FRUS*, 1941, III: on independence, for example, pp. 176–7; on economic arrangements, for example, pp. 191ff. On Southeast Asia, see Hull, *Memoirs*, (n. 36), vol. 2, pp. 1600–1.

38 Iriye, *The Cold War in Asia* (n. 2), p. 87.

39 Hull, *Memoirs*, (n. 36), vol. 2, chapters 109 and 110.

40 Although the project was never realized, the plans are most interesting. See especially the Memorandum of the Interdivisional Petroleum Commission of the Department of State, reprinted in *FRUS*, 1944, V, pp. 27ff., and the Memorandum of Understanding, *FRUS*, 1944, III, pp. 111ff.

41 *FRUS*, 1948, VI, p. 44.

42 Ibid., pp. 28–9.

43 Dwight D. Eisenhower, *Mandate for Change, 1953–1956* (Doubleday, 1963), p. 372.

44 *FRUS*, 1948, VI, p. 116.

45 Ibid., passim.

46 Neil Sheehan et al., *The Pentagon Papers* (Bantam Books, 1971), chapter 1; Walter LaFeber, "Roosevelt, Churchill and Indochina: 1942–1945," *American Historical Review*, 80, 5, December 1975; Thorne, *Allies of a Kind* (n. 19), chapters 7, 13, 20, 27; Dallek, *Franklin D. Roosevelt* (n. 30), pp. 512ff.

47 *FRUS*, 1948, VI, p. 48.

48 Ibid., p. 551.

49 Ibid., p. 49.

50 L. S. Stavrianos, *Greece: American Dilemma and Opportunity* (Henry Regnery, Chicago, 1952), pp. 186–9 and passim.

51 Department of State, *China White Paper* (Washington, 1949), p. 652.

52 Degras, *The Communist International: Volume II* (n. 32) pp. 342, 460. Stalin's famous phrase might be recalled: The CCP was eventually to abandon the United Front and "squeeze them (the KMT) like a lemon." See Adam Ulam, *Expansion and Coexistence: The History of Soviet Foreign Policy, 1917–1967* (Praeger, 1968), pp. 167ff.

53 In this and the following three paragraphs, I am largely following the discussion in Iriye, *The Cold War in Asia* (n. 2), chapters 3 and 4; also, Tsou, *America's Failure in China* (n. 2).

54 *China White Paper* (n. 51), pp. xiv, xvi.

55 Dean Acheson, *Present at the Creation: My Years in the State Department* (Norton, 1969), p. 344; Mao Tse-tung, *Selected Readings from the Works of Mao Tse-tung* (Foreign Language Press, Peking, 1971), pp. 345ff.

56 Ibid., and *China White Paper* (n. 51), p. 723.

57 Michael Schaller, *The U.S. Crusade in China, 1938–1945* (Columbia University Press, 1978). For an opposing view, see Ulam, *Expansion* (n. 52), pp. 470ff.

58 Department of State, *Bulletin*, 32, 551, p. 115.

59 *FRUS*, 1949, IX, p. 309.

60 See, for example, the British correspondence in ibid., pp. 57–61.

61 Department of State, *Bulletin*, 32, 550, January 16, 1950, p. 79. See also John W. Spanier, *The Truman-MacArthur Controversy and the Korean War* (Norton, 1965), chapter 3.

62 James A. Nathan and James K. Oliver, *United States Foreign Policy and World Order* (Little, Brown, 1976), pp. 128ff.

63 Robert W. Tucker, *The Radical Left and American Foreign Policy* (Johns Hopkins University Press, 1971), p. 109.

64 Dwight D. Eisenhower, *Waging Peace, 1956–1961* (Doubleday, 1965), pp. 42–4, 176.

65 Townsend Hoopes, *The Devil and John Foster Dulles: The Diplomacy of the Eisenhower Era* (Little, Brown, 1973), chapters 21 and 22.

66 Eisenhower, *Waging Peace* (n. 64), p. 99.

67 John S. Badeau, *The American Approach to the Arab World* (Harper & Row, 1968), pp. 7–8.

68 Eisenhower, *Mandate for Change* (n. 43), pp. 363, 373. Secretary of State Dulles was of the same opinion. Eisenhower quotes him as writing in 1954: "We would want to have a success. We could not afford thus to engage the prestige of the United States and suffer a defeat which would have world-wide repercussions." (*Mandate for Change*, p. 345).

69 On Yemen, see Badeau, *The American Approach* (n. 67), chapter 7; on the other cases, see the accounts in Arthur M. Schlesinger, Jr., *A Thousand Days: John F. Kennedy in the White House* (Houghton Mifflin, 1965), passim.

70 John F. Kennedy, *The Strategy of Peace* (Harper & Row, 1960), p. 60.

71 Schlesinger, *A Thousand Days* (n. 69), p. 276.

72 Kennedy, *Strategy for Peace* (n. 70), p. 61.

73 Daniel Ellsberg, *Papers on the War* (Pocket Books, 1972), pp. 99–101.

74 For a sample of American writing on the subject, including speeches by high government officials, see T. N. Greene, ed., *The Guerrilla – and How to Fight Him: Selections from the Marine Corps Gazette* (Praeger, 1966). For a review of the period, see Douglas S. Blaufarb, *The Counterinsurgency Era: U.S. Doctrine and Performance, 1950 to the Present* (Free Press, 1977). For an interesting study of counterinsurgency in the French case, see John Steward Ambler, *Soldiers Against the State: The French Army in Politics* (Doubleday, 1968), part 3.

75 Blaufarb, *The Counterinsurgency Era* (n. 74), chapters 3 and 4; Schlesinger, *A Thousand Days* (n. 69), pp. 340ff.

76 *Public Papers of the Presidents of the United States: John F. Kennedy, 1961* (Government Printing Office, 1962), p. 205.

77 Schlesinger, *A Thousand Days* (n. 69), p. 259. See also Leslie H. Gelb with Richard K. Betts, *The Irony of Vietnam: The System Worked* (Brookings Institution, 1979), chapter 3.

78 Sheehan, *The Pentagon Papers* (n. 46), p. 128, and Arthur M. Schlesinger, Jr., *The Bitter Heritage: Vietnam and American Democracy, 1941–1961* (Houghton Mifflin, 1966), p. 21.

79 *Public Papers of the President of the United States: Richard Nixon, 1969* (Government Printing Office, 1970), p. 548.

80 *Public Papers of the President of the United States: Richard Nixon, 1970* (Government Printing Office, 1971), pp. 116, 118.

81 Ibid., p. 120.

82 Henry A. Kissinger, *White House Years* (Little, Brown, 1979), p. 915.

83 Henry A. Kissinger, "The Process of Détente" (1974), in Kissinger, *American Foreign Policy* (Norton, 1977, 3rd ed.), p. 147.

84 Henry A. Kissinger, "The Permanent Challenge of Peace: U.S. Policy Toward the Soviet Union" (1976), in ibid., pp. 317–18, 321.

85 Public address by Zbigniew Brzezinski at Harvard University, February 19, 1980, and interview in the *New York Times*, March 30, 1980.

86 *FRUS*, 1945, VII, pp. 107, 113–14.

87 See David P. Calleo and Benjamin M. Rowland, *America and the World Political Economy: Atlantic Dreams and National Realities* (Indiana University Press, 1973), part 2; Robert Gilpin, *U.S. Power* and the *Multinational Corporation: The Political Economy of Foreign Direct Investment* (Basic Books, 1975), chapters 3 and 4; Varg, "The Economic Side of the Good Neighbor Policy," (n. 16); and Irwin F. Gellman, *Good Neighbor Diplomacy: United States Policies in Latin America, 1933–1945* (Johns Hopkins University Press, 1979). For a comparison of British and American policies, see Stephen D. Krasner, "State Power and the Structure of International Trade," *World Politics*, 28, 3, April 1976. See also Peter J. Katzenstein, "Conclusion: Domestic Structures and Strategies of Foreign Economic Policy," in Katzenstein, ed., *Between Power and Plenty: Foreign Economic Policies of Advanced Industrial States* (University of Wisconsin Press, 1978), which first appeared as the Autumn 1977 edition of *International Organization*, 31, 4.

88 Even the study favoring most strongly the analysis of U.S. policy as based on considerations of state, rather than on those of self-interested, particularistic groups, is quick to admit that this country has a relatively weak state deeply penetrated by business interests. See Krasner, *Defending the National Interest* (n. 28). Whereas Krasner's central focus is on the distinction between the Congress and the presidency with respect to American policy, Blasier, *The Hovering Giant* (n. 11), chapter 7, makes an equally useful distinction by pointing to the different results when American policy is directed by the president or when, instead, it is left in the hands of middle-rank individuals such as ambassadors. On splits that may occur within the business community and that give the state special advantages, see Joan Hoff Wilson, *American Business and Foreign Policy, 1920–1933* (University Press of Kentucky, 1971), chapter 1; and Charles H. Lipson, "Corporate Preferences and Public Policies: Foreign Aid Sanctions and Investment Protection," *World Politics*, 28, 3, April 1976.

89 Edward S. Mason and Robert E. Asher, *The World Bank since Bretton Woods* (Brookings Institution, 1973), p. 434.

90 Richard Stuart Olson, "Economic Coercion in World Politics: With a Focus on North-South Relations," *World Politics*, 31, 4, July 1979, pp. 485ff.; and Steven J. Rosen, "The Open Door Imperative and U.S. Foreign Policy," in Steven J. Rosen and James R. Kurth, eds., *Testing Theories of Economic Imperialism* (Heath, 1974).

91 The Rockefeller Panel Reports, *Prospect for America* (Doubleday, 1961), p. 13.

92 R. Peter DeWitt, Jr., *The Inter-American Development Bank and*

Political Influence: With Special Reference to Costa Rica (Praeger, 1977).

93 Gabriel Kolko and Joyce Kolko, *The Limits of Power: The World and United States Foreign Policy, 1945–1954* (Harper & Row, 1972), p. 2.

94 Ibid., pp. 254, 263.

95 *FRUS*, 1949, IX, pp. 57–61 and passim.

96 Mira Wilkins, *The Maturing of Multinational Enterprises: American Business Abroad from 1914 to 1970* (Harvard University Press, 1974), pp. 397–8.

97 Krasner, *Defending the National Interest* (n. 28), p. 218. See, too, James R. Kurth, "Testing Theories of Economic Imperialism," in Rosen and Kurth, *Testing Theories of Economic Imperialism* (n. 90); see also efforts to distinguish the reason for different American responses to expropriations in Blasier, *The Hovering Giant* (n. 11), chapter 7 and passim.

98 Richard N. Gardner, *Sterling-Dollar Diplomacy: The Origins and the Prospects of Our International Economic Order* (McGraw-Hill, 1969), especially "Introduction: A Twenty-Five Year Perspective" in the 2nd ed., and chapters 15 and 16 on the necessary postwar political adjustments. Charles S. Maier, "The Politics of Productivity: Foundations of American International Economic Policy after World War II," in Katzenstein, *Between Power and Plenty* (n. 87).

99 The alliance's charter is reprinted in State Department, *Bulletin*, September 1961.

100 Richard Barnet, *Roots of War: The Men and Institutions behind U.S. Foreign Policy* (Penguin Books, 1971); Gelb with Betts, *The Irony of Vietnam* (n. 77); Daniel Ellsberg, "The Myth of the Quagmire Machine," in Ellsberg, *Papers on the War* (n. 73).

101 Edmund Burke, "Letters on a Regicide Peace," in *Edmund Burke: Selected Works*, ed. W. J. Bate (Random House, 1960), pp. 478–82.

102 Text reprinted in Joseph Marion Jones, *The Fifteen Weeks (February 21–June 5, 1947)* (Harcourt Brace Jovanovich, 1955), pp. 269ff.

103 Eisenhower, *Mandate* (n. 43), p. 347.

104 Cited in Nathan and Oliver, *United States Foreign Policy* (n. 62), p. 356.

105 Kissinger, *White House Years* (n. 82), pp. 655–7.

106 Robert A. Packenham, *Liberal America and the Third World: Political Development Ideas in Foreign Aid and Social Science* (Princeton University Press, 1973), especially pp. 25–49.

107   John D. Martz, *Acción Democrática: Evolution of a Modern Political Party in Venezuela* (Princeton University Press, 1966).

108   Schlesinger, *A Thousand Days* (n. 69), p. 769.

109   Ibid., pp. 223, 187, 195.

110   On the organization of hemispheric defense against fascism, see Dallek, *Franklin D. Roosevelt* (n. 30), pp. 175ff.

111   Rusk is cited in Nathan and Oliver, *United States Foreign Policy* (n. 62), p. 182. And see Roger Hilsman's foreword to Vo Nguyen Giap, *People's War, People's Army* (Praeger, 1968), as well as his speech reprinted in Greene, *The Guerrilla* (n. 74).

112   On Lenin, see Degras, *Communist International: Volume II* (n. 32), cited p. 346; on Stalin, *Foundations of Leninism* (n. 15), part 6; on Lin Piao, "Long Live the Victory of People's War!" (Foreign Language Press, Peking, 1967), pp. 48–9.

113   U.S. Congress, Senate, Committee on Foreign Relations, Subcommittee on U.S. Security Agreements and Commitments Abroad, *U.S. Security Agreements and Commitments Abroad* (1971), vol. 2, p. 2417.

114   Gale W. McGee, *The Responsibilities of World Power* (The National Press, 1968), p. 83.

115   Cited in the *New York Times*, September 10, 1979.

116   This has been most effectively discussed in Stanley Hoffmann, *Primacy or World Order: American Foreign Policy since the Cold War* (McGraw-Hill, 1978).

117   Kissinger, *White House Years* (n. 82), p. 65.

118   Walter J. Levy, "Oil and the Decline of the West," *Foreign Affairs*, 58, 5, Summer 1980; J. B. Kelley, *Arabia, the Gulf and the West* (Basic Books, 1980), chapters 7–8.

Chapter 5. American imperialism in the early 1980s

1   George Liska, *Imperial America: The International Politics of Primacy* (Johns Hopkins University Press, 1967), preface and p. 180.

2   Some theoretical works had anticipated such developments as these, however. See Samuel P. Huntington, *Political Order in Changing Societies* (Yale University Press, 1968), chapter 3.

3   National Security Adviser Zbigniew Brzezinski was explicitly cited to this effect on October 31, 1979: see the *New York Times*, November 1, 1979.

4   Barry M. Blechman and Stephen S. Kaplan, "U.S. Military Forces as a Political Instrument," *Political Science Quarterly*, 95, 2, Summer 1979.

5 Stockholm International Peace Research Institute, *The Arms Trade with the Third World* (Almqvist and Wiksells Boktyckeri, Stockholm, 1971), p. 166. Another source puts the number of Latin Americans trained in the United States between 1945 and 1972 at 200,000, with another 30,000 in Panama. See Miles D. Wolpin, *Military Aid and Counterrevolution in the Third World* (Heath, 1972), p. 73.

6 U.S. Arms Control and Disarmament Agency, *World Military Expenditures and Arms Transfers, 1967–1976*, July 1978, table 7.

7 Central Intelligence Agency, National Foreign Assessment Center, *Communist Aid to Less Developed Countries of the Free World, 1977* (1978), tables 2 and 6; and United States Arms Control and Disarmament Agency, *World Military Expenditures and Arms Transfer, 1968–1977* (Government Printing Office, 1979), table IV.

8 Organization for Economic Cooperation and Development, *Economic Outlook*, 27, July 1980, p. 5; United Nations, *Monthly Bulletin of Statistics*, June 1980, table 52.

9 Department of Commerce, "OPEC Transactions in the U.S. International Accounts, 1972–1977," *Survey of Current Business*, April 1978, p. 21, table 1.

10 See, for example, Stephen Krasner, "Oil is the Exception," *Foreign Policy*, 15, Summer 1974; Raymond F. Mikesell, "More Third World Cartels Ahead?" *Challenge*, 17, 5, November-December 1974; The Brookings Institution, "Trade in Primary Commodities: Conflict or Cooperation?" *Tripartite Report by 15 Economists from Japan, the European Community and the United States*, October 1974.

11 Carlo M. Cipolla, *The Economic History of World Population* (Penguin Books, 6th ed., 1976), pp. 43ff.

12 United Nations, *Monthly Bulletin of Statistics*, August 1979 (corrected).

13 Albert Hirschman, *National Power and the Structure of Foreign Trade* (University of California Press, 1969), p. 36.

14 Richard Graham, *Britain and the Onset of Modernization in Brazil, 1850–1914* (Cambridge University Press, 1968), pp. 73, 320.

15 Edward Hallett Carr, *The Bolshevik Revolution, 1917–1923* (Macmillan, 1961), vol. 3, p. 61.

16 World Bank, *Annual Report*, 1979, p. 136.

17 C. Fred Bergsten et al., *American Multinationals and American*

Interests (Brookings Institution, 1978), passim; and Robert Gilpin, *U.S. Power and the Multinational Corporation* (Basic Books, 1975).

18 Dale Johnson, "Dependence and the International System," in James D. Cockcroft et al., *Dependency and Underdevelopment: Latin America's Political Economy* (Doubleday, Anchor Books, 1972), p. 75n, 94n.

19 Department of Commerce, "U.S. Direct Investment Abroad in 1976," and "Sales by Majority-Owned Foreign Affiliates of U.S. Companies, 1974," in *Survey of Current Business*, August 1977 and May 1976 respectively. The point is crucial in establishing the role of the multinationals in capital accumulation on the periphery. Raymond Vernon, *Storm Over Multinationals* (Harvard University Press, 1977), p. 124, reports that the United States government collected $1 billion in taxes from American enterprises abroad in 1972, whereas foreign governments obtained $13 billion. See also Vernon, *Restrictive Business Practices: The Operations of United States Enterprises in Developing Countries: Their Role in Trade and Development* (UNCTAD, 1972), p. 14; and Raymond Mikesell, *Foreign Investment in the Petroleum and Mineral Industries* (Johns Hopkins University Press, 1971), p. 428.

20 Department of Commerce, "Sources and Uses of Funds for a Sample of Majority-Owned Foreign Affiliates of U.S. Companies," *Survey of Current Business*, July 1975.

21 Richard J. Barnet and Ronald E. Mueller, *Global Reach: The Power of the Multinational Corporations* (Simon & Schuster, 1974), pp. 154–5. On a different yet related topic, see Stanley Lebergott, "The Returns to U.S. Imperialism, 1890–1929," *The Journal of Economic History*, 40, 2, June 1980.

22 James W. Vaupel and Joan P. Curhan, *The Making of Multinational Enterprise* (Graduate School of Business Administration, Harvard University, 1969), pp. 240–1 for expansion; pp. 376–7 and 505 for losses.

23 Department of Commerce, "U.S. Direct Investment Abroad in 1976," *Survey of Current Business*, August 1977, tables 4 and 5.

24 For example, on Mexico, see Richard Weinert, "The State and Foreign Capital," in José Luis Reyna and Weinert, eds., *Authoritarianism in Mexico* (Institute for the Study of Human Issues, Philadelphia, 1977); on Southeast Asia, see Franklin Weinstein, "Multinational Corporations and the Third World: The Case of Japan and Southeast Asia," *International Organization*, 30, 3, Summer 1976; on Nigeria, see *African Development*, 10, 12, December 1975. Raymond Vernon has described this general process as the "obsolescing bargain" (see n. 19), whereas Theodore H. Moran writes of the "learning curve" whereby over time host states become progressively stronger relative to multinational corporations: See his "Multinational Corporations and Dependency: A Dialogue for Dependentistas and Non-Dependentistas," *International Organization*, 32, 1, Winter 1978. See also David A. Jodice, "Sources of Change in Third World Regimes for Foreign Direct Investment, 1968–1976," *International Organization* 34, 2, Spring 1980.

25 Whereas the North accounted for some 70 percent of southern trade between 1972 and 1978, the South was responsible for less than 25 percent of northern commerce. See United Nations, *Monthly Bulletin of Statistics*, annual June edition. On aid, see World Bank, *Annual Report*, various years; and the annual Organization for Economic Cooperation and Development (OECD) publication *Development Cooperation: Efforts and Policies of the Members of the Development Assistance Committee*.

26 This development is suggested in statistics on manufacturing investment and sales and their increase over time provided by the Department of Commerce in articles such as "U.S. Direct Investment Abroad in 1977," and "Sales by Majority-Owned Foreign Affiliates of U.S. Companies," *Survey of Current Business*, August 1978 and May 1976 respectively.

27 "Covert Action in Chile, 1963–1973," Staff Report of the Select Committee to Study Governmental Operations with Respect to Intelligence Activities, United States Senate (Government Printing Office, 1975).

28 See Peter A. Goldberg, "The Politics of the Allende Overthrow in Chile," *Political Science Quarterly*, 90, 1, Spring 1975, especially pp. 108ff.

29 Stanley Hoffmann, "Notes on the Elusiveness of Modern Power," *International Journal*, Spring 1975; and, in the same edition of this journal, Susan Strange, "What Is Economic Power, and Who Has It?".

30 For example, see various issues of *Foreign Trade*, published by the Ministry of Foreign Trade, Moscow. In Western writing, see, among others, Elizabeth Kridl Valkenier, "The USSR, the Third World, and the Global Economy," *Problems of Communism*, 28, 4, July–August 1979; and Richard Lowenthal, "A Strategy of Counter-Imperialism," reprinted in his *Model or Ally? The Communist Powers and the Developing Countries* (Oxford University Press, 1977).

31 United Nations, *Monthly Bulletin of Statistics*, July 1980.

32 Organization for Economic Cooperation and Development, *Development Cooperation*, 1979, pp. 139, 131.

33 For example, see the discussions in O. V. Kuusinen et al., *Fundamentals of Marxism-Leninism* (Foreign Language Publishing House, Moscow, 1963, 2nd rev. ed.), chapter 25; and Shalva Sanakoyev, *The World Socialist System: Main Problems, Stages of Development* (Progress Publishers, Moscow, 1972).

34 For a general account, see Roger E. Kanet, ed., *The Soviet Union and the Developing Nations* (Johns Hopkins University Press, 1974); and Hugh Seton-Watson, *The Imperialist Revolutionaries: Trends in World Communism in the 1960s and 1970s* (Hoover Institution Press, 1978), chapters 3, 6, 7. See also the documents collected in Jane Degras, ed., *The Communist International: Volume I, 1919–1923* (Oxford University Press, 1956).

35 See also Lenin's *Theses on the National and Colonial Questions* (1920).

36 United States Arms Control and Disarmament Agency, *World Military Expenditures and Arms Transfer, 1968–1977* (Government Printing Office, 1979).

37 Central Intelligence Agency (National Foreign Assessment Center), *Communist Aid to Less Developed Countries of the Free World, 1977* (1978), tables 2 and 6.

38 Shao Chuan Leng and Norman D. Palmer, *Sun Yat-sen and Communism* (Praeger, 1960); and Richard Lowenthal, "The Soviet Model of One-Party Rule and Its Impact," in his *Model or Ally?* (n. 30).

39 Babrak Karmal, "The Afghan People Will Stand Firmly on Guard of the Revolution," *World Marxist Review* (also published as *Problems of Peace and Socialism*), 23, 4, April 1980, p. 3; and Alvaro Ramírez, "Nicaragua: From Armed Struggle to Construction," *World Marxist Review*, 23, 1, January 1980, p. 52.

40 For an overall assessment, see David D. Finley, *Some Aspects of Conventional Military Capability in Soviet Foreign Relations* (Working Paper 20, Center for International and Strategic Affairs, University of California, Los Angeles, February 1980). On the Soviet navy, see James M. McConnell and Bradford Dismukes, "Soviet Diplomacy of Force in the Third World," *Problems of Communism*, 28, 1, January–February 1979.

41 On the Soviet affirmations, see various issues of the digest of Soviet word and action in *USSR and Third World* (formerly published as *Mizan*) (Central Asian Research Centre, London).

42 United Nations, *Monthly Bulletin of Statistics*, June 1979.

43 Organization for Economic Cooperation and Development, *Economic Outlook*, 25, July 1979, table 1.

44 Campbell R. McConnell, "Why is U.S. Productivity Slowing Down?" *Harvard Business Review*, 57, 2, March–April 1979, comparative table, p. 38.

45 See, for example, Edward N. Luttwak, "After Afghanistan, What?" *Commentary*, 69, 4, April 1980; and Raymond Aron in various issues of *L'Express* (as in July 1980).

46 V. Nekrasov, *Pravda*, June 9, 1980, cited in *The Current Digest of the Soviet Press*, 32, 23, July 9, 1980.

47 Miles Kahler, "Rumors of War: The 1914 Analogy," *Foreign Affairs*, 58, 2, Winter 1979–80.

48 For assessments discounting the importance of Soviet military gains relative to those of the United States, see Barry R. Posen and Stephen W. Van Evera, "Overarming and Underwhelming," *Foreign Policy*, 40, Fall 1980; and Arthur Macy Cox, "The CIA's Tragic Error," *The New York Review of Books*, November 6, 1980.

49 Dimitri K. Simes, "The Death of Detente?" *International Security*, 5, 1, Summer 1980; Robert Legvold, "Containment Without Confrontation," *Foreign Policy*, 40, Fall 1980.

50 Stanley Hoffmann, *Primacy or World Order: American Foreign Policy since the Cold War* (McGraw-Hill, 1978), pp. 243, 263.

51 Ellen Frey-Wouters, *The European Community and the Third World: The Lomé Convention and Its Impact* (Praeger, 1980).

52 On the growing domestic and regional problems of the Third World at the beginning of the 1980s, see Fouad Ajami, "The Fate of Nonalignment," *Foreign Affairs*, 59, 2, Winter 1980–1. For indications of likely American future action prevalent at the time, see Robert W. Tucker, "The Purposes of American Power," *Foreign Affairs*, 59, 2, Winter 1980–1; Jeane Kirkpatrick, "U.S. Security and Latin America," *Commentary*, 71, 1, January 1981; and Norman Podhoretz, *The Present Danger* (Simon & Schuster, 1980).

Appendix: A note concerning moral issues and American imperialism

1 Friedrich Engels in the Chartist newspaper *Northern Star*, January 22, 1848. Marx's 1853 articles for the *New York Daily Tribune* on Britain in India are better-known statements of this same view.

2 The text is reprinted in United Nations, *UNCTAD, Second Session, New Delhi*, vol. 1, *Report and Annexes*, p. 431.

3 United Nations, *UNCTAD, Third Session, Santiago de Chile*, vol. 1.

4 Algerian Mission to the United Nations, *Petroleum, Raw Materials and Development*, April 1974, p. x.

5 The charter is reprinted in U.S. Department of State, *Selected Documents*, "The Challenge of the Third World: Seventh Special Session of the U.N. General Assembly," September 1–2, 1975, pp. 8ff.

6 The Manila Declaration and Programme of Action, reprinted in United Nations, *Proceedings of the United Nations Conference on Trade and Development* (Nairobi), vol. 1, annex 5, 1977, p. 110.

7 Cited in the *New York Times*, October 13, 1979. See also Robert W. Tucker, *The Inequality of Nations* (Basic Books, 1977).

8 Organization for Economic Cooperation and Development, *Development Cooperation: Efforts and Policies of the Members of the Development Assistance Committee*, 1979, annex 4. See also Morris D. Morris, *Measuring the Condition of the World's Poor: The Physical Quality of Life Index* (Pergamon Press, 1979). See, too, Graciela Chichilnisky, "Development Patterns and International Order," *Journal of International Affairs*, 31, 2, Fall/Winter 1977.

9 See, for example, Peter Singer, "Reconsidering the Famine Relief Argument," in Peter C. Brown and Henry Shue, eds., *Food Policy: The Responsibility of the United States in the Life and Death Choices* (Free Press, 1977). For a generally similar approach, see the essays collected in William Aiken and Hugh La Follette, eds., *World Hunger and Moral Obligation* (Prentice-Hall, 1977).

10 Frantz Fanon, *The Wretched of the Earth* (Grove Press, 1966), p. 76.

11 For a similar point of view expressed by North Americans, see Frances Moore Lappé and Joseph Collins with Gary Fowler, *Food First: Beyond the Myth of Scarcity* (Houghton Mifflin, 1977); and Michael Harrington, *The Vast Majority: A Journey to the World's Poor* (Simon & Schuster, 1977).

12 Charles R. Beitz, *Political Theory and International Relations* (Princeton University Press, 1979).

13 Under Robert McNamara the World Bank has been instrumental in analyzing these problems and trying to address them. Two books published under its auspices are Irma Adelman and Cynthia Taft Morris, *Economic Growth and Social Equity* (Stanford University Press, 1973); and Hollis Chenery et al., *Redistribution with Growth* (Oxford University Press, 1974). On efforts by the bank to improve the position of the small farmer in the developing countries see World Bank, *Annual Report*, 1978, pp. 17ff.; and *World Development Report*, 1979, pp. 88ff.

14   The documentation is abundant. See, for example, Keith Griffin, *The Political Economy of Agrarian Change: An Essay on the "Green Revolution"* (Harvard University Press, 1974); and Gunnar Myrdal, *The Challenge of World Poverty: A World Anti-Poverty Program in Outline* (Pantheon Books, 1970), chapters 3 and 4.

15   On the spread of export crops relative to those for domestic consumption, see Cheryl Christensen, "World Hunger: A Structural Approach," *International Organization*, 32, 3, Summer 1978; also, Lappé, *Food First* (n. 11), part 8. On investment, see Peter Evans, *Dependent Development: The Alliance of Multinational, State, and Local Capital in Brazil* (Princeton University Press, 1979); on South Africa, E. J. Kahn, Jr., "Annals of International Trade," *The New Yorker*, May 14, 1979, and on Brazil, Sylvia Ann Hewlett, *The Cruel Dilemmas of Development: Twentieth-Century Brazil* (Basic Books, 1980).

16   James Petras, *Politics and Social Structure in Latin America* (Monthly Review Press, N.Y., 1970), part 3, section 3.

17   Department of State, *Bulletin*, September 1961, pp. 463ff.

18   Abraham F. Lowenthal, " 'Liberal,' 'Radical,' and 'Bureaucratic' Perspectives on U.S. Latin American Policy: The Alliance for Progress in Retrospect," and Richard R. Fagen, "Commentary on Einaudi," in Julio Cotler and Fagen, eds., *Latin America and the United States: The Changing Political Realities* (Stanford University Press, 1974).

19   Cited in Harry Magdoff, *The Age of Imperialism: The Economics of U.S. Foreign Policy* (Monthly Review Press, N.Y., 1969), p. 121.

20   Ibid., pp. 120–1.

21   Organization for Economic Cooperation and Development, *Development Cooperation* (n. 8), 1979, calculated from annex 4.

22   Carlo M. Cipolla, *The Economic History of World Population* (Penguin Books, 6th ed., 1976). See also Joel Migdal, *Peasants, Politics and Revolution: Pressures toward Political and Social Change in the Third World* (Princeton University Press, 1974), pp. 92ff.

23   See Stanley Hoffmann, "The Hell of Good Intentions," *Foreign Policy*, 29, Winter 1977–8.

24   See Ernst B. Haas, "Human Rights," in Kenneth A. Oye et al., *Eagle Entangled: U.S. Foreign Policy in a Complex World* (Longman, 1979).

25   Arthur Schlesinger, Jr., "Human Rights and the American Tradition," *Foreign Affairs*, 57, 3, 1978.

26   Myrdal, *The Challenge of World Poverty* (n. 14), pp. 362–3, 372.

Selected bibliography

The period of British hegemony (Chapters 1 to 3)

Allen, G. C. A Short Economic History of Modern Japan: 1867–1937. Praeger, 1962.

Amin, Samir. Accumulation on a World Scale: A Critique of the Theory of Underdevelopment. Monthly Review Press (New York), 1974.

Arendt, Hannah. The Origins of Totalitarianism, part 2. Harcourt Brace Jovanovich, 1951.

Aron, Raymond. Immuable et changeante: de la IVe à la Ve République. Calmann-Lévy (Paris), 1959.

Bailey, Frank Edgar. British Policy and the Turkish Reform Movement: A Study in Anglo-Turkish Relations, 1826–1853. Howard Fertig (New York), 1970.

Barale, Jean. La Constitution de la IVe République à l'épreuve de la guerre. Librarie Générale de Droit et de Jurisprudence, 1963.

Baran, Paul. The Political Economy of Growth, 2nd ed. Monthly Review Press (New York), 1962.

Barratt-Brown, Michael. After Imperialism. Humanities Press, 1970.

Bartlett, C. J. Great Britain and Sea Power, 1815–1853. Oxford University Press, 1963.

Bauer, P. T. "The Economics of Resentment: Economics and Underdevelopment." Journal of Contemporary History, 4, 1, January 1969.

Beloff, Max. "The Special Relationship: an Anglo-American Myth." In Martin Gilbert, ed., A Century of Conflict, 1850–1950: Essays for A. J. P. Taylor. Hamish Hamilton (London), 1966.

Berg, Elliot J. "The Economic Basis of Political Choice in French West Africa." American Political Science Review, LIV, 1960.

Cameron, Rondo, ed. *Banking and Economic Development: Some Lessons of History*. Oxford University Press, 1972.

Cardoso, Fernando Henrique. "Dependent Capitalist Development in Latin America." *The New Left Review*, 74, July-August 1972.

"Associated-Dependent Development: Theoretical and Practical Implications." In Alfred Stepan, ed., *Authoritarian Brazil: Origins, Policies and Future*. Yale University Press, 1973.

Cayrac-Blanchard, Françoise. *Le Parti communiste indonésien*. Armand Colin (Paris), 1973.

Chao, Kang. *The Development of Cotton Textile Production in China*. Harvard University Press, 1977.

Churchill, Winston S. *The World Crisis, 1911–1914*. Scribner, 1924.

Clark, Edward C. "The Ottoman Industrial Revolution." *International Journal of Middle East Studies*, V, January 1974.

Cohen, Benjamin J. *The Question of Imperialism: The Political Economy of Dominance and Dependence*. Basis Books, 1973.

Cohen, Paul A. "Ch'ing China: Confrontation with the West, 1850–1900." In James B. Crowley, ed., *Modern East Asia: Essays in Interpretation*. Harcourt Brace Jovanovich, 1970.

Cohen, William. "The French Colonial Service in West Africa." In Prosser Gifford and William Roger Louis, eds., *France and Britain in Africa: Imperial Rivalry and Colonial Rule*. Yale University Press, 1971.

Craig, Gordon A. *Germany, 1866–1945*. Oxford University Press, 1978.

Crozier, Michel. *The Bureaucratic Phenomenon*. University of Chicago Press, 1964.

Dallek, Robert. *Franklin D. Roosevelt and American Foreign Policy, 1932–1945*. Oxford University Press, 1979.

Dalton, Hugh. *High Tide and After: Memoirs, 1945–1960*. Frederick Muller (London), 1962.

De Gaulle, Charles. *La France sera la France*. F. Bouchy et Fils (Paris), 1951.

The Complete War Memoirs of Charles de Gaulle. Simon & Schuster, 1967.

De Porte, A. W. *De Gaulle's Foreign Policy, 1944–1946*. Harvard University Press, 1968.

Dernberger, Robert F. "The Role of the Foreigner in China's Economic Development, 1840–1949." In Dwight H. Perkins, ed., *China's Modern Economy in Historical Perspective*. Stanford University Press, 1975.

Deschamps, Hubert. "French Colonial Policy in Tropical Africa between the Two World Wars." In Prosser Gifford and William Roger Louis, eds., *France and Britain in Africa: Imperial Rivalry and Colonial Rule*. Yale University Press, 1971.

Dewey, Clive. "The End of the Imperialism of Free Trade: The Eclipse of the Lancashire Lobby and the Concession of Fiscal Autonomy to India." In Dewey and A. G. Hopkins, eds., *The Imperial Impact: Studies in the Economic History of Africa and India*. Athlone Press, 1978.

Diáz Alejandro, Carlos F. *Essays on the Economic History of the Argentine Republic*. Yale University Press, 1970.

Dike, K. Onwuka. *Trade and Politics in the Niger Delta, 1830–1885: An Introduction to the Economic and Political History of Nigeria*. Oxford University Press, 1956.

Dutt, Romesh. *The Economic History of India: In the Victorian Age, 1837–1900*, 2nd ed. Government of India, Ministry of Information and Broadcasting, 1970.

Eckstein, Alexander, et al. "The Economic Development of Manchuria: The Rise of a Frontier Economy." *The Journal of Economic History*, 34, 1, March 1974.

Eden, Anthony. *Full Circle*. Houghton Mifflin, 1960.

Eisenstadt, S. N. "Post-Traditional Societies and the Continuity and Reconstruction of Tradition." *Daedalus*, 102, Winter 1973.

Elgey, Georgette. *La République des illusions*. Fayard (Paris), 1965.

Epstein, Leon D. *British Politics in the Suez Crisis*. University of Illinois Press, 1964.

Evans, Peter. *Islamic Roots of Capitalism: Egypt, 1760–1840*. University of Texas Press, 1979.

Fairbank, John King. *The United States and China*, 2nd ed. Viking Press, 1958.

Feis, Herbert. *Europe, the World's Banker, 1870–1914: An Account of European Foreign Investment and the Connection of World Finance with Diplomacy before the War*. Yale University Press, 1930.

Ferns, H. S. *Britain and Argentina in the Nineteenth Century*. Oxford University Press, 1960.

Fieldhouse, K. K. "'Imperialism': An Historiographical Revision." *The Economic History Review*, second series, 14, 2, 1961.

    Economics and Empire, 1830–1914. Cornell University Press, 1973.

Fischer, Fritz. *Germany's Aims in the First World War*. Norton, 1967.

World Power or Decline: The Controversy over Germany's Aims in the First World War. Norton, 1974.

Ford, A. G. "British Investment and Argentine Economic Development, 1880–1914." In David Rock, ed., *Argentina in the Twentieth Century.* University of Pittsburgh Press, 1975.

Frank, André Gunder. "The Development of Underdevelopment." In James D. Cockcroft et al., *Dependence and Underdevelopment: Latin America's Political Economy.* Doubleday (Anchor Books), 1972.

"Economic Dependence, Class Structure, and Underdevelopment Policy." In James D. Cockcroft et al., *Dependence and Underdevelopment: Latin America's Political Economy.* Doubleday (Anchor Books), 1972.

"Sociology of Underdevelopment and Underdevelopment of Sociology." In James D. Cockcroft et al., *Dependence and Underdevelopment: Latin America's Political Economy.* Doubleday (Anchor Books), 1972.

Gallagher, John, and Ronald Robinson. "The Imperialism of Free Trade." *Economic History Review,* second series, 6, 1, 1953.

"The Partition of Africa." In *The New Cambridge Modern History,* vol. 11. Cambridge University Press, 1962.

Africa and the Victorians: The Climax of Imperialism. Doubleday, 1968.

Galtung, Johan. "A Structural Theory of Imperialism." *Journal of Peace Research,* 8, 2, 1971.

Geertz, Clifford. *The Religion of Java.* University of Chicago Press, 1960.

Gerschenkron, Alexander. *Economic Backwardness in Historical Perspective.* Harvard University Press, 1962.

Europe in the Russian Mirror: Four Lectures in Economic History. Cambridge University Press, 1970.

Gillard, David. *The Struggle for Asia, 1828–1914: A Study in British and Russian Imperialism.* Holmes and Meier, 1977.

Goldsworthy, David. *Colonial Issues in British Politics, 1945–1961.* Oxford University Press, 1971.

Graham, Gerald S. *Tides of Empire: Discussions on the Expansion of Britain Overseas.* McGill-Queen's University Press, 1972.

Graham, Richard. *Britain and the Onset of Modernization in Brazil, 1850–1914.* Cambridge University Press, 1968.

"Robinson and Gallagher in Latin America: The Meaning of Informal Imperialism." In William Roger Louis, ed., *Imperialism:*

The Robinson and Gallagher Controversy. Franklin Watts (New York), 1976.

Green, Martin. Dreams of Adventure, Deeds of Empire. Basic Books, 1979.

Grosser, Alfred. La Politique extérieure de la Ve République. Seuil (Paris), 1965.

Grunwald, Kurt, and Joachim O. Ronall. Industrialization in the Middle East. Council for Middle Eastern Affairs Press, 1960.

Gutkind, Peter C. W., and Immanuel Wallerstein, eds. The Political Economy of Contemporary Africa. Sage, 1976.

Handbook for the Ivory Coast. U.S. Department of State, 1973.

Hershlag, Z. Y. Introduction to the Modern Economic History of the Middle East. E. J. Brill (Long Island City, N.Y.), 1964.

  Turkey: The Challenge of Growth. E. J. Brill (Long Island City, N.Y.), 1968.

Hintze, Otto. The Historical Essays of Otto Hintze, ed. Felix Gilbert. Oxford University Press, 1975.

Hirschman, Albert O. "The Turn to Authoritarianism in Latin America and the Search for its Economic Determinants." In David Collier, ed., The New Authoritarianism in Latin America. Princeton University Press, 1980.

Hobsbawm, E. J. Industry and Empire. Pelican, 1969.

Hobson, J. A. Imperialism: A Study, 1st ed., 1902. University of Michigan Press, 1965.

Hoffman, J. S. Great Britain and the German Trade Rivalry. Russell and Russell (New York), 1964.

Hoffmann, Stanley, ed. In Search of France. Harper & Row, 1965.

Hopkins, A. G. An Economic History of West Africa. Longman, 1973.

Hurewitz, J. C. Diplomacy in the Near and Middle East: A Documentary Record: 1535–1914. Van Nostrand, 1956.

Hutchins, Francis. India's Revolution: Gandhi and the Quit India Movement. Harvard University Press, 1973.

Imlah, Albert H. Economic Elements in the Pax Britannica. Harvard University Press, 1958.

Issawi, Charles. Egypt in Revolution: An Economic Analysis. Oxford University Press, 1963.

  ed. The Economic History of the Middle East, 1800–1914. University of Chicago Press, 1966.

Jervis, Robert. Perception and Misperception in International Politics. Princeton University Press, 1976.

Kahin, George. *Nationalism and Revolution in Indonesia.* Cornell University Press, 1952.

and John W. Lewis. *The United States in Vietnam.* Dial Press, 1967.

Kahler, Miles Edwin. "External Sources of Domestic Politics: Decolonization in Britain and France." Ph.D. dissertation, Harvard University, 1977.

Kaufman, Robert R., et al. "A Preliminary Test of the Theory of Dependency." *Comparative Politics,* VII, 3, April 1975.

"Industrial Change and Authoritarian Rule in Latin America: A Concrete Review of the Bureaucratic-Authoritarian Model." In David Collier, ed., *The New Authoritarianism in Latin America.* Princeton University Press, 1980.

Keatley, Patrick. *The Politics of Partnership.* Penguin Books, 1963.

Kehr, Eckart. *Economic Interest, Militarism and Foreign Policy: Essays on German History.* University of California Press, 1977.

Kindleberger, Charles P. *Economic Growth in France and Britain, 1851–1950.* Harvard University Press, 1964.

Kolko, Gabriel. *The Politics of War: The World and United States Foreign Policy, 1943–1945.* Random House, 1968.

Kuznets, Simon. *Modern Economic Growth: Rate, Structure and Spread.* Yale University Press, 1966.

Landes, David S. *Bankers and Pashas: International Finance and Economic Imperialism in Egypt.* Harvard University Press, 1958.

The Unbound Prometheus: Technological Change and Industrial Development in Western Europe from 1750 to the Present. Cambridge University Press, 1969.

Latham, A. J. H. *Old Calabar, 1600–1891: The Impact of the International Economy upon a Traditional Society.* Oxford University Press, 1973.

The International Economy and the Underdeveloped World, 1865–1914. Rowman and Littlefield (Totowa, N.J.), 1978.

Leites, Nathan. *On the Game of Politics in France.* Stanford University Press, 1959.

Lenin, Vladimir. *Imperialism, the Highest Stage of Capitalism.* 1917.

Lewis, W. Arthur. *Growth and Fluctuations, 1870–1913.* Allen & Unwin, 1978.

Leys, Colin. *Underdevelopment in Kenya: The Political Economy of Neo-Colonialism, 1964–1971.* University of California Press, 1974.

Liska, George. *Quest for Equilibrium: America and the Balance of Power on Land and Sea.* Johns Hopkins University Press, 1977.

Lukács, Georg. *Histoire et conscience de classe.* Editions de Minuit (Paris), 1960.

McAlister, John T. *Viet Nam: The Origins of Revolution.* Knopf, 1969.

McGowan, Patrick J. "Economic Dependency and Economic Performance in Black Africa." *The Journal of Modern African Studies,* XIV, 1, 1976.

Macmillan, Harold. *Riding the Storm: 1956–1959.* Macmillan, 1971.

MacRae, D. *Parliament, Parties and Society in France, 1946–1958.* St. Martin's Press, 1967.

McVey, Ruth. "The Social Roots of Indonesian Communism." Speech published by the Centre d'Etude du Sud-Est Asiatique et de l'Extrême-Orient, l'Université Libre de Bruxelles.

Maddison, Angus. *Economic Growth in Japan and the USSR.* Allen & Unwin, 1969.

  Class Structure and Economic Growth: India and Pakistan since the Moghuls. Allen & Unwin, 1971.

Marshall, D. Bruce. *The French Colonial Myth and Constitution-Making in the Fourth Republic.* Yale University Press, 1973.

Mommsen, Wolfgang J. "Domestic Factors in German Foreign Policy before 1914." In James J. Sheehan, ed., *Imperial Germany.* Franklin Watts (New York), 1976.

Monger, George. *The End of Isolation: British Foreign Policy, 1900–1907.* Thomas Nelson (New York), 1963.

Monroe, Elizabeth. *Britain's Moment in the Middle East, 1914–1956.* Johns Hopkins University Press, 1963.

Moore, Barrington, Jr. *Social Origins of Dictatorship and Democracy: Lord and Peasant in the Making of the Modern World.* Beacon Press, 1966.

Morgenthau, Ruth S. *Political Parties in French-Speaking West Africa.* Oxford University Press (Clarendon Press), 1964.

Morris, Morris D. "Towards a Reinterpretation of Nineteenth-Century Indian Economic History." *The Indian Economic and Social History Review,* V, March 1968.

Mortimer, Rex. "Class, Social Cleavage, and Indonesian Communism." *Indonesia* (Cornell University Press), no. 8, October 1969.

Moulder, Frances V. *Japan, China, and the Modern World-Economy: Toward a Reinterpretation of East Asian Development.* Cambridge University Press, 1977.

Munro, J. Forbes. *Africa and the International Economy, 1800–1960*. Rowman and Littlefield (Totowa, N.J.), 1976.

Murphy, Rhodes. *The Treaty Ports and China's Modernization: What Went Wrong?*. *Michigan Papers in Chinese Studies*, 7, 1970.

The Outsiders: The Western Experience in India and China. University of Michigan Press, 1977.

Nkrumah, Kwame. *Neo-Colonialism: The Last Stage of Imperialism*. International Publishers (New York), 1966.

O'Donnell, Guillermo. *Modernization and Bureaucratic-Authoritarianism: Studies in South American Politics*. Institute of International Studies (Berkeley), 1973.

"Corporatism and the Question of the State." In James M. Malloy, ed., *Authoritarianism and Corporatism in Latin America*. University of Pittsburgh Press, 1977.

"Reflections on the Patterns of Change in the Bureaucratic-Authoritarian State." *Latin American Research Review*, 13, 1, 1978.

Owen, E. R. J. "Lord Cromer and the Development of Egyptian Industry, 1883–1907." *Middle Eastern Studies*, II, 4, July 1966.

"The Attitudes of British Officials to the Development of Egypt's Economy, 1882–1922." M. A. Cook, ed., *Studies in the Economic History of the Middle East*. Oxford University Press, 1970.

Pelaez, Carlos Manuel. "The Theory and Reality of Imperialism in the Coffee Economy of Nineteenth-Century Brazil." *Economy History Review*, second series, 29, 2, May 1976.

Platt, D. C. M. *Finance, Trade, and Politics in British Foreign Policy, 1815–1914*. Oxford University Press, 1968.

"Further Objections to an 'Imperialism of Free Trade,' 1830–60." *Economic History Review*, second series, 26, 1, February 1973.

Latin America and British Trade, 1806–1914. Harper & Row, 1973.

"Dependency in Nineteenth Century Latin America." *Latin American Research Review*, 15, 1, 1980.

Platt, D. C. M., ed. *Business Imperialism, 1840–1930: An Inquiry Based on British Experience in Latin America*. Oxford University Press, 1977.

Ray, David. "The Dependency Model and Latin America: Three Basic Fallacies." *The Journal of Interamerican Affairs and World Studies*, XV, 1, February 1973.

Rodney, Walter. *How Europe Underdeveloped Africa*. Bogle-l'Ouverture (London), 1973.

Rosenberg, Hans. "Political and Social Consequences of the Great Depression of 1873–1896 in Central Europe." Reprinted in James J. Sheehan, ed. *Imperial Germany*. Franklin Watts (New York), 1976.

Rosovsky, Henry. *Industrialization in Two Systems: Essays in Honor of Alexander Gerschenkron*. Wiley, 1966.

Rungta, Radhe Shyam. *The Rise of Business Corporation in India, 1851–1900*. Cambridge University Press, 1970.

Sartre, Jean-Paul. *Critique de la raison dialectique*. Gallimard (Paris), 1960.

Schumpeter, Joseph. *The Sociology of Imperialism*. First published 1919; first English edition, 1951.

Semmel, Bernard. *Imperialism and Social Reform: English Social-Imperial Thought, 1895–1914*. Harvard University Press, 1960.
The Rise of Free Trade Imperialism: Classical Political Economy and the Empire of Free Trade and Imperialism, 1750–1850. Cambridge University Press, 1970.

Serra, Jose. "Three Mistaken Theses Regarding the Connection between Industrialization and Authoritarian Regimes." In David Collier, ed., *The New Authoritarianism in Latin America*. Princeton University Press, 1980.

Shaw, Stanford J. "The Nineteenth-Century Ottoman Tax Reforms and Revenue System." *International Journal of Middle East Studies*, VI, October 1975.

Skocpol, Theda. "France, Russia, China: A Structural Theory of Social Revolution." *Comparative Studies in Society and History*, 18, 2, 1976.
"Wallerstein's World Capitalist System: A Theoretical and Historical Critique." *American Journal of Sociology*, 82, 5, March 1977.
States and Social Revolutions: A Comparative Analysis of France, Russia and China. Cambridge University Press, 1979.

Smith, Tony. "Idealism and People's War: Sartre on Algeria." *Political Theory*, I, 4, November 1973.
The End of the European Empire: Decolonization after World War II. Heath, 1975.
The French Stake in Algeria, 1945–1962. Cornell University Press, 1978.
"The Logic of Dependence Theory Revisited," *International Organization* (in press).

Staley, Eugene. *War and the Private Investor: A Study in the Rela-*

tions of International Politics and International Private Invest-ment. Howard Fertig (New York), 1935; reprinted 1967.

Stein, Stanley J., and Barbara H. Stein. *The Colonial Heritage of Latin America: Essays on Dependency in Perspective.* Oxford University Press, 1970.

Sterling, Richard W. *Macropolitics: International Relations in a Global Society.* Knopf, 1974.

Temin, Peter. "The Relative Decline of the British Steel Industry, 1880–1913." In H. Rosovsky, ed., *Industrialization in Two Systems: Essays in Honor of Alexander Gerschenkron.* Wiley, 1966.

Thompson, Leonard. "France and Britain in Africa: A Perspective." In Prosser Gifford and William Roger Louis, eds., *France and Britain in Africa: Imperial Rivalry and Colonial Rule.* Yale University Press, 1971.

Tignor, Robert L. "Bank Misr and Foreign Capitalism." *International Journal of Middle East Studies,* 8, 2, April 1977.

Tomlinson, B. R. *The Political Economy of th Raj, 1914–1917: The Economics of Decolonization in India.* Macmillan, 1979.

Trimberger, Ellen Kay. *Revolution from Above: Military Bureaucrats and Developments in Japan, Turkey, Egypt and Peru.* Transaction Books (New Brunswick, N. J.), 1977.

Turner, Henry Ashby. "Bismarck's Imperialist Venture: Anti-British in Origin?" In Prosser Gifford and William Roger Louis, eds., *Britain and Germany in Africa.* Yale University Press, 1967.

Veblen, Thorstein. *Imperial Germany and the Industrial Revolution.* Macmillan, 1915.

Véliz, Claudio. *The Centralist Tradition of Latin America.* Princeton University Press, 1980.

Von Albertini, Rudolph. *Decolonization.* Doubleday, 1971.

Wahl, Nicholas. "The French Political System." In Samuel Beer and Adam Ulam, eds., *Patterns of Government.* Random House, 1962.

Wakeman, Frederic, Jr. "High Ch'ing: 1638–1839." In James B. Crowley, ed., *Modern East Asia: Essays in Interpretation.* Harcourt Brace Jovanovich, 1970.

Wall, Irwin M. "The French Communist and the Algerian War." *The Journal of Contemporary History,* 12, 3, July 1977.

Wallerstein, Immanuel. "Dependence in an Interdependent World: The Limited Possibilities of Transformation within the Capitalist World Order." *African Studies Review,* XVII, 1, April 1974.

The Modern World-System: Capitalist Agriculture and the Origins of the European World-Economy in the Sixteenth Century. Academic Press, 1974.

"The Rise and Future Demise of the World Capitalist System." *Comparative Studies in Society and History,* XVI, 4, September 1974.

"Class Formation in the Capitalist World-Economy." *Politics and Society,* 5, 3, 1974.

Wehler, Hans-Ulrich. "Bismarck's Imperialism, 1862–1890." *Past and Present,* 48, August 1970.

Wiarda, Howard J. "Toward a Framework for the Study of Political Change in the Iberic-Latin Tradition: The Corporative Model." *World Politics,* 25, 2, January 1973.

Williams, Philip. *Crisis and Compromise: Politics in the Fourth Republic.* Doubleday (Anchor Books), 1966.

Woodruff, William. *Impact of Western Man: A Study of Europe's Role in the World Economy, 1850–1960.* St. Martin's Press, 1967.

Wright, Mary Clabaugh. *The Last Stand of Chinese Conservatism: The T'ung-Chih Restoration, 1862–1874.* Stanford University Press, 1962.

Zolberg, Aristide. *One Party Rule in the Ivory Coast.* Princeton University Press, 1969.

The period of U.S. hegemony (Chapters 4, 5, and the Appendix)

Acheson, Dean. *Present at the Creation: My Years in the State Department.* Norton, 1969.

Adelman, Irma, and Cynthia Taft Morris. *Economic Growth and Social Equity.* Stanford University Press, 1973.

Aiken, William, and Hugh La Follette, eds. *World Hunger and Moral Obligation.* Prentice-Hall, 1977.

Ajami, Fouad. "The Fate of Nonalignment." *Foreign Affairs,* 59, 2, Winter 1980–1.

Ambler, John Steward. *Soldiers against the State: The French Army in Politics.* Doubleday, 1968.

Badeau, John S. *The American Approach to the Arab World.* Harper & Row, 1968.

Barnet, Richard. *Roots of War: The Men and Institutions behind U.S. Foreign Policy.* Penguin, 1971.

Barnet, Richard J., et al. *Global Reach: The Power of the Multinational Corporations.* Simon & Schuster, 1974.

Beitz, Charles R. *Political Theory and International Relations.* Princeton University Press, 1979.

Bemis, Samuel Flagg. *The Latin American Policy of the United States: An Historical Interpretation.* Harcourt Brace Jovanovich, 1943.

Bergsten, C. Fred, et al. *American Multinationals and American Interests.* Brookings Institution, 1978.

Blasier, Cole. *The Hovering Giant: U.S. Responses to Revolutionary Change in Latin America.* University of Pittsburgh Press, 1976.

Blaufarb, Douglas S. *The Counterinsurgency Era: U.S. Doctrine and Performance, 1950 to the Present.* Free Press, 1977.

Blechman, Barry M., and Stephen S. Kaplan. "U.S. Military Forces as a Political Instrument." *Political Science Quarterly,* 95, 2, Summer 1979.

Borg, Dorothy. *American Policy and the Chinese Revolution, 1925–1928.* Macmillan, 1947.

The United States and the Far Eastern Crises of 1933–1938. Harvard University Press, 1964.

Burke, Edmund. "Letters on a Regicide Peace." In *Edmund Burke: Selected Works,* ed. W. J. Bate. Random House (Modern Library), 1960.

Calleo, David P., and Benjamin M. Rowland. *America and the World Political Economy: Atlantic Dreams and National Realities.* Indiana University Press, 1973.

Campbell, Charles S. *The Transformation of American Foreign Relations, 1865–1900.* Harper & Row, 1976.

Carr, Edward Hallett. *The Bolshevik Revolution, 1917–1923.* Macmillan, 1961.

Central Intelligence Agency, National Foreign Assessment Center. *Communist Aid to Less Developed Countries of the Free World, 1977.* Washington, D.C., 1978.

Chenery, Hollis, et al. *Redistribution with Growth.* Oxford University Press, 1974.

Chichilnisky, Graciela. "Development Patterns and International Order." *Journal of International Affairs,* 31, 2, Fall/Winter 1977.

Christensen, Cheryl. "World Hunger: A Structural Approach." *International Organization,* 32, 3, Summer 1978.

Cipolla, Carlo M. *The Economic History of World Population,* 6th ed. Penguin Books, 1976.

Clemens, Diane Shaver. *Yalta.* Oxford University Press, 1970.

Clyde, Paul Hibbert. *United States Policy toward China: Diplomatic* and *Public Documents, 1839–1939.* Russell and Russell (New York), 1964.

Cox, Arthur Macy. "The CIA's Tragic Error." *New York Review of Books,* November 6, 1980.

Cumberland, Charles C. *Mexico: The Struggle for Modernity.* Oxford University Press, 1968.

Dallek, Robert. *Franklin D. Roosevelt and American Foreign Policy, 1932–1945.* Oxford University Press, 1979.

DeConde, Alexander. *A History of American Foreign Policy.* Scribner, 1971.

Degras, Jane, ed. *The Communist International: Volume I, 1919–1923.* Oxford University Press, 1956.

Dewitt, Jr., R. Peter. *The Inter-American Development Bank and Political Influence: With Special Reference to Costa Rica.* Praeger, 1977.

Diamond, William. *The Economic Thought of Woodrow Wilson.* Johns Hopkins University Press, 1943.

Divine, Robert A. *American Immigration Policy, 1924–1952.* Yale University Press, 1957.

Eisenhower, Dwight D. *Mandate for Change, 1953–1956.* Doubleday, 1963.

Waging Peace, 1956–1961. Doubleday, 1965.

Ellsberg, Daniel. *Papers on the War.* Pocket Books, 1972.

Emerson, Rupert. *From Empire to Nation: The Rise to Self-Assertion of Asian and African Peoples.* Beacon Press, 1964.

Evans, Peter. *Dependent Development: The Alliance of Multinational, State, and Local Capital in Brazil.* Princeton University Press, 1979.

Fagen, Richard R. "Commentary on Einaudi." In Julio Cotler and Fagen, eds., *Latin America and the United States: The Changing Political Realities.* Stanford University Press, 1974.

Fanon, Frantz. *The Wretched of the Earth.* Grove Press, 1966.

Finley, David D. *Some Aspects of Conventional Military Capability in Soviet Foreign Relations,* Working Paper 20. Center for International and Strategic Affairs, University of California (Los Angeles), February 1980.

Frey-Wouters, Ellen. *The European Community and the Third World: The Lomé Convention and Its Impact.* Basic Books, 1980.

Friend, Theodore. *Between Two Empires: The Ordeal of the Philippines, 1921–1946.* Yale University Press, 1965.

Gaddis, John Lewis. *The United States and the Origins of the Cold War, 1941–1947.* Columbia University Press, 1972.

Gardner, Richard N. *Sterling-Dollar Diplomacy: The Origins and the Prospects of Our International Economic Order.* McGraw-Hill, 1969.

Gelb, Leslie H., and Richard K. Betts. *The Irony of Vietnam: The System Worked.* Brookings Institution, 1979.

Gellman, Irwin F. *Good Neighbor Diplomacy: United States Policies in Latin America, 1933–1945.* Johns Hopkins University Press, 1979.

Gilpin, Robert. *U.S. Power and the Multinational Corporation: The Political Economy of Foreign Direct Investment.* Basic Books, 1975.

Goldberg, Peter A. "The Politics of the Allende Overthrow in Chile." *Political Science Quarterly,* 90, 1, Spring 1975.

Graham, Richard. *Britain and the Onset of Modernization in Brazil, 1850–1914.* Cambridge University Press, 1968.

Greene, T. N., ed. *The Guerrilla – and How to Fight Him: Selections from the Marine Corps Gazette.* Praeger, 1966.

Griffin, Keith. *The Political Economy of Agrarian Change: An Essay on the "Green Revolution".* Harvard University Press, 1974.

Haas, Ernst B. "Human Rights." In Kenneth A. Oye et al., *Eagle Entangled: U.S. Foreign Policy in a Complex World.* Longman, 1979.

Harrington, Michael. *The Vast Majority: A Journey to the World's Poor.* Simon & Schuster, 1977.

Herwig, Holger H. *Politics of Frustration: The United States in German Naval Planning, 1889–1901.* Little, Brown, 1976.

Hewlett, Sylvia Ann. *The Cruel Dilemmas of Development: Twentieth-Century Brazil.* Basic Books, 1980.

Hilsman, Roger. Forward in Vo Nguyen Giap, *People's War, People's Army.* Praeger, 1968.

Hirschman, Albert. *National Power and the Structure of Foreign Trade.* University of California Press, 1969.

A Bias for Hope: Essays on Development in Latin America. Yale University Press, 1971.

Hoffmann, Stanley. "Notes on the Elusiveness of Modern Power." *International Journal,* Spring 1975.

"The Hell of Good Intentions." *Foreign Policy,* 29, Winter 1977–8.

Primacy or World Order: American Foreign Policy since the Cold War. McGraw-Hill, 1978.

Hoopes, Townsend. *The Devil and John Foster Dulles: The Diplomacy of the Eisenhower Era.* Little, Brown, 1973.

Hull, Cordell. *The Memoirs of Cordell Hull,* vol. 2. Macmillan, 1948.

Huntington, Samuel P. *Political Order in Changing Societies.* Yale University Press, 1968.

Iriye, Akira. *The Cold War in Asia: A Historical Introduction.* Prentice-Hall, 1974.

Jodice, David A. "Sources of Change in Third World Regimes for Foreign Direct Investment, 1968–1976." *International Organization,* 34, 2, Spring 1980.

Johnson, Dale. "Dependence and the International System." In James D. Cockroft et al., *Dependence and Underdevelopment: Latin America's Political Economy.* Doubleday (Anchor Books), 1972.

Jones, Joseph Marion. *The Fifteen Weeks (February 21–June 5, 1947).* Harcourt Brace Jovanovich, 1955.

Kahler, Miles. "Rumors of War: The 1914 Analogy." *Foreign Affairs,* 58, 2, Winter 1979–80.

Kahn, E. J., Jr. "Annals of International Trade." *The New Yorker,* May 14, 1979.

Kanet, Roger E., ed. *The Soviet Union and the Developing Nations.* Johns Hopkins University Press, 1974.

Karmal, Babrak. "The Afghan People Will Stand Firmly on Guard of the Revolution." *World Marxist Review* (also published as *Problems of Peace and Socialism*), 23, 4, April 1980.

Katzenstein, Peter J. "Conclusion: Domestic Structures and Strategies of Foreign Economic Policy." In Katzenstein, ed., *Between Power and Plenty: Foreign Economic Policies of Advanced Industrial States.* University of Wisconsin Press, 1978.

Kelly, J. B. *Arabia, the Gulf and the West.* Basic Books, 1980.

Kennedy, John F. *The Strategy of Peace.* Harper & Row, 1960.

Kirkpatrick, Jeane. "U.S. Security and Latin America." *Commentary,* 71, 1, January 1981.

Kissinger, Henry A. *American Foreign Policy,* 3rd ed. Norton, 1977. *White House Years.* Little, Brown, 1979.

Kolko, Gabriel, and Joyce Kolko. *The Limits of Power: The World and United States Foreign Policy, 1945–1954.* Harper & Row, 1972.

Krasner, Stephen D. "Oil is the Exception." *Foreign Policy,* 15, Summer 1974.

"State Power and the Structure of International Trade." *World Politics,* 28, 3, April 1976.

Defending the National Interest: Raw Materials Investments and U.S. Foreign Policy. Princeton University Press, 1978.

Kuusinen, O. V., et al. *Fundamentals of Marxism-Leninism,* 2nd rev. ed. Foreign Language Publishing House (Moscow), 1963.

LaFeber, Walter. *The New Empire: An Interpretation of American Expansion, 1860–1895.* Cornell University Press, 1963.

"Roosevelt, Churchill and Indochina; 1942–1945." *American Historical Review,* 80, 5, December 1975.

Lappé, Frances Moore, and Joseph Collins with Gary Fowler. *Food First: Beyond the Myth of Scarcity.* Houghton Mifflin, 1977.

Lebergott, Stanley. "The Returns to U.S. Imperialism, 1890–1929." *The Journal of Economic History,* 40, 2, June 1980.

Legvold, Robert. "Containment without Confrontation." *Foreign Policy,* 40, Fall 1980.

Leng Shao-Chuan, and Norman D. Palmer. *Sun Yat-sen and Communism.* Praeger, 1960.

Lenin, Vladimir. *Theses on the National and Colonial Questions.* 1920.

Levy, Walter J. "Oil and the Decline of the West." *Foreign Affairs,* 58, 5, Summer 1980.

Lin Piao. "Long Live the Victory of People's War!" Foreign Language Press (Peking), 1967.

Link, Arthur S. *Wilson: The New Freedom.* Princeton University Press, 1956.

Lipson, Charles H. "Corporate Preferences and Public Policies: Foreign Aid Sanctions and Investment Protection." *World Politics,* 28, 3, April 1976.

Liska, George. *Imperial America: The International Politics of Primacy.* Johns Hopkins University Press, 1967.

Louis, William Roger. *British Strategy in the Far East, 1919–1939.* Oxford University Press, 1978.

Imperialism at Bay: The United States and the Decolonization of the British Empire, 1941–1945. Oxford University Press, 1978.

Lowenthal, Abraham F. " 'Liberal,' 'Radical,' and 'Bureaucratic' Perspectives on U.S. Latin American Policy: The Alliance for Progress in Retrospect." In Julio Cotler and Richard R. Fagen, eds., *Latin America and the United States: The Changing Political Realities.* Stanford University Press, 1974.

Lowenthal, Richard. *Model or Ally? The Communist Powers and the Developing Countries.* Oxford University Press, 1977.

Lundestad, Geri. *The American Non-Policy Towards Eastern Europe, 1943–7.* Humanities Press, 1975.

Luttwak, Edward N. "After Afghanistan, What?" *Commentary*, 69, 4, April 1980.

McConnell, Campbell R. "Why is U.S. Productivity Slowing Down?" *Harvard Business Review*, 57, 2, March-April 1979.

McConnell, James M., and Bradford Dismukes. "Soviet Diplomacy of Force in the Third World." *Problems of Communism*, 28, 1, January-February 1979.

McGee, Gale W. *The Responsibilities of World Power.* The National Press, 1968.

Magdoff, Harry. *The Age of Imperialism: The Economics of U.S. Foreign Policy.* Monthly Review Press, 1969.

Mao Tse-tung. *Selected Readings from the Works of Mao Tse-Tung.* Foreign Language Press (Peking), 1971.

Martz, John D. *Acción Democrática: Evolution of a Modern Political Party in Venezuela.* Princeton University Press, 1966.

Mason, Edward S., and Robert E. Asher. *The World Bank since Bretton Woods.* Brookings Institution, 1973.

May, Ernst R. *American Imperialism: A Speculative Essay.* Atheneum, 1968.

Migdal, Joel. *Peasants, Politics and Revolution: Pressures toward Political and Social Change in the Third World.* Princeton University Press, 1974.

Mikesell, Raymond F. *Foreign Investment in the Petroleum and Mineral Industries.* Johns Hopkins University Press, 1971.

"More Third World Cartels Ahead?" *Challenge*, 17, 5, November-December 1974.

Mitchell, Christopher. "Dominance and Fragmentation in U.S. Latin American Policy." In Julio Cotler and Richard R. Fagen, eds., *Latin America and the United States: The Changing Political Realities.* Stanford University Press, 1974.

Moran, Theodore H. "Multinational Corporations and Dependency: A Dialogue for Dependentistas and Non-Dependentistas." *International Organization*, 32, 1, Winter 1978.

Morris, Morris D. *Measuring the Condition of the World's Poor: The Physical Quality of Life Index.* Pergamon Press, 1979.

Munro, Dana G. *Intervention and Dollar Diplomacy in the Caribbean, 1900–1921.* Princeton University Press, 1964.

Myrdal, Gunnar. *The Challenge of World Poverty: A World Anti-Poverty Program in Outline.* Pantheon Books, 1970.

Nathan, James A., and James K. Oliver. *United States Foreign Policy and World Order.* Little, Brown, 1976.

Olson, Richard Stuart. "Economic Coercion in World Politics: With a Focus on North–South Relations." *World Politics,* 31, 4, July 1979.

Organization for Economic Cooperation and Development. *Economic Outlook* (biannual).

Development Cooperation (annual).

Packenham, Robert A. *Liberal America and the Third World: Political Development Ideas in Foreign Aid and Social Science.* Princeton University Press, 1973.

Petras, James. *Politics and Social Structure in Latin America.* Monthly Review Press, 1970.

Podhoretz, Norman. *The Present Danger.* Simon & Schuster, 1980.

Public Papers of the Presidents of the United States: John F. Kennedy, 1961. Government Printing Office, 1962.

Public Papers of the President of the United States: Richard Nixon, 1969. Government Printing Office, 1970.

Ramírez, Alvaro. "Nicaragua: From Armed Struggle to Construction." *World Marxist Review,* 23, 1, January 1980.

Rippy, J. Fred. *British Investments in Latin America, 1822–1949: A Case Study in the Operations of Private Enterprise in Retarded Regions.* University of Minnesota Press, 1959.

Rosen, Barry R., and Stephen W. Van Evera. "Overarming and Underwhelming." *Foreign Policy,* 40, Fall 1980.

Rosen, Steven J. "The Open Door Imperative and U.S. Foreign Policy." In Steven J. Rosen and James R. Kurth, *Testing Theories of Economic Imperialism.* Heath, 1974.

Sanakoyev, Shalva. *The World Socialist System: Main Problems, Stages of Development.* Progress Publishers (Moscow), 1972.

Schaller, Michael. *The U.S. Crusade in China, 1938–1945.* Columbia University Press, 1978.

Schlesinger, Arthur M., Jr. *A Thousand Days: John F. Kennedy in the White House.* Houghton Mifflin, 1965.

The Bitter Heritage: Vietnam and American Democracy, 1941–1961. Houghton Mifflin, 1966.

"Human Rights and the American Tradition." *Foreign Affairs,* 57, 3, 1978.

Schmitt, Karl M. *Mexico and the United States, 1821–1973.* Wiley, 1974.

Schroeder, Paul W. *The Axis Alliance and Japanese-American Relations, 1941*. Cornell University Press, 1958.

Seton-Watson, Hugh. *The Imperialist Revolutionaries: Trends in World Communism in the 1960s and 1970s*. Hoover Institution Press, (Stanford, CA), 1978.

Sheehan, Neil, et al. *The Pentagon Papers*. Bantam Books, 1971.

Simes, Dimitri K. "The Death of Detente?" *International Security*, 5, 1, Summer 1980.

Singer, Peter. "Reconsidering the Famine Relief Argument." In Peter G. Brown and Henry Shue, eds., *Food Policy: The Responsibility of the United States in the Life and Death Choices*. Free Press, 1977.

Smith, Robert Freeman. *The United States and Revolutionary Nationalism in Mexico, 1916–1932*. University of Chicago Press, 1972.

Smith, Tony. "Changing Configurations of Power in North-South Relations since 1945," *International Organization*, Winter 1977.

Spanier, John W. *The Truman–MacArthur Controversy and the Korean War*. Norton, 1965.

Staley, Eugene. *War and the Private Investor: A Study in the Relations of International Politics and International Private Investment*. University of Chicago Press, 1935.

Stalin, Joseph. *Foundations of Leninism*. Moscow, 1924.

Stavrianos, L. S. *Greece: American Dilemma and Opportunity*. Henry Regnery (Chicago), 1952.

Steel, Ronald. *Pax Americana*, 2nd ed. Viking, 1970.

Stockholm International Peace Research Institute. *The Arms Trade with the Third World*. Almqvist and Wiksells Boktyckeri (Stockholm), 1971.

Strange, Susan. "What is Economic Power, and Who Has It?" *International Journal*, Spring 1975.

Thorne, Christopher. *Allies of a Kind: The United States, Britain and the War Against Japan, 1941–1945*. Oxford University Press, 1978.

Treaties and Conventions Concluded between the United States of America and Other Powers since July 4, 1776. Government Printing Office, 1889.

Tsou, Tang. *America's Failure in China*. University of Chicago Press, 1936.

Tucker, Robert W. *The Radical Left and American Foreign Policy*. Johns Hopkins University Press, 1971.

The Inequality of Nations. Basic Books, 1977.
"The Purposes of American Power." *Foreign Affairs,* 59, 2, Winter 1980–1.
Ulam, Adam. *Expansion and Coexistence: The History of Soviet Foreign Policy, 1917–1967.* Praeger, 1968.
United Nations. *Monthly Bulletin of Statistics.*
UNCTAD Second Session, New Delhi.
UNCTAD Third Session, Santiago de Chile.
Proceedings of the United Nations Conference on Trade and Development, Nairobi.
United States Arms Control and Disarmament Agency. *World Military Expenditures and Arms Transfers, 1967–1976.* July 1978.
United States Congress, Senate, Committee on Foreign Relations, Subcommittee on United States Security Agreements and Commitments Abroad, *U.S. Security Agreements and Commitments Abroad.* 1971.
United States Department of Commerce. *Survey of Current Business* (monthly).
United States State Department. *Bulletin* (monthly).
Foreign Relations of the United States (annual volumes).
USSR and Third World (formerly published as *Mizan*). Central Asian Research Centre (London).
Valkenier, Elizabeth Kridl. "The USR, the Third World, and the Global Economy." *Problems of Communism,* 28, 4, July–August 1979.
Varg, Paul A. "The Economic Side of the Good Neighbor Policy: The Reciprocal Trade Program and South America." *Pacific Historical Review,* 95, 1976.
The Making of a Myth: The United States and China, 1897–1912. Michigan State University Press, 1978.
Vaupel, James W., and Joan P. Curhan. *The Making of Multinational Enterprise.* Graduate School of Business Administration, Harvard University, 1969.
Vernon, Raymond. *Restrictive Business Practices: The Operations of United States Enterprises in Developing Countries: Their Role in Trade and Development.* UNCTAD, 1972.
Storm Over Multinationals. Harvard University Press, 1977.
Weinert, Richard. "The State and Foreign Capital." In José Luis Reyna and Weinert, eds., *Authoritarianism in Mexico.* The Institute for the Study of Human Issues (Philadelphia), 1977.
Weinstein, Franklin. "Multinational Corporations and the Third

World: The Case of Japan and Southeast Asia." *International Organization*, 30, 3, Summer 1976.

Wilkins, Mira. *The Emergence of Multinational Enterprise: American Business Abroad from the Colonial Era to 1914.* Harvard University Press, 1970.

The Maturing of Multinational Enterprises: American Business Abroad from 1914 to 1970. Harvard University Press. 1974.

Williams, Benjamin H. *Economic Foreign Policy of the United States.* Howard Fertig (New York), 1967.

Williams, William Appleman. *The Tragedy of American Diplomacy.* Dell, 1962.

Wilson, David A. "Principles and Profits: Standard Oil Responses to Chinese Nationalism, 1925–1927." *Pacific Historical Review*, XLVI, 4, 1977.

Wilson, Joan Hoff. *American Business and Foreign Policy, 1920–1933.* University Press of Kentucky, 1971.

Wolpin, Miles D. *Military Aid and Counterrevolution in the Third World.* Heath, 1972.

Wood, Bryce. *The Making of the Good Neighbor Policy.* Columbia University Press, 1961.

World Bank. *Annual Report.*

World Development Report (annual).

Wright, Mary Clabaugh. *The Last Stand of Chinese Conservatism: The T'ung-Chih Restoration, 1862–1874.* Stanford University Press, 1962.

Yergin, Daniel. *Shattered Peace: The Origins of the Cold War and the National Security State.* Houghton Mifflin, 1977.

Index

Philippines, 19, 36, 143, 150–1, 162, 166, 167, 171, 194
Platt, D. C. M., 22–6, 34, 38, 57, 62, 253 n. 32
Poland, 91, 159–60
Portugal, 18, 19, 92
Prebisch, Rául, 235
Puerto Rico, 36

Qaddafi, Muammar, 122, 241

railways, 42, 43, 62–3
Ramadier, Paul, 107
Ramírez, Alvaro, 222
Rassemblement Démocratique Africain, 113, 115–16, 119
Rockefeller Foundation, 187
Roosevelt, Franklin, 101–2, 144, 146, 156, 158–61, 165, 167, 183, 185, 246
Roosevelt, Theodore, 153, 154
Rusk, Dean, 198
Russia, 31, 33, 35, 38, 42, 43, 45, 46, 47, 63, 65, 68, 81, 87, 88; see also Great Britain; Soviet Union

Sahel, 238
Sartre, J. P., 79
Saudi Arabia, 132
Schlesinger, Arthur, 175, 196–7, 245
Senegal, 33, 86, 115–16
Senghor, Léopold, 119
Singapore, 20, 28, 33, 90
Skocpol, Theda, 68, 80
Smith, Adam, 26
South Africa, 33, 92, 131, 149, 247
South Yemen, 206, 216, 228
Soviet Union: foreign economic policy, 41, 210, 215, 221; military capacity after 1970, 203, 204, 205, 206, 216, 217, 218–21, 223–4; relations with China, 169–71; relations with the Third World, 173, 206, 216–24; relations with the United States, 91, 158–60, 179–80, 181, 190, 191, 193, 194–5, 197–200, 216–25, 228–34; see also Comintern; Russia
Spain, 18, 19, 60, 89
Spanish-American War, 142, 143
Staley, Eugene, 30
Stalin, Joseph, 149, 158–9, 167, 199, 210, 271 n. 52
Sudan, 52
Suez (crisis of 1956), 93, 94, 104, 105, 131–2, 133, 173
Sukarno, 112, 121, 127, 163, 218
Sun Yat-sen, 146, 219, 221
Sweden, 245
Syria, 138, 180, 206, 228

Taft, William, 153
Taiping Rebellion, 47
Teheran Conference, 159, 188

Thailand, 205
Third World: defined, 7–10; described, 138–9; nationalism, 110–32, 164–5
Tito, Joseph, 169
Touré, Sékou, 119–20
Trilateral Commission, 238
Truman, Harry, 91, 164, 168, 170–1, 184
Truman Doctrine, 141, 168, 194
Tucker, Robert W., 171
Tunisia, 22, 52, 97, 111, 113, 121
Turkey, 64, 86, 102, 194, 216, 221; see also Ottoman Empire
Turner, H. A., 38

United Nations, 9, 160, 183, 217, 236, 237; UNCTAD, 235
United States, 36, 44, 45, 60, 85, 92, 93, 94, 95, 138–249; compared with Britain, 1–5, 17, 148, 182–3, 184, 189, 190, 193, 211, 226; foreign economic policy, 38, 144–8, 150–2, 154–7, 185–90, 201, 211–15, 225, 268 n. 4, 274 n. 88; period 1898–1939, 141–58; period 1940–1950, 158–71; period 1951–1981, 171–82; relations with other countries, see China, France, Great Britain, Japan, Latin America, Soviet Union, Vietnam; see also decolonization, imperialism; Monroe Doctrine, Open Door Policy; and under individual presidents

Véliz, Claudio, 58
Venezuela, 45, 196
Vietnam, 33, 52, 92, 93, 94, 102, 180, 218, 223; war against France, 113, 117, 122, 124–7, 130–1, 133–4; war against the United States, 139, 140–1, 162–5, 173–4, 175–9, 189–90, 194, 198, 204–5, 226, 239, 245

Wallerstein, Immanuel, 73–4, 77, 80–2, 260 n. 34
Wehler, H. U., 38
Wilkins, Mira, 189
Wilson, Woodrow, 32, 144, 146, 152, 154, 158
World Bank, 9, 91, 186–7, 238, 282 n. 13
World War I, 86–9, 95, 230
World War II, 90, 101–4, 158–9, 197
Wright, Mary, 63

Yalta, 159, 188
Young, Andrew, 181
Yugoslavia, 162, 222

Zaire, 205, 216; see also Congo
Zimbabwe, 181, 224
Zolberg, Aristide, 117

308

DATE DUE

DEC 09 2005
DEC 08 2005
JAN 17 2006

GAYLORD

PRINTED IN U.S.A.